UFO Case Files Of Scotland (Volume 3)

By

Malcolm Robinson

The author gratefully acknowledges the permission granted to reproduce the copyright material in this book. Every effort has been made to trace copyright holders and to obtain their permission for the use of copyright material. The author apologises for any errors or omissions in the book and would be grateful if notified of any corrections that should be incorporated in future reprints or editions of this book.

Copyright © 2025 Malcolm Robinson. All rights reserved. without limiting the rights under copyright reserved above, no part of this publication may be reproduced, stored in, or introduced into a retrieval system, or transmitted in any form by any means (electronics, mechanical, photocopying, recording or otherwise) without the prior written permission of both the copyright owners and the publisher of this book. Names and specific locations, when necessary, have been changed to protect the identity of the individuals who are still living at the time of this publication. All stories are based on true events.

*Book cover design copyright © Jason Gleaves.
jasonufonly@outlook.com
www.facebook.com/ufonly
www.youtube.com/ufonly
www.twitter.com/@jasonufonly*

Non-fiction / Body, Mind & Spirit / Parapsychology / UFOs / Unexplained Phenomena

ISBN: 978-1-918038-86-6

This book is dedicated to those UFO witnesses who have come forward with their accounts. Without you, this subject would be all the poorer.

CONTENTS

Foreword:

Introduction: Scotland. 1

1 The Scottish Borders. 9

2 Dumfries and Galloway. 16

3 Ayrshire Region. 25

4 Strathclyde Region. 43

5 Edinburgh and Lothian Region. 64

6 Central Scotland Region. 120

7 Tayside, Perth & Kinross Region. 172

8 Aberdeenshire, Northeast & West Scotland. 197

9 Scottish Highlands and Islands. 209

10 Updates on the Polmont Reservoir UFO Photo. 219

11 Updates on the Dechmont Woods UFO Incident. 244

12 Summing Up. 305

References: 308

Further Reading: 309

About the Author: 312

To Contact the Author: 314

OTHER BOOKS BY THE AUTHOR

UFO Case Files of Scotland (Volumes 1 - 2)

Paranormal Case Files of Great Britain (Volumes 1-2-3-4)

The Monsters of Loch Ness (The History and the Mystery)

The Dechmont Woods UFO Incident (An ordinary day, An extraordinary event)

The Sauchie Poltergeist (And other Scottish Ghostly Tales)

Please Leave Us Alone (The true and terrifying story of an Irish family and their desperate fight against the 'Hat Man' and supernatural forces)

The A70 UFO Incident (Scotland's first officially reported UFO Abduction)

The Falkland Hill UFO Incident (Scotland's most controversial UFO case)

The Bonnybridge UFO Enigma (A Modern Day Mystery) With Ron Halliday.

(Available from Amazon and Lulu)

FOREWORD

This is the third volume of UFO sightings across Scotland, and I hope just like the previous two volumes, you may wonder, as I do, at these strange aerial vehicles as they flit across the Scottish skies.

Since the last volume of UFO Case Files of Scotland, I've had a number of people coming forward to me with their UFO sightings, and its only right and proper that rather than file them away where no one will see them, that they see the light of day in this book. I've always said that it's no good people coming to me with their UFO sightings only for me to just to file them away. These sightings need to get 'out there', so that people like you the reader, can see what is going on in the skies above the Scotland. I've been working in the field of UFO and Paranormal research for well over 45 years, and needless to say, in that time, I've seen and heard many strange tales, a number of which I aim to share with you throughout this book.

Anyone who knows me, knows that I started out sceptical, that I honestly felt that there was no validity in UFO sightings or ghostly visions etc, that it was all nonsense. *"These things don't happen do they"?* Well, I set out in 1979 to disprove them all, how naïve was I? Over the years after speaking with many people, it soon became apparent that there are indeed strange things flitting about our skies. I would inform the reader, that as I have written extensively about other major UFO reports in Scotland, namely the A70 UFO Incident, The Bonnybridge UFO events, the strange events near Newton of Falkland in Fife, and also the Dechmont Woods UFO Incident, that I won't be going into great detail about those here. I may mention them in passing, but these cases have been covered extensively in my previous books. Please see the section, 'Further Reading' at the end of this book should you wish to purchase them. That said, there are updates on the Dechmont Woods UFO Incident which I'm sure you will find of interest. New witnesses and a whole lot more, including a strange creature that was sighted in Dechmont Woods. All that is coming up later. I should also mention that some people were happy to share their UFO experiences with me but didn't want their real name used for fear of ridicule, so with some, (not all) people mentioned in this book, I have used a pseudonym. I have all the real names of everyone mentioned in this book in a file at home, and these will be open to any serious researcher who may wish to explore that sighting further, with the proviso that they 'must' keep the identity of that person private.

This book I hope, will show you how diverse these UFO sightings can be. Not only that, but I do hope that they show you how bizarre a lot of them are. Are UFOs our own technology? In other words, black budget projects? For me a lot of them are. This of course means that a lot of these so called 'black budget projects' are being misidentified as UFOs, and I'm pretty sure that the Military and Air Force are quite happy about this, as it takes away from what they really are. But dear reader, I wouldn't still be in this wonderful subject, if I honestly didn't believe that we are dealing with a very real and genuine phenomenon. A phenomenon that is not based on this Earth.

I'd like to point out to the reader that quite a large number of case files that I feature here in this book, come from letters and UFO sighting account forms that were sent to me back in the early 1980's and early 1990's. Some of these letters were hard to read and some had missing pages. This was due to my many house moves over the years, during which letters and files have been mislaid. Of course, the early 1980's was a time before the wide use of the internet, and in those days, you wrote a letter to the witness or various agencies seeking out answers, be that the police, the airports, the meteorological stations, the Ministry of Defence and so on. Sometimes you didn't even get a reply. Things of course are so different these days, you can send an e-mail to the other part of the world and get an instantaneous reply. Then there are visual platforms like Zoom, Steamyard, and Teams amongst others, which allow you to speak and visually appear, to people all over the world. My how things have changed, so much different from when I started out in 1979. Now, I'd like to point out to the reader, that like the previous two volumes of Scottish UFO case files, I have broken these UFO reports into their respective parts of the country. Like any UFO sighting, we have to take them with a pinch of salt, and I would ask the reader to do so here. Why? Simply because 'some' of the sightings contained within this book may have other alternative explanations, but then again that's the case with many UFO sightings the world over. Before we get to those UFO sightings, let us take a look at Scotland as a nation, and some of the people who have made it as it is today.

SCOTLAND

An Introduction to Scotland

As a Scot, I am very proud of my country, and I would just like to share with the reader, but some of the many facts about my homeland, many of which you may already know, some of which you may not. Did you know for instance, that the world's oldest football was found wedged in the rafters at Stirling Castle in Central Scotland? It was found by renovation workers in 1981 and was made from pig bladder covered in leather and is now on display in the Stirling Smith Art Gallery and Museum. The football is thought to date back to somewhere between 1540–1570 and rumours even point to the idea it could have belonged to Mary Queen of Scots.

Wikipedia tells us that as of 2019, the population of Scotland was 5,463,300. Scotland has 790 islands. 660 of which are uninhabited. The capital of Scotland is Edinburgh, and our patron Saint is Saint Andrew. Ben Nevis is the highest peak in the British Isles, standing at 4,413 feet. There are 600 square miles of freshwater lakes across Scotland the most famous of which is of course Loch Ness. There are over 2,000 castles that have been built in Scotland, most of which are still standing. Famous castles include Stirling Castle, Balmoral and Edinburgh Castle. Usually, these castles were built as defensive mechanisms. The symbol of Scotland is the Scottish thistle. This dates back to the era of Viking conquests of Scotland. According to one legend, a Norse army was trying to sneak up on a Scottish camp at night, as they did so, one Norseman stood on a thistle, causing him to shout out in pain and give up their position.

The unofficial Scottish national anthem is "Flower of Scotland" composed in 1967 by folk musician Roy Williamson; it refers to Battle of Bannockburn fought in 1314. The town of St Andrews is considered the home of golf and is one of the oldest golf clubs in the world, founded in 1843. Did you know that 11% of Scottish people have red hair which is a higher percentage than in any other country. 61% of American Presidents are of Scots or

Scots-Irish descent. Around five million Americans and Canadians identify with Scotland. The shortest scheduled flight in the world is one-and-a-half miles long from Westray to Papa Westray in the Orkney Islands of Scotland. The journey takes just 1 minute 14 seconds to complete. Edinburgh was the first city in the world which had its own fire brigade.

Needless to say, Scotland has produced many thousands of famous people. People who have rose to the top of their profession and made Scotland what it is today. The following are but a few famous Scottish people which I drew from an enormous list of famous Scottish people from that font of knowledge which is Wikipedia. These are my top 56, (In no particular order)

NOTABLE SCOTTISH PEOPLE (Both living and dead)

1. **Robert the Bruce** (1274 – 1329) Born north of Girvan in Ayrshire. King of Scots (1309-1329). Leader of the revolt against English rule during wars of Scottish independence.

2. **Alexander Fleming** (1881-1955) Born Darvel, East Ayrshire. Biologist, pharmacologist and botanist who discovered penicillin. Later shared Nobel Prize in Medicine (1945) with Howard Florey and Ernst Boris Chain.

3. **John Logie Baird** (1888 – 1946) Born Helensburgh, in Argyll and Bute. Baird was an engineer and inventor, who demonstrated the first televised moving objects and later colour television.

4. **William Wallace** (13th Century) Born Elderslie, Renfrewshire. Scottish independence leader during the war of Scottish independence. Defeated an English army at the Battle of Stirling Bridge in 1297. Died aged 35 on the 23rd of August 1305.

5. **Alexander Graham Bell** (1847–1922) Born in Edinburgh. Bell was an inventor of the telephone and worked on developments in understanding hearing.

6. **Robert Burns.** Poet (1759 – 1796) Born Alloway. Burns was a romantic poet, considered the National Poet of Scotland. Burns often based his poetry on traditional folk songs. He wrote 'Auld Lang Syne'.

7. **James Watt** (1736–1819) Born Greenock. Watt was a mechanical engineer, who improved the Newcome steam engine creating an efficient steam engine, which was essential for the industrial revolution.

8. **James Clerk Maxwell** (1831-1879) Physicist, born Edinburgh. Maxwell made a significant contribution to understanding electromagnetism. His research in electricity and kinetics laid the foundation for quantum physics.

9. **J.K. Rowling Writer.** (1965 –) Born in England, moved to Scotland in 1993. Author of the Harry Potter Series which has become the best-selling book series of all time. Her first book was Harry Potter and the Philosopher's Stone (1997). Rowling has also published adult fiction, such as The Casual Vacancy (2012) and The Cuckoo's Calling (2013)

10. **Andy Murray** (1987 –) (Born in Glasgow, Scotland. Great Britain, tennis) Olympic gold medallist 2012. First British winner of Wimbledon since Fred Perry.

11. **Sir Walter Scott** (1771 – 1832) Born in Edinburgh. Scott was a historical novelist, playwright, and poet associated with the romantic era. Notable works include Ivanhoe, Rob Roy, The Lady of the Lake, and Waverley. Scott was also a member of the Highland Society and President of the Royal Society of Edinburgh.

12. **Sir Arthur Conan Doyle** (1859 – 1930) Born Edinburgh. Doyle was an author of historical novels and plays. Most famous for his short stories about the detective Sherlock Holmes, such as The Hound of the Baskervilles (1902) and Sign of Four (1890).

13. **Alex Ferguson** (1941–) Football manager, born in Glasgow. Ferguson achieved unprecedented success with Aberdeen and Manchester United completing a record 26 years at Manchester Utd.

14. **Billy Connolly** (1942 –) Comedian. Born in Glasgow, he worked in the Glasgow shipyards before making a career as folk singer and later comedian. Also, become actor starting in films such as Mrs Brown (1997)

15. **Sean Connery** (1930 – 2020) Born in Fountainbridge, Edinburgh. Connery was an Oscar-winning actor. Connery was the first actor to play in the James Bond film franchises. He won the Academy Award for best supporting actor in The Untouchables.

16. **Thomas Carlyle** (1795 – 1881) Born in Ecclefechan, Dumfriesshire. Carlyle was a Writer, historian, mathematician and philosopher. Carlyle was biting satirist in the inequities of the nineteenth century.

17. **Sir James Dewar** (1842 – 1923) Born Kincardine-on-Forth, Fife. Dewar was chemist and physicist. He invented the vacuum flask, which he used in the study of the liquidation of gases.

18. **Robert Stevenson** (1772 – 1850) Born in Glasgow. Stevenson was a civil engineer and designer. He was noted for his innovative and effective construction of lighthouses on inaccessible places, such as the Bell Rock Lighthouse.

19. **Robert Louis Stevenson** (1850 – 1894) Born in Edinburgh. Author of Treasure Island and the Strange Case of Dr Jekyll and Mr Hyde. The 26th most translated author in the world.

20. **Isabella MacDuff** – Countess of Buchan (1286–1313) MacDuff who played a key role in Scottish Wars of Independence. When her husband sided with the English, she defied him and rode to Scone to crown Robert the Bruce.

21. **Robert William Thomson** (1822 – 1873) Born in Stonehaven. Thomson was a self-taught chemist, engineer and studied modern sciences. He invented the original vulcanised rubber pneumatic tyre. He also invented the fountain pen.

22. **John Boyd Dunlop** (1840 – 1921) Born in Dreghorn, North Ayrshire. Dunlop re-invented and improved the pneumatic tyre. He was a vet for nearly 10 years before inventing an improved pneumatic, inflatable tyre for his son's tricycle.

23. **Andrew Carnegie** (1835 – 1918) Born in Dunfermline, Fife. Carnegie emigrated to the US aged 12. He became powerful U.S. steel magnate and later philanthropist.

24. **James Chalmers** (1782 – 1853) Born in Dundee. Chalmers was a bookseller and newspaper publisher. He proposed reforms to speed up mail from Edinburgh to London and was recognised as the inventor of the adhesive postage stamp.

25. **James Braid** (1795 – 1860) Born Portmoak, Kinross-shire. Braid was a surgeon who developed the process of Hypnosis.

26. **Jackie Stewart** (1939 –) Born Milton, Dunbartonshire. Stewart was World Champion Racing Driver 1969, 1971, 1973.

27. **Bill Shankly** (1913 – 1981) Born Glenbuck, Ayrshire. Football player who represented Scotland five times, but most famous as the manager of Liverpool F.C. 1959-74.

28. **Mary, Queen of Scots** (1542 – 1587) Born Linlithgow, West Lothian. Queen of Scotland (1542 – 1567). After 18 years in custody in England she was beheaded due to perceived threat to Elizabeth I.

29. **George Cleghorn** (1716 – 1794) Doctor who helped discover Quinine as a cure for Malaria.

30. **Sir Ralph Alexander Cochrane** (1895 – 1977) Air Chief in World War Two. Planned Dambusters raid in 1943.

31. **Kenny Dalglish** (1951 –) Scottish Football player. Played for Celtic and Liverpool.

32. **John Knox** (1505 – 1572) Instrumental in Protestant Reformation in Scotland.

33. **Air Chief Marshall Hugh Dowding** (1882 – 1970) Commander in Chief of Fighter Command during Battle of Britain and noted Spiritualist.

34. **Sir Patrick Geddes** (1854 – 1932) Father of Town Planning.

35. **Charles Mackintosh** (1766 – 1843) Invented Mac Raincoat.

36. **James Gregory** (1638 – 1675) Inventor of the first reflecting telescope.

37. Earl Douglas Haig (1861 – 1928) Commander of Allied troops on Western Front in World War. Later founded the Poppy fund for ex-servicemen.

38. Kenneth Grahame (1859 – 1932) Author. Including "The Wind in the Willows."

39. James Lind (1716 – 1794) Naval doctor. Helped prevent scurvy on naval expeditions.

40. Joseph Lister (1827 – 1912) At the University of Glasgow, pioneered use of antiseptics reducing infections after operations.

41. David Livingstone (1813 – 1873) Explorer.

42. John McAdam (1756 – 1836) Surveyor and builder of roads.

43. Sir Chris Hoy (1976 –) Olympic cyclist.

44. Sir Robert McAlpine (1847 – 1934) Construction Firm.

45. Ronald Balfour Corbett (Ronnie Corbett), (1930) Comedian.

46. Flora MacDonald (1722 – 1790) Born in Milton, South Uist. She helped Bonnie Prince Charles evade capture after the Battle of Culloden.

47. Mary Somerville (1780 – 1872) Scottish science writer and polymath. The first female to become a member of the Royal Astronomical society.

48. Kirkpatrick Macmillan (1813 – 1878) Inventor of the bicycle.

49. Robert Watson-Watt (1892-1973) invented radar.

50. Robbie Coltrane (1950 – 2022) Actor.

51. Donovan (1946 –) Singer.

52. Annie Lennox (1954) Individual Singer.

53. Lulu Kennedy-Cairns (1948 –) Born Marie McDonald Lawrie in Lennoxtown, Stirlingshire. Pop singer.

54. Sir John Sholto Douglas 8th Marquis of Queensberry. (1844 – 1900) Devised the 'Queensberry Rules' for boxing in 1867.

55. Susan Boyle (1961 –) Scottish singer who appeared on Britain's Got Talent and experienced a meteoric rise to fame as a singer.

56. Thomas Telford (1757–1834) Civil engineer and stonemason. Telford was an innovative civil engineer, who helped build Menai suspension bridge, A5 road and numerous canals.

I could have picked many more famous Scottish people. But the above people, in my opinion, helped to make Scotland a great and powerful nation.

CHAPTER ONE

The Scottish Borders

INCIDENT AT NORTH BERWICK

Author's Comment. We start our book where contributor Jeff Nisbett discusses a sequence of photographs which he believes to be a UFO. These were taken over Lamb Island in North Berwick. I felt that rather than dissect Jeff's photograph, I should present it as written to me by Jeff. (His photographs of his sighting can be found in the photographic section of this book)

Jeff Writes.

"Anytime I find myself back in Scotland, I try to spend at least one day in North Berwick, a picturesque coastal town about 20 miles to the east of Edinburgh. The views of the offshore islands are glorious. The gulls cry, the waves lap, and it's a great place to sample some of the fine local seafood. It is also one of the strangest places on the face of the planet. I had known for some time that the area from North Berwick west to the town of Bonnybridge, is considered to be a UFO 'hotspot' which, considering the population, has had more sightings than anywhere else on Earth. In Canada, the ratio of sightings to inhabitants is one per 61,200, and one per 136,450 in the United States. There are 300 registered sightings in Scotland each year, which translates into one per 17,000 inhabitants. Sceptics have blamed the whisky. If you had asked me just a few months ago how much thought I had given to the phenomenon, I would have said 'not much', but that was then".

"I made two trips to Scotland in 2004, and on the second trip I was accompanied for the first time by all of my immediate family and their respective spouses. On Sunday morning, July 4th, I naturally dragged them all out to North Berwick. We had a nice stroll about the town, visited the new Seabird Center beside the harbour, took photographs of the glorious views, and sampled some of the fine local seafood before heading back to Edinburgh in the late afternoon. It was a grand day for all. A few weekends after returning home to the U.S. I was reviewing my vacation photos while my daughter was visiting. I had one photograph on my computer screen where I pointed to an object in the sky and said, *"Look, Sarah, a UFO!"* Well of course she thought I was either playing a prank on her or that there had been dirt on my lens. But a few hours later she emailed me a photo taken that same day on her own camera, which showed a similar object. Needless to say, my photo had suddenly gained many points in my daughter's credibility department".

"It was my 'movies; that did it!"

"My Nikon digital camera has the ability to shoot 35-second QuickTime movies. The QuickTime technology is relatively new, but it is not exclusive to Nikon. In fact, many other cameras that have entered the consumer market over the past couple of years share the same technology. And the fact that digital cameras topped the 2003 Christmas gift wish list means that there are now scads of QuickTime-enabled cameras hanging from the necks of tourists pretty much everywhere. But if they have used their cameras to shoot QuickTime movies, it's unlikely that many would have bothered to click through them frame-by-frame. I have! During my first 2004 trip to Scotland, in April, I shot two of those 35-second movies from the same vantage point as the photos my daughter and I shot later in July. The first was a slow pan from North Berwick out to Bass Rock Island, and the second panned from Craigleith Island back to North Berwick. While the first of these movies is by far the more spectacular, with several of the aforementioned objects appearing in the same frame. I have been able to calculate the objects' minimum airspeed, as well as discover where these objects come from. And so, I feel that these eight brief moments in time will be the most interesting to the readers of your book".

"While viewing my second movie, I suddenly realized it began with a complete view of Craigleith, and therefore with a known quantity the fact that Craigleith is a quarter mile long. The object first appeared about three seconds into the movie and remained visible in the next two frames. Although the object appears three times in the movie, the QuickTime imaging technology only captures an image once every one-fifteenth of a second (as opposed to video, at 24 fps, and film, at 35 fps), so the duration of time the object is actually visible in the movie covers a period of just two-fifteenths of a second less than the blink of an eye. Using Craigleith's quarter-mile length as a 'benchmark' of distance, I was able to calculate that the object was traveling at an astonishing 1.25 miles per second if it was flying directly over the island. But since it is traveling on an oblique angle, and may also be a considerable distance beyond Craigleith, that calculation may actually be quite conservative".

"Conservative or not, 1.25 miles per second translates to a blistering 4,500 miles per hour, which is 6.6 times the speed of sound Mach 6.6 in air-force jargon. Chicago to Vienna in just under an hour, think of it! Imagine flying over the Atlantic in less time than it took to check your luggage. It is indeed a sobering thought that the official aircraft world speed record is held by the Lockheed SR-71 Blackbird that, on July 28, 1978, clocked in at just half that speed, or Mach 3.3. In the meantime, there are objects that are moving at twice that speed in the lower-atmosphere skies above North Berwick, too fast for the naked eye to catch. And, as my movies show, they are not always flying in a straight line. A particularly memorable sequence shows one following a S-curved path across the sky in just 14 frames less than a second and another performing a graceful loop-de-loop! They are quite the aerial hot-rods. All that said, there is no reason to believe that my Mach 6.6 airspeed estimate proves that their pedals have been pushed anywhere near the metal. So, what are these objects? Who or what might be in them? And where did they come from?".

"There are many diverse theories held by as many diverse groups, none of which has ever managed to slip past the ever-vigilant guardians of acceptable mainstream thought. The sceptics are able to shake off most reported sightings by trotting out, often with a chuckle, one or more of the following time-honoured explanations, weather balloons; swamp gas; earth lights; reflections in a window; experimental aircraft; the whisky. And the list goes on. True believers have their own unique set of problems when it comes to putting forth their theories. They do not constitute a unified front and have little or no power over the mainstream press, which tends to report the few sightings that make it past the news desk with a wink-and-grin delivery. Disappointing, but hardly surprising considering the disparate theories held by the believers. Some believers tend to focus less on the extraterrestrial vehicles than on their pilots. And since none of those vehicles has ever been officially found, there is an additional layer of mystery added to their speculations that is not likely to be penetrated anytime soon".

"The few Christian Fundamentalists who also happen to believe in extraterrestrial vehicles quite understandably believe that Satan and his band of fallen angels pilot the craft. What other explanation could they allow themselves to have? Those who believe that Earth's human population did not spring from the loins of the biblical Adam and Eve, but instead came from the stars, have their own set of insurmountable problems to contend with as you might well imagine. There are also those who feel that extraterrestrials may have actually been the Gods mentioned in the world's various mythologies, which came down to Earth and took the daughters of men as their wives which would understandably be a very unpopular theory indeed. The incomprehensibly vast distances of space throw yet another spanner in the works, and have spawned the theories that either the vehicles have the ability to enter a 'portal' or 'wormhole' that immediately transports them to star systems that would otherwise take many light years to get to, or that they have in fact always been with us, and actually exist below the surface of the earth, from whence they come and go at will. Hmm. Let's take one of these two theories at a time and think how easy it would be to fit my little QuickTime movie into either scenario".

• *"The 'Beam me UP, Scotty'* scenario: A few frames of my first movie actually show objects that appear to have expanded, and so it doesn't take too great a leap of the imagination, if you have one, to speculate that they may actually be in the process of atomically dematerializing in order to rematerialize someplace else perhaps at some far-flung point in the universe".

• *"The 'Beam me DOWN, Scotty'* scenario. Let's consider that from the Bass Rock westward to Edinburgh's Castle Rock there are no fewer than six 'extinct' volcanic plugs. As most of us here know, live volcanoes are ever connected to the molten core of the earth by a tube. Is it possible that these ancient tubes have become flyways of sorts, and is that where the 'expanded' objects are heading?"

"I will consider, for now, the second scenario".

"As I have toggled back and forth along several microsecond sequences in my movies, it has become apparent that these objects are not coming down to us from above but are instead emerging from below. At least three sequences in my movies show that these objects are rising out of the sea. You will notice that, perhaps most amazingly, the object shows no sign of having to visibly accelerate from the surface of the water in order to reach its cruising speed in the air. Instead, it appears to be operating at top speed from its first appearance! My observations are supported by a Pravda news article, which reports, 'In 1963, the U.S. Navy was conducting training not far from Puerto Rico. Suddenly, the training session had to be stopped. Sonar operators determined that one of the submarines was changing its coordinates and was following a strange object. The object was moving at an incredible speed, 150 knots. No modern submarine is capable of traveling at such rapid speed. (On average, subs cannot exceed 45 knots).' The article goes on to say that 'American scientist A. Sanderson, who devoted many years of his life to studying ocean depths, writes the following about a mysterious occurrence which he observed from the deck of an icebreaker in the Atlantic. *'Suddenly, something emerged from the waters, breaking thick ice; the huge silver object disappeared in the sky."*

"Let's assume it is unlikely that I, with my 4.2-megapixel camera, have been the first to discover the origin of these objects or to calculate their speed. While non-traditional investigators such as myself would dearly love to have made such discoveries, I find it inconceivable that the top governments in the world, with their ultra-high-tech hardware and software, would be utterly in the dark about these objects, and so I think it's fair to assume they are not. Most disturbingly, the claim has been made that the memberships of certain 'shadow governments' have been in touch with diverse extraterrestrial life forms for quite a while some benevolent and some considerably less so while the rest of us have been allowed to toddle on in ignorance. The eminently credentialed Dr. Michael E. Salla has published an extensive and highly interesting paper on this subject at www.exopolitics.org. While space forbids me to excerpt too much of Salla's data, I can do no less than to say that two of the extraterrestrial races he mentions are thought to live below the surface of the Earth and have done so for many millennia. If one considers that humankind has always set its sights on the stars, and that it took us millennia to break out of the thin pocket of atmosphere that surrounds our planet, one might also begin to consider, with newfound wonder, the mysteries that have ever lain beneath our feet. Now, how does the idea of extraterrestrial life square with the idea of a God? It should come as a comfort to many of you that the two are not mutually exclusive. On more than one occasion Monsignor Corrado Balducci, a Vatican demonologist, has stated his belief in the existence of extraterrestrial life. Here is what he said in an interview with Zecharia Sitchin".

"That life may exist on other planets is certainly possible. The Bible does not rule out that possibility. On the basis of scripture and on the basis of our knowledge of God's omnipotence, His wisdom being limitless, we must affirm that life on other planets is possible, credible, and even probable".

"On February 17th, 1600, the Inquisition burned Giordano Bruno to death in the centre of Rome for having the temerity to suggest, among other 'heresies,' the very same thing, having first taken the final precaution of driving a nail through Bruno's tongue to stop it from blaspheming further. The times do change. So, for you ever-growing legions of amateur QuickTime cinematographers out there, why not put my claims to the test? Just pick up your cameras, head on over to the UFO hotspot nearest you, and let 'em roll! It's time to meet the neighbours".

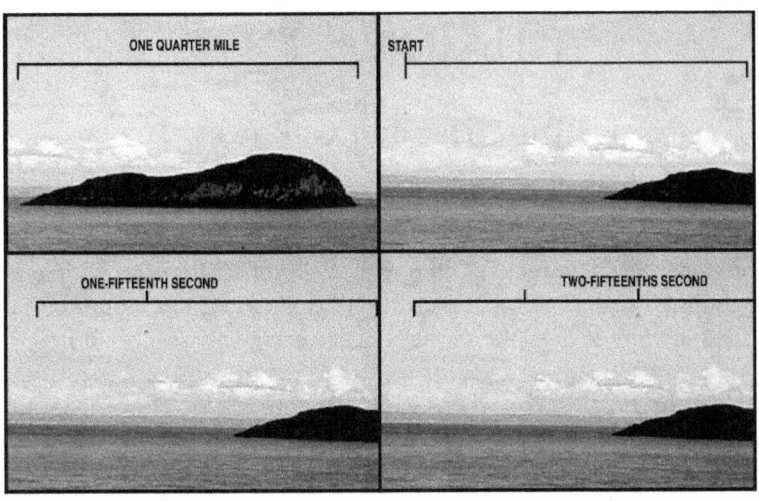

Four-part sequence of a UFO travelling in from the left-hand side. Jeff Nisbett North Berwick UFO July 4th, 2004

CHAPTER TWO

Dumfries and Galloway

Author's Comment. Many UFO sightings are nothing but moving lights across a dark night sky, as is the case here in our next case file. However, there is a slight difference with this account, in that it 'appeared' to play 'tig' with a commercial airline. Here is how the witness Harriot Watson described it.

"I live on a farm (no outside lights) in Dumfries and Galloway, away from any village or town overlooking the Solway Firth so experience a very dark sky and last night was no exception. It was clear and very frosty. The date was Saturday 18th December 2021 and the time was 8.45pm. I went out with my dog onto my drive and heard a plane so looked up to see where it was. As I looked, the plane was high, and its lights were clearly visible flashing. It was flying in a south easterly direction over the Solway Firth towards Cumbria England. Just below the plane was a moving white light going in the opposite direction. At first, I thought it was going to collide. The pilots and passengers must have seen it. However, the plane kept on route, but this light remained high up in the same area and zigzagged back and forth in short bursts of speed in a westerly direction (above wild open hill country) I watched it for about five minutes, and during that time, it split into two and joined up again on two occasions it then just faded out".

"It is not the first time I have seen this happen. In September 2021, again about 9:00pm, I watched a white light follow a commercial plane (much lower in the sky) heading north towards Glasgow and Edinburgh this light also zigzagged right behind the plane's tail then flew over it and below it. Again, I watched for a few minutes till I lost sight of both craft, but I could still hear the plane. It was hard to believe what I was watching; I am not sure what to think. I am not an oddball, just an old lady letting my dog have her final outside visit before bedtime. I dismissed it the first time, although I did tell a neighbour and now wished I had rung him last night".

"Thanks for responding and listening". Harriot Watson (Mrs)

Author's Comment. Our next case file (well a few actually!) was sent to me by Jim Jones, and whilst the first four UFO sightings are from the Dumfries and Galloway Region, the others are from Central Scotland, but as he was the witness, I felt it only best to mention his other sightings in the same section.

SPINNING LIGHTS AND BALL LIGHTNING!

Hi Malcolm,

"I recently saw a Facebook post in which you were looking to hear from people who may have seen any UFOs in the Stirling area. First of all, I would like to state that I have some knowledge about UFOs because I had some sightings when I was young that got me interested in the topic. I am extremely sceptical about most of the cases I read about and believe that there are a lot of charlatans in the UFO scene, and this stops me from digging too deep into the subject, but I am open minded about the topic, purely down to my own personal sightings. I have had a number of sightings over the years, some of which have left a huge impression on me, although I tend not to speculate too much on what they were because I simply don't know, and there is so much we don't know about the world and even our minds. I'll write a brief list of some of the sightings below. One of my greatest regrets is that I did not report any of them. Some of the sightings were in Stirling".

1983/84 (Not sure of the exact year) "I witnessed a silver cylinder rotating on its axis above a field near Brydekirk, in Dumfries and Galloway. My mother was driving me to hospital at the time".

1984/85 (Again, not quite sure of the exact year) "I observed a silent, fast red light travelling across the sky, quite low on the horizon near Brydekirk".

1990 "I witnessed spinning circular lights moving erratically in the sky, seen with a friend in Annan".

1991 "Seemingly the same spinning lights flying quite low over me and a friend while camping by the river Annan. These two sightings are the ones that have baffled and amazed me the most".

"The following three sightings were all seen from around the Stirling University grounds about 1993/94".

"While having a barbecue in Hermitage Wood, about ten of us saw a very big, orange ball that was like a mini sun hovering over Stirling that seemingly came out of nowhere. It started moving slowly in our direction before suddenly getting small and then disappearing".

"Another night me and two friends saw a white luminous oval shape travel slowly across the sky over Stirling, it was in view for about five minutes".

"And finally for Stirling, another night me and another two friends were walking up to the Wallace Monument. I heard a fizzing sound and turned around and looked up, there was a crackling ball of light (white) flying over us and the monument".

2010 "I saw a silent white ball of light which travelled over my flat and quite low over the town that I was staying in near Gifu, Japan. This was also witnessed by my wife".

"These are the ones that I have tended to think about the most. I'd be very interested in hearing if you have had similar reports. Anyway, thanks for reading this".
Regards, Jim Jones.

Author's Comment. The crackling ball of white light that Jim and his two friends seen flying over them at the Wallace Monument near Stirling, is reminiscent of what's known as 'ball lightning' which is a very rare phenomenon which can range in size from pea size to the size of a basketball. They are usually observed in thunderstorms (but not always) Other names for ball lightning are, 'St Elmo's Fire', 'Will-o'-the wisp'.

Three UFO sightings in Dumfries and Galloway over the past three years

In previous books I have mentioned some UFO incidents that have been featured in the newspapers. The following piece was initially featured in an Ayrshire newspaper which was then picked up by the Scottish Daily Record newspaper and reprinted on the 1st of May 2024. Written by Marc McLean. He states.

"Some eagle-eyed residents have shared their close encounters with mysterious flying objects in the sky. Three UFO sightings in Dumfries and Galloway have been recorded and officially documented over the past three years. The first was a circular UFO spotted in the skies above the Solway Coast on February 6th, 2021. Witnesses described it as 'a round-shaped aircraft, quite flat and dark coloured with lights at the back'. It was moving very slowly and must have been closer than most UFO experiences as they even commented that it was around 12 feet wide".

"On December 11th, 2022, witnesses in Dumfries reported seeing a 'star-like UFO', and described it as a bright light, changing colour as it was pulsating. They were gobsmacked as the flying object was moving slightly left and right, and then up and down. Around 11 months later, on October 21st, 2023, another UFO was reportedly spotted from Galloway Park. The witness report states: 'Three orbs appeared and seemed to be playing in an X formation, circling each other and shooting off and coming back'. These sightings have been compiled by research group UFO Identified, which has documented 1,789 sightings of unexplained objects in the skies above the UK since

2020. That includes 395 sightings last year alone. Information was taken from social media, newspaper reports, and Freedom of Information requests, as well as from reports made directly to UFO spotter groups around the UK. The group's research shows that people living in the Southeast of England have the best chance of seeing a UFO, with 233 documented sightings since 2020, followed by the Northwest (218) and the South West (193). However, there have also been other sightings closer to Dumfries and Galloway as two were also recorded in Carlisle. The first was an orb-shaped UFO spotted on January 7th, 2021, which 'changed colours when looking at it through camera'. The other UFO was spotted by a shocked motorist on October 25th, 2023. The driver, who was on the M6 towards the Scotland border, said they saw an object made up of bright lit-up white blocks hovering in one place, not moving".

Author's Comment. Eleven years before the above account, the Scottish Daily Record was informing their readers about more UFO sightings in the Dumfries and Galloway region. In 2013 staff writer Trish Lewis presented the following.

Close Encounters of the Dumfries Kind.
UFO fever has hit Dumfries and Galloway following last week's article about mysterious lights in the sky

"The Standard has received numerous letters and emails following the report of an apparent UFO sighting in Dumfries last week. And the Standard's sister paper the Galloway News, has also received emails about a possible sighting. The paper was also contacted by a man in Yorkshire who claimed he had seen similar lights in the night sky near where he lives a few days later. One researcher emailed in saying that a potential UFO was also sighted at Saltcoats in Ayrshire on December 23rd. So, are we really being visited by extraterrestrials, or is there a more logical explanation for what has been going on? One eyewitness to the Boxing Day sighting over Dumfries, Phil Gibb, emailed in and offered one explanation, he said".

"We also saw the UFOs whilst out walking on Boxing Day evening near Park Farm. There were four in total travelling very slowly towards Cargenbridge. They were not very high in the sky, and as they moved westwards the glow diminished. After careful thought, we concluded that these were nothing more than metallised helium balloons the orange glow being a reflection from street lights."

"Another theory which some readers have suggested and which the MoD has echoed, is that the strange lights may not have been helium balloons, but rather Chinese paper lanterns. These large paper balloons do give off a subdued orange and yellow glow once lit and from the distance can be easily mistaken for something else. Understandably, paper lanterns are not a commonly used means to celebrate holidays like Boxing Day and New Year in Scotland like fireworks are, so it is possible that people who have never seen them before may have mistaken them for UFOs. An anonymous reader contacted the Standard claiming responsibility for the Boxing Day lights, saying that they sent four paper lanterns up into the sky to celebrate the holidays".

The reader said:

"The UFOs in question were actually Chinese lanterns made from tissue paper and have a small square of flammable material at the bottom. These lanterns act like small hot air balloons and once inflated drift into the sky until the flames die down. Four of these lanterns were set off from the Hardthorn area of town on Boxing Day."

"But lanterns would not explain some witness accounts that claimed the lights were moving in different directions and sometimes at great speed. Surely all the lanterns would have travelled at the same incredible pace as one another if it was simply the wind? When the Standard reported on the Boxing Day lights, witness Macaulay Moodycliffe told the paper that he had seen a plane in the sky not that far away from the lights and the two seemed to be moving far faster than the aircraft was. Matt

Benson, who contacted us about seeing lights near his home in Barbly in Yorkshire on New Year's Day also claimed that one of the three lights he saw was moving faster than the other two he witnessed that evening. He said".

"I saw three circular orange balls, one sped away from the other two at some speed, the other two moved slower. There was no noise whatsoever and they were bright orange. They were not fireworks, and they didn't burn out, simply moved south and out of sight."

"The lights spotted in Dumfries on Boxing Day and close to the Haugh of Urr on New Year's Eve by different witnesses, were described as shrinking into the distance as well before finally disappearing. If these were lanterns in every case, they would simply drift off into the distance. But although this special type of firework can answer certain questions like the lack of engine noise and the colour of the so-called UFOs, it still does not answer how in some instances objects were seen to dart off faster than their counterparts. But these lanterns would not explain every case of strange lights seen in the skies over Britain this week. The incident that occurred at Conisholme in Lincolnshire where a 290ft wind turbine had one of its 65ft blades torn off by what eyewitnesses described as a streaking light, cannot so easily be explained away. Numerous witnesses reported seeing orange and yellow spheres hovering around the wind farm before the collision and authorities and wind turbine company, Ecotricity, who own the wind farm, were left baffled without an explanation".

Author's Comment. Back in 2013 releasing Chinese Lanterns were all the rage, thankfully these days you see very little of this. It sounds to me, that the above descriptions given of these 'so called UFOs', were indeed the result of the release of Chinese Lanterns. The descriptions given, have all the hallmarks of them. When these lanterns are viewed from a distance, they can look suspiciously like a strange flying object, which to many, would presumably be a UFO!

Doing research for this chapter on the internet, I came across an e-mail that was sent in 2010 to the Dumfries and Galloway Constabulary by a Kirsty Drain. It was sent as she was concerned about the UFO sightings across Dumfries and Galloway. Here is what she wrote.

REQUEST TO POLICE ON UFO SIGHTINGS

Dear Dumfries and Galloway Constabulary.

"I am writing to request figures for the number of UFO sightings that have been recorded in the region of Dumfries and Galloway in the last ten years. I look forward to hearing from you".
Yours faithfully, Kirsty Drain.

The following is the reply that Kirsty received from the police.

Dear Ms Drain.

FREEDOM OF INFORMATION (SCOTLAND) ACT 2002.
REQUEST FOR INFORMATION

"I refer to your email of 2nd March in relation to UFO sightings and advise that your request has been allocated the above reference number which should be quoted in all related correspondence"
"Under the terms of the Act, the force has 20 working days to respond to each request, effective from the date on which it was received and therefore you will receive further correspondence in due course"
"You should be aware that there may be a fee payable for the retrieval, collation and provision of the information you have requested. You will be advised if a fee applies and, in this case, no information will be provided without payment".
"If you have any queries in the meantime, please contact me".
Regards Steven Irving.

Freedom of Information Officer, Force Information Directorate. Strategic Development and Governance. Dumfries and Galloway Constabulary.

Author's Comment. I wonder if Kirsty ever got her reply? I have written a number of Freedom of Information requests, not just to the police, but to the British Government, all to no avail!

CHAPTER THREE

Ayrshire Region

Author's Comment. When I give lectures around the British Isles, I often get people coming up to me after my lecture to inform me about their own UFO sighting. This was the case in 2024 at the Scottish UFO and Paranormal Conference which we hold each year at the Queen Margaret Union in Glasgow University. One man approached me as I came off the stage, I could see as he walked up to me that he was in tears and was stood in line behind other people who were standing waiting to speak to me. When he finally got to the front of the line he was crying. This was most unusual, I've never ever had anyone anywhere speak to me at a UFO Conference in tears. I really felt for the guy. Needless to say, he was drawing stares from people around him. I took him to one side where he proceeded to tell me a remarkable tale. The following is his written account of what he saw that day. (photos in the photographic section)

MUSHROOM SHAPED OBJECT OVER PADDOCK

Dear Malcolm,

"Thank you for your excellent talk. It was captivating and very well delivered. I was also very pleased to have had the short opportunity to talk to you right afterwards, even if I did get a bit emotional. I very much appreciated your kind manner in our brief exchange, thank you".

"I apologise, but this is quite a lengthy email, so please grab a coffee! I've attached some google map images of where it occurred, and I have also done a crude sketch of what I recall seeing from the window. It's not very good, the proportions are slightly out, as are the lights on it, and it remained perfect horizontal, not slightly angled like I have drew it. But the drawing gives a basic impression regardless. So, please allow me to properly introduce myself. My name is Norman Cale, and I had what I feel was a fairly significant sighting/experience in Ayrshire, a little over twenty years ago. (2001/2) I presently reside in Inverclyde, and for nearly the last decade, I have worked for a specialised Greenock social support service that deals primarily with severe mental health in the community, forensic psychology, addictions, and criminal justice rehabilitation and reintegration. For the last four years I was one of the two seniors/supervisors in the service. I've only ever mentioned my life changing experience to about, maybe four or five people. So, to volunteer it to yourself in a public space was a huge step for me. It felt like I was 'coming out.' My experience is not a long account, but the proximity of it and the qualitative aspect of the experience I believe is what makes it hold some significance".

"I unfortunately have zero evidence, other than my word and the word of my ex. My ex became a PhD grad and worked on particle colliders around the world, so quite the sober headed scientist type and super smart. (I hold a degree in Sociology, so not a total half-wit). She shared in all the experience with me, apart from about the first 30 seconds of it. I'm short on some of the specifics e.g. precise time, but the basic account is thus".

What happened

"It was approximately 2-3am, and I was sitting at the computer in the study writing an email, to a friend in Spain, I'm a night owl, have been since a young child, so my being up this late was not unusual. My ex was sleeping in bed in the next room. The computer was next to the window, with my left side parallel to the window. Due to the back garden being a sheep paddock, the curtains were open. There are only three houses here; us, my landlord and the next-door neighbour, so very quiet and private, which is why we lived there. As you can see from the images I've attached, there is the cottage, then a sheep paddock (1 acre square I believe), then a high old stone wall which must have been 10-12 feet tall, then a thin band of woods which runs around the property. Behind this was the neighbouring farmer's land. He was a middle-aged man who lived there only with his mother, if I am recalling correctly. His name I don't recall. That night I was happily typing away and casually turned my head to the left to look out the window, only to see behind the thin band of leafless woods, what I describe as a mushroom shaped craft hovering silently, approximately 15-20 feet below the top of the tree line".

"The main body/dome of the craft I estimate was a bit shorter than the length of a typical Scottish bus, and possibly up to twice the height. It looked like the top third of a circle. It was smooth with nothing visible protruding that I could see. It appeared to be a dark metallic colour, though given it was night and the bottom was illuminated, it could have been lighter in colour. From the underneath there was a much shorter and narrower central column, like a little mushroom stalk. Underneath the main body, running around the full circumference there were elongated red and blue lights. They were quite vivid and impacting in the night. There was also a circle of lights on the base of the stalk too. The entire craft was very clearly visible and not far away at all. It was not concealed by the trees and was highly apparent. I estimate it was 130-150 metres away from my position when I first noticed it".

"On seeing it I did one of the smartest moves of my life, I immediately ran through to the next room and woke up my sleeping partner with a hard shake and the exclamation *"UFO!"* I'm so pleased I had the presence of mind to wake her. At that moment I thought nobody was going to believe it if it was just me telling this account. I ran back into the study, and she followed. We stood at the old sash window, with myself on the left-hand side and her on the right. Within two minutes (maximum) extreme fear kicked in, and I really do mean extreme. I have never felt fear like this. It has taken me years of reflection upon this experience to gain some kind of understanding of this aspect of it. I recall at the time thinking the fear I was feeling was not natural, but it was so totally overwhelming. In hindsight I now have the suspicion that this fear was 'broadcast' to us. It is very difficult to describe, but it felt as if the fear was coming from the outside in, rather from inside out. I now question if this was a defensive electro-magnetic field of some kind or some kind of mental ability? The fear felt like a force coming from the woods.

Like a silent noise blasting us into terror. I'm obviously speculating here, but these are my best guesses at this time. Whether this is just my internal reaction being misinterpreted by myself I cannot say with 100% certainty, that possibility remains, as I know how this must read! But my strong feeling is that there was a powerful vibrational fear influence of some nature. So, the situation rapidly turned from one of amazement and astonishment, to one of terror and hardcore panic. Indeed, so much so, that we hid behind the cottage wall in the study. I was so afraid. This is an old Scottish cottage (allegedly Robert Burn's father lived and worked in it) and the cottage had very thick stone walls. I recall hoping that this would shield our presence from being detected. A desperate hope I knew even then. But we both stood frozen with our backs towards the wall, doing quick glances out the window".

"At this point the craft began to slowly rise to just above the tree line and then slowly (maybe 10 mph or thereabouts) started to move in the direction of the cottage. I have no recollection beyond this point. My ex said that she recalled a blue light coming down onto the paddock as the craft moved in our direction. However, I cannot recall this. My memory picks up the next day. I spoke to my dad on the phone later that morning and told him about the sighting. I got about two sentences in, and he shot me down. I thought to myself that if this is how family are going to react to the news, then the rest of the world would be potentially worse, so we kept silent about the sighting for years, even after we split up (we were together for a total of 15 years). Due to no memory beyond a certain point, I don't make claims of anything further happening, and I actually deeply hope this is the truth of the matter. It seems as if I have 'missing time', but this could be down to nothing more poor memory or even shock/trauma. But I unfortunately do find it most odd to have a vivid memory of the experience and then it suddenly stops cold, to nothing at all. I've considered regression, but to honest, I don't think I want full recall. The thought of it terrifies me".

"The following weeks, months, and years after the event is very strange too, because the experience very easily slipped into the background of our life and became something that we hardly ever mentioned. I don't know if this was because it was too difficult to reconcile or if it was due to it being such a fearful experience. Yet, at the same time, for myself the experience was a paradigm crash. My worldview shattered at that moment in time. I had previously considered this impossible. I had been a sincerely spiritual person since I was 16/17 years old, but I was not a UFO guy in any shape or form whatsoever. I knew nothing of this field, beyond watching the X-files (which I took as purely entertainment). I had previously mentally ruled out the notion of visitation due to factors of distance, that 'they' wouldn't have an immune system for our environment, nor would they be used to our gravitational force, and so forth. All the factors seemed logically against it to my mind. I thought there must be life elsewhere but took a 'realistic' view of it. Well, it seems I was probably wrong about all of this, because here I was staring a craft (which I am presuming was not man-made) that I could almost hit with a stone, and it was heading in my direction".

"My last point, and thank you for reading this far, is that I don't have a precise date. That might sound odd. It seems very odd to me! But I don't know what day it was, what month it was, and if it was 2001 or 2002. It was winter because the trees were bare, I recall that clearly. The other timeline event I recall from that precise time, was that there was a report in the news of a prisoner who had been taken to the local hospital (Crosshouse) and had escaped into the Kilmarnock community. I believe this was either on the day of my sighting, or possibly the day before. I have since tried to find this info in news archives to identify the date, but I have been unable to locate the info. I imagine you get told a lot of accounts probably not unlike mine. What you do with them (other than books) I don't know. Such experiences are very isolating. They are difficult to share (if shared at all) and leave you feeling displaced in the world. So, for the time being I'm just pleased to have been able to have finally speak about it, and for that Malcolm, I thank you".

Yours Sincerely, Norman Cale.

Author's Comment. After reading Norman's e-mail. I replied with.

Hi Norman,

"I am so glad that you have got in touch. It's very difficult to have a proper talk at a conference due to the quick turnaround of the speakers. I could see behind me when I was speaking to you, that the next speaker was due to come on, hence I didn't have time for a proper chat. But so glad that you picked up one of my cards and got in touch. Well clearly, I can see that your UFO sighting has had a profound impact on you. Which is something that many people experience. When you see something 'not of this world. Having read your report and looked over your drawings (which I am so glad you did as it brings home the sighting much clearer) I can see that this did not look like a conventional aircraft. In point of fact, it looked similar to a UFO that was photographed over Westall in Australia some years ago. This mushroom like UFO had a shorter stem than the one you witnessed, but who knows, it may have retracted it upwards into the main body before it took off (speculation on my part) At the end of the day Norman, I can offer no answer to account for what you saw, speculations yes, but no definitive answers. I 'believe you'. I truly do. Can I ask if I could have your permission to feature your sighting in a future book that I aim to write next year? I can give you a false name should you wish, and not give away the true location of your sighting? Do let me know. If hypnosis is something that you would like to explore regarding your sighting, let me know. If you have any questions for me Norman, please get in touch. You are a very brave man to come forward, how I wish we had more like you, but sadly lots of people don't come forward for fear of ridicule. So well done to you".

Best wishes. Malcolm Robinson.

Author's Comment. Norman replied with.

Hello there Malcolm,

"Thank you for your response, much appreciated. I was a little familiar with that case in Oz, but not of the craft shape. The pics you sent (thank you btw!) are by far the closest I have seen to what I witnessed. I don't recall the little protuberance on top, and I believe the shape seemed flatter, but other than that pretty darn similar! It's quite stunning to see something so close. Yes, by all means, you can use my experience in a book. Any further questions or info required please just ask whenever the time is right to do so. One detail I think I forgot to mention was that it was silent, didn't hear a peep. Lastly, thank you again for the opportunity to openly speak of this. It really has been quite cathartic for me".

Kind regards, Norman Cale.

MYSTERY OVER PRESTWICK, SCOTLAND, (September 2010)

Author's Comment. This case file was originally sent to me via Philip Mantle. I'll let the witness Alan Gore, tell you what happened in his own words.

"Allow me to introduce myself, my name is Alan Gore, I'm 32 years old (completely sane and responsible father of one) I witnessed something at 9:45pm on a Saturday night (25th September 2010) which has left me numb and a bit spooked. I saw a bright orange ball in the sky (very clear night on Saturday) the shape within seconds got bigger and looked as though it was on fire, it then pulsed into a cross/star shape and then back into a ball. It passed directly over my head and was clearly a disc shape, however at times it seemed to look transparent but still visible. Now that was strange, but here is where it gets even stranger".

"After it passed over, it moved away and stopped, maybe about a mile away, I'm really not sure how to calculate the distance, but as I say it stopped. A reddish/orange light appeared from underneath it almost like a lighthouse light but more spread out, perhaps like the spray feature on a watering hose you would use in a garden. It was pointing downwards and moving around, and then a small red ball appeared to come out of the top of the object. It then hovered for a minute or less. The ball then started moving upwards towards space. The red spray looked to be getting more intense. Then a second and third red ball appeared from either side of the object and began moving away horizontally left and right at a moderate speed. The spray stopped, and the main object looked like it was lowering towards the ground, and then a fourth red ball appeared from underneath the main object and proceeded towards the ground faster than the main object. A second bright orange object then appeared overhead briefly, and then both objects faded and vanished. I have hunted the internet to find similar reports, and yes, between the 24th and 26th of September, I have found twelve sightings of the orange objects around the U.K. All of which seem to be sightings from a distance, and really only speak about the shape and colour of the objects. I can't find anything that sounds remotely close to what I witnessed! I feel that someone official should be aware of this as I have searched the internet for similar descriptions but have found 'NOTHING'. The whole experience has freaked me out, but more so the search light bit, what was it doing? I hope this helps in some way".

"I also forgot to mention that about 10 mins or so after the incident I heard an extremely loud airplane engine pass over head, my mother lives not far from Prestwick Interpretational airport, so I know the sound of commercial airplanes only too well. What I heard was not a commercial plane, the boom of a fighter jet engine perhaps? Thanks again for your time and patience".

Yours Truly, Alan Gore.

Author's Comment. What I find surprising about this account, is that this object, whatever it was, displayed a characteristic that is uncommon with many UFO sightings, and that was this spray like effect that was coming down from beneath this object. The witness of course initially described the object changing shape, and small ball-like structures were coming out of it. Here we have yet another strange aspect of observable UFOs.

Out next case file concerns the close proximity of a UFO surrounding a fighter jet. We could ask ourselves the question, was this fighter jet in pursuit of this UFO, or was it just a 'chance encounter'. Here is what the witness to that event, Eddie Kleboe had to say.

THE FIGHTER JET AND THE UFOS

"Hi. You may be interested in a UFO experience that I had. An experience that has remained vivid in my memory as if it happened only yesterday. I guess the biggest problem is pinpointing exactly when it happened. I was on a summer holiday trip with a family friend just outside Ballantrae in South Ayrshire. I was staying in a caravan on a local farm. The farmer had taken us to the shoreline on his tractor and trailer where he parked up on the sand. It was the fighter jet that first caught our attention as it flew upward from the horizon. As we watched it, we noticed it was heading towards a white disc shape which was sitting at the edge of a white cloud much bigger than the jet, at least four times as big. As we watched, three small discs 'emerged' from the larger one and fanned out, as if to surround the jet, which, to our amazement, just suddenly disappeared. The smaller discs then returned to the larger one which slowly merged into the cloud. Being very young we concluded that they must be making a movie. Sadly, my friend died very young, and we only met each other occasionally, but we did speak about our experience and wondered what exactly we had seen that day. I have been trying to remember what age I was when this happened, but as mentioned, everyone on that holiday has since passed. I think I must have been at least seven- to ten-year-old at the time, which would put the date 1969 - 72. I remember it being a nice summer weather, but can't recall any significant events, like the football world cup. So think it more probable after 1969. I have always wondered if an RAF jet had gone missing around that time and how I could find out. Hope my experience is of interest".

Kind regards. Eddie Kleboe

Author's Comment. This is not the first time that jets have been set out in pursuit of UFOs, UFOlogy is full of stories such as this.

FOLLOWED HOME BY STRANGE LIGHTS!

Hi Malcolm,

"Here is my account of all the sightings I have had since October 2010".

"My first encounter was on the 7th of October 2010, which I reported along with the later one I had on November 15th on UK-UFO. I was out walking with my dog that first night at around 7:00pm, it was just beginning to get dark, and I headed on foot to Millenium Park, Dunlop. For no reason, I at once headed straight up the little hill with the Dunlop monument and weathervane on it and sat on the ledge looking out to the fields and sky which had a few stars. I noticed a very bright larger star and looked at how bright it was. Immediately, I noticed a small light come out from what appeared to be behind it, and move in a smooth, curving way, and blink on and off for a few seconds. It then moved to the right of my vision, blinked again, and moved upwards but within my field of vision. I stood up from where I was sitting and felt the need to wave at it! Just as soon as I did this, I then saw another one exactly the same. A small star like orb, appear from the big bright star and do the same as the other one did, they both moved at angles for a few minutes. I heard a plane break the sound barrier, and both blinking lights seemed to disappear then reappear as the plane was far out in the distance. I waved again, and I was sure they were friendly and just saying hello, (how ridiculous do I sound). I then observed them close to each other and slightly higher in the sky, moving away together in an undulating way like the way a dolphin swims. I couldn't believe my eyes, I was so excited, I couldn't see them anymore, so I walked back down the hill with my dog, went through the gate to the larger field and out the other way that takes me onto the main little one-track road. During this time, I kept my eyes on the sky but couldn't see them anymore. I got to the single-track road. By now it was dark, and I looked in the direction I had seen them in and noticed an orange light moving slowly through the trees at exactly the same pace as I was walking at. It was bigger and more orange in colour than the other little starry objects, but it did move, but when I got to beyond the trees to get a better look, it just disappeared!"

"Nothing more happened that evening, not until November 15th, when I was heading home from work just after 6:00am, I travelled to Stewarton (2 miles from Dunlop) first to get petrol for my next nights work, and on the route from Stewarton to Dunlop A735, I noticed on my left in the sky, a big orange light stationary in the sky. Then I saw it 'drop' out of the sky like a yoyo, in a very controlled fashion. I continued driving, but less than four seconds later, I was immediately aware that it was heading in my direction, and straight away, as soon as I thought this, a large bright orange 'orb' with some small flames coming out of the back of it, came tearing past the front of my car, no higher than a telegraph pole, it seemed to glow, and I have that image etched in my mind of when it first came into my view. I did not need to brake to miss it, I felt no fear, it had just covered acres of fields and did not cause me to brake, instead it gave me the perfect image of it, which will stay with me forever, its timing was perfect. It was faster than anything that I have ever seen move. It shot straight up the road that heads to Neilston, (the road I have seen other sightings). I would have had no hope of following it if that had crossed my mind, but it didn't at the time. There was a car behind me, which immediately overtook me and drove quickly away. I had slowed down, hoping the driver would stop to talk about it, but no, off he/she went in a big hurry! I do remember now, feeling some heat through the windscreen as the orange ball passed. It must have been the size of a large van, but it was round. When I think back, it would hold one person comfortably".

"After that, I had a personal loss, my dog died in March, so I wasn't getting out on walks, although still driving home after a night shift. I always drive home the same route up the Kingston Road from Neilston to Dunlop. I never saw anything at all, nothing, until about the middle of August, when on my way home at around 7:00am, it was light, I noticed a star like object following me from the right hand side at about 1 mile distance. It was bright and noticeable as it was daylight. It travelled alongside me all the way from the moors in Neilston till Dunlop. I waved at it during my journey! I made the right turn towards Dunlop, travelled about 200 yards, then noticed it dip very sharply downwards. I braked in order to see where it gone, as it hadn't done any sharp movements until that point. As soon as I started thinking this, I rounded a bend and immediately in front of me was a bin lorry parked in the middle of the road. If I hadn't braked and slowed down, I would have went into the back of that stationary lorry or swerved to avoid it and hurtled down an 80-foot embankment full of old trees! I immediately realised that the sudden movement of that light was maybe a warning of danger ahead. I said thank you! I noticed it over the fields when I parked the car, and I walked into my house, while it moved out of sight".

"After that I have seen a light appear outside my workplace, (just once) and was there all the way home. I have seen lights following me regularly on that road, then a few weeks ago, heading home on the same Kingston Road (Neilston to Dunlop) it must have been the middle of October, I saw two starlike objects that I had been waving at low down in the sky. It was becoming daylight, I felt they were in closer proximity, and I became aware of something else to my right. I looked up and saw a triangle or boomerang shaped object flying very slowly almost directly above my car, it had red, green, white and blue lights pulsating round it. I particularly noticed the blue one and what a nice colour it was. I slowed right down and tried to see where it was again, but it had vanished. It may have been directly above, but I couldn't see for the car roof. I waved anyway even though it was out of my vision. I have seen bright star like objects even when it is overcast when normally no stars can be seen. I was amazed when I saw one on an overcast morning at about 6.30am. It was October 30th hanging low in the sky just at the edge of Neilston where there are no more houses, and I still have a 7-mile drive to Dunlop through hilly terrain. It was there and stayed there till I reached Dunlop".

"More recently, I was heading into work last weekend, Saturday night 3rd December at about 6:50pm. It had been snowing, I was halfway between Dunlop and Lugton, when I noticed a craft, not a starlike object, but a craft with lights pulsating around it, sitting in the sky not flying anywhere, just staying almost stationary. It was low in the sky, and I suddenly got a bit panicked about travelling the road to work in Glasgow as my window wipers had failed. I thought I should stop at Lugton. Meanwhile this craft is still directly in front, it couldn't be missed, I stopped at Lugton, turned off the engine, turned it back on, and the wipers had indeed failed and wouldn't go back on, I headed home and phoned work, trains cancelled so I took the night off, it began snowing again, I don't know what would have happened if I had travelled either to or home from work".

"As you can see, I'm getting used to seeing these types of things now in the sky, I've never had a camera on me when they appear, I've never felt the need to film them or even if my little digital camera would film in the dark or the sky. It's made me interested in everything to do with UFOs and their origins, and how long they have been here, what they are doing, who they are etc. I don't believe in negative things, it's not good for people, I do believe they have good intentions and are not out to do anything suspect to us. I have never felt one shred of fear seeing any of these sightings, only happiness, hope and excitement, that's why I'm always compelled to wave at these crafts/lights and will continue to for as long as I keep seeing them which I hope is for as long as I live!"
Sincerely, Helen Moore.

THE ROOF TOP UFO

Hi Malcolm,

"I originally sent this email to Nick Pope, not knowing of you until I saw you on Craig Charles T.V. show recently. I don't know if it's of any use to you, but it was a defining moment for me, one that I will never forget".

From Danny Hanley to Nick Pope.

Dear Mr Pope,

"My name is David Hanley, and I live in a town called Kilwinning in North Ayrshire in Scotland. I would like to share with you, an event that happened to me in October 2013".

"It was one night, either the 3rd or 7th of October just as it was getting dark outside. I was sitting in the living room just staring out the window from my chair looking at the street, when I suddenly noticed a set of lights in the sky. I said to my wife *"What the fxxk is that"?* The lights were attached to an object very dark in colour which was moving just above the roof tops of the houses in the street towards my house. As it was moving, the lights disappeared but the object was still there. I ran outside to the balcony of my conservatory and stood in disbelief as this object stopped and hovered above the road. I could make out that it was triangular in shape and looked like a stealth fighter from the front with no obvious cockpit screen. This object made no noise whatsoever, no downdraft, no exhausts or heat source. As it hovered, it was perfectly still, no little corrective movements".

"I lit a cigarette while I watched this object which was facing my house, thinking that this thing is watching me, so I decided to wave to it! After another couple of minutes, it turned and headed away to my left very slowly and eventually disappeared. Judging by its size I reckon it was around 50 feet wide because it was the same width as the street and triangle shaped. To the best of my knowledge no one has technology anything like this. But the one

thing that really amazed me that night, was the way it appeared. One second it wasn't there, and the next it just appeared. I know it must sound stupid, but it was like it had jumped through time, like the way you would see it in a science fiction film. This event has always puzzled me, and I've never told anyone. My wife was so scared that night, that she wouldn't leave the living room and my step daughter ran through to her bedroom when this object appeared. I've contacted you just because you are a leading authority on UFOs and thought you might be interested. Please feel free to contact me if you would like to discuss this event some more".
Thanks. David Hanley.

Author's Comment. Below is how Nick Pope responded.

Hi David,

"Thank you for telling me about your UFO sighting. It sounds fascinating and no obvious conventional explanation comes to mind. While I still comment on UFOs and the unexplained from time to time in the media, now that I've retired from the Ministry of Defence and moved to the U.S., I no longer research or investigate any of this. If you'd like to discuss your sighting with someone or want it investigated, I recommend that you contact an organisation such as BUFORA or ASSAP. I'm not sure that they'll be able to undertake a detailed investigation so long after the event, but if nothing else, they may be able to check to see if they have any reports which by date, location or description might tie in with your own sighting".
Best wishes, Nick Pope.

Author's Comment. As David only sent me this e-mail in 2020 regarding an event that happened in 2013, I still sent e-mails off to various agencies hoping to elicit some kind of answer, none were forthcoming!

THE DISAPPEARING LIGHT!

It was Saturday October 10th, 2010, around 7:05pm, when 47-year-old witness Eric Long happened to glance up into the dark Kilmarnock sky only to see a strange globe of light moving slowly about the sky. This light initially took a straight course to the right, then travelled back on itself, then dropped down and disappeared. Thankfully he had a mind to quickly take some video footage of it with his camera and managed to record six minutes of footage before it was lost to view. Eric sent me the footage which I must admit, it did look a bit strange, similar to other type of footage that has been sent to me over the years, the vast majority of which have turned out to be aircraft. This footage was slightly different, in the course that it took. That's not to say that it might have been some kind of normal aerial object, as busy Prestwick Airport is only a few miles from the location. The witness had a flight tracker on his phone which did 'not' show any aircraft in the vicinity at that particular time. He is well aware of seeing aircraft and helicopters and this, he said, was none of those, plus there was no sound coming from it. I'm always wary of sightings like these as they do often turn out to have natural explanations. For the moment however, this one is unexplained.

Norman Cale's drawing of a UFO he witnessed in 2003

UFO Direction of travel. Norman Cale 2003 UFO sighting

Westall UFO Australia. Similar to Norman Cale UFO

CHAPTER FOUR

Strathclyde Region

STRANGE OBJECT CAPTURED ON RADAR

Author's Comment. It's always great when one of these so-called UFOs can be tracked on radar by a trained and competent radar operator. But when that object is not seen visually, one can no doubt wonder, what was picked up. In June of 2025, I received an e-mail from one Jim Webb who had this to say.

Dear Sir,

"I have just read your latest book on the UFO sightings around Bonnybridge. Having lived in Bonnybridge for over five years, I can honestly say, I was never aware of any unusual activities. I am somewhat surprised that you didn't include the incident at Cumbernauld airport which caused a real furore with Glasgow ATC. It was around 1997/8, and I was a student pilot at the time. A student with instructor were coming into land on runway 27, and as number 2 in the circuit, we were asked to report when visual with aircraft ahead. Its landing light (assumed) was on. The instructor reported negative then all hell broke loose".

"The incoming 'vehicle' streaked down the runway at a rate of knots seeming to give out smoke and was glowing. It then disappeared into Glasgow controlled airspace and proceeded to accelerate to an enormous speed and climbed to over 50000 feet out into the upper atmosphere where Glasgow radar lost it. This was confirmed to me by one of the controllers on duty. The incident was duly recorded as a controlled airspace infringement. The phones from Glasgow ATC were asking Cumbernauld what the hell was going on. Rebecca who is now a pilot with Logan air, was on the radio with ATC duties at Cumbernauld at the time of the incident. She was visibly shocked as were a few others. I got my pilots licence at the end of 1999, and in 12 years of flying around Europe I have never even sniffed a UFO. My only other experience was some strange movements in the sky circa 1955. I was seven at the time and Dan Dare daft".

Regards, Jim Webb.

Author's Comment. I wrote back saying that I had to admit, that I had never heard of this account. I then asked Jim, was he saying that the 'aircraft' that was coming down was 'not' a normal aircraft? Or was it an aircraft in trouble. He wrote back.

Hi Malcolm,

"It was not an aircraft. The flying club had a visit some years later to Glasgow ATC. And the controller on duty the night of the incident was quite clear about what happened. The 'object', he said, left the controlled airspace at a phenomenal speed and was gone in seconds. It flew down the runway from east to west. Glasgow controlled airspace is about 2.5 miles from the end of the runway. It just continued straight ahead. The account of what took place was related to me in Cumbernauld control tower by four people who were there, one-of them was the flying instructor who incidentally was my flying instructor. He was behind it and said he saw nothing and couldn't understand what all the fuss was about. But fuss there was. The incident was real enough. Hope this helps".

Regards, Jim Webb.

Author's Comment. I then asked Jim for more information, he replied.

Malcolm,

"This was a general conversation fielded by one of the groups. You may not like this in the sense it was prompted by the alleged sightings of UFOs over High Bonnybridge. The consensus was that the UFO sightings were due to the white powder the residents blew up their noses and the amount of Buckfast that went down their throats. It was that sort of place. That's when they got round to the event they had witnessed. The persons involved were, as I recall, Mike Anderson (instructor), Lenny, Kenny and Becky. All probably long-gone, lord knows where, after all it was over 25 years ago. The only thing I can add, is that since there had been a controlled airspace infringement, a statuary MOR (mandatory occurrence report) had to have been raised. If so, it should be on file somewhere. At that time the CAA headquarters in Scotland was at Prestwick. If you were the owner of an aircraft every month the CAA would send you a small booklet with a list of 'incidents' as recorded by the air accident investigation board (AAIB). I don't know if these reports are kept on file on the CAA web site. It's worth a look. As a trainee at that time and not an owner, I didn't receive anything. As regards your question and I'm not at all certain in my answers".

A) "I think it was January. 1997/98"

b) "It was about dusk".

c) "As to the report being sent to the MoD, I have no idea, but I doubt it".

d) "As I said previously, even although Mike was following the object, he didn't see a thing! Strange as it may seem".

"As regards the Bonnybridge UFOs. I have had only one other incident that I would give any credence to. I was the managing director of a catering company in Denny. My secretary a very level-headed woman who had an encounter with a UFO which left her traumatised. She wouldn't give details but whatever it was it certainly shook her to the core. I'll have a look at the CAA web site to see if anything is recorded there but I'm not holding my breath. There not the sharpest tacks in the box".

Regards. Jim Webb.

Author's Comment. Well Jim came back and said the following.

Hi Malcolm,

"I have checked UFO incidents in Glasgow controlled air space for 1997/98 and basically hit a brick wall. The incidents were mainly reported by airline pilots and a few members of the public. Now what's known as an Airprox (danger of collision) is a serious situation and has to be investigated. In every case no investigation was carried out as there was no radar record to confirm the presence of another craft. How convenient is that! In some cases, I think that this scenario was factually correct as the radars at Glasgow up until wind farms appeared, were no better than those in use at the end of the war! The replacements were not much better. I can confirm that in talking to one of the controllers, he definitely stated that the radar tracked the object until it entered the upper atmosphere at, as he said, 'supersonic speed'. I think you'll get nothing from the authorities".

Regards, Jim Webb.

Author's Comment. I did look into this but never got anywhere. I wonder what this object was that was tracked on radar but not observed by the pilot flying behind it? Another strange mystery over the skies of Scotland.

CLOSE ENCOUNTER
FOR GEORGE AND HIS FRIENDS

This was the headline from the Kirkintilloch Herald newspaper of September 16th, 2009, upon which a number of other local residents called in to the newspaper with their own UFO sightings. But first, let me present what staff reporter Jill Castle wrote about this strange encounter.

'A shocked driver has described what he believes could have been an encounter with a UFO. George Donnan, (64), was driving with his friends Alistair and Doreen McMillan, when his car was hit by a beam of yellow, green and blue light. The ordeal unfolded as they approached a roundabout on Glen Road, Lennoxtown. George says the beam appeared to be coming from the hillside and lasted around two minutes. He has reported the incident which happened at midnight on Thursday, September 10th to the police. George says.'.

"The zig-zagging beam was made-up of coloured squares which lit up the grass and trees in the surrounding area as well as the road".

'He and his passengers instantly thought it was an ambulance, and he pulled over to let it pass. However, they checked the road and there were no other vehicles in sight. The trio left the scene but returned 5 minutes later to find that the lights had gone. George said it was a terrifying experience'.

"My friends wanted to get out of the car and investigate but I locked the door and told them to stay inside. It was scary, I've never seen anything like it before. We all saw the same thing at the same time. We were absolutely bamboozled by it. I've never seen a UFO before. I never looked for one, because I'm not that type of person. But I suppose in the back of my mind I think that there is something up there".

'The sighting was the second alleged UFO encounter to be reported in the Kirkintilloch area that day. At 8:50pm, a large orange ball which resembled flames was spotted in the sky. It disappeared after two minutes'

Author's Comment. The following week, there was another report in the Kirkintilloch Herald where again staff writer Jill Castle reported more UFO sightings. It read.

'The Herald has been inundated with calls from readers who believe they may have spotted a UFO in the skies above Kirkintilloch. In last week's edition we told how driver George Donnan and his passengers were hit by a strange beam of coloured light as he travelled along Glen Road in Lennoxtown. The beam lit up the surrounding area and vanished after several minutes. Now numerous Herald readers have contacted us with reports of unexplainable sightings throughout the area. Claims include a ball of flames in the sky over Lenzie on Friday

September 11th. A bright orange light over Lennox Forest on Easter Sunday. And red globes over Waterside village on Saturday, September 12th. Experts say sightings like these are not uncommon. Brian McNulty, a member of Strange Phenomena Investigations, (SPI) Scotland, has witnessed many UFO sightings over the years, including an orange ball descending into the Campsie Hills. He has urged members of the public to report sightings so that they can be properly investigated. Brian said'.

"Any strange light or object on or near the ground should never be approached. With mobile phone cameras wildly available, a quick picture from a safe distance would be useful for identification. All UFO sightings should be reported to local or National UFO Investigation groups. Investigators will attempt to identify the cause and log all information. The recent sighting at Lennoxtown reminded me of strange lights seen in Wester Ross in the early 90s. Two witnesses who were flashing their torches at the clear night sky, said that after a few minutes, ladder shaped colour lights unfolded down towards them. This was similar to the zigzagging movement reported a few days ago in this area".

Author's Comment. I think what Brian was referring to above about the Wester Ross sighting, was in fact myself with a fellow UFO witness we were indeed flashing our torches into the dark night sky and were stunned to see a column of light descend from the sky, then stop, then shoot right back up into the sky and was gone in seconds. My good friend Brian McMullan (Jnr) lives in the Lennoxtown area and saw these newspaper reports and sent the following information into the Kirkintilloch Herald for the attention of Jill Castle. He wrote.

Hi Jill.

"An Unidentified Flying Object is exactly what it says it is! These days with our skies filled with various man-made objects and junk, it becomes difficult to identify what is really up there! Aircraft, satellites, weather balloons, party balloons even astronomical objects such as meteors, planets, the moon, and

Venus in the morning sky, have all been mistaken for UFOs. We do get used to viewing these, and most objects become identifiable, but in the case of the recent sighting in Lennoxtown, where witnesses viewed strange lights seemingly targeting their car, then circumstances change. These particular lights were causing fear and alarm, and it was the right decision to report this to the Police. Unless there is a 'flap' or a 'wave' as occurred in the Bonnybridge sightings, then there is really no such thing as a typical sighting for a particular area. Over a period of years other sightings have connections to this area. In July 1985 three witnesses saw an 'amber ball' descending eventually becoming a saucer shape. This appeared to come from the area of the Campsie Fells. They viewed this from the north of Glasgow".

"Another case in 2007 was near Bishopbriggs, where two witnesses in a car saw what they believed to be a 'cow' being lowered into a farmer's field. It was about 20 feet up, moving along, before being lowered. Nothing could be seen 'holding' the animal in the air. It was at dusk, so the mobile camera revealed nothing. They stopped the car as they approached the field and saw other cows 'running' and making a bit of a racket!"

"In December 2002 in the Robroyston area, two witnesses in a car viewed a diamond shaped stationary object with coloured lights high in the night sky above their car. This same object was also seen by other witnesses in March 2003 in same area! Although we lived in Glasgow until recently, we tended to put in some skywatching time in the Campsie Hills. We would park the van and climb to a high point where we had a good view of the surrounding skyline. On one occasion, we saw an amber coloured ball of light to the north. As it flew overhead, we noticed that a large passenger plane heading towards Glasgow airport seemed to be on a direct collision course with the object. The object speeded up and did a sharp 90-degree turn missing the plane before disappearing in a flash into the night sky. An impossible manoeuvre for an earthly craft and amazing to watch! Should Kirkintilloch and its surrounding areas produce a high number of UFO sightings we can call on extra investigators from SPI Scotland".

"I would say in Scotland there are around a couple of hundred sightings a month. Many of these are spread out among other groups. There are of course many more sightings we don't hear about. Witnesses view all sorts of UFOs and have experiences but sadly through criticism and ridicule, they tend to keep things to themselves. All UFO groups have a privacy policy, and only if the witness wishes then his or her names will be logged in a report. Only the group and the witness can view these reports. Lots of witness sightings still tend to be identifiable but there still remain a small but interesting percentage of unexplainable true UFOs".

"One thing is certain though. Strange things are happening to ordinary people every day. Situations completely out with our control and understanding and always occurring when least expected. The scientific world always asks 'how' but never 'why'.
Brian McMullan. SPI Scotland. Gabriel Society.

AN ENORMOUS CRAFT JUST SUDDENLY APPEARED!

Author's Comment. Our next case file to some, may seem more than out of the ordinary, and that the witness may have misinterpreted a normal airliner. That said, his testimony would seem to say something different, and yet, he still refers to it as a spacecraft! Here is what he had to say to me.

"It was August 2019, and I was sitting on the back doorstep at my home in East Kilbride looking through a large gap that formed in the clouds, The light was failing as it was about eight or nine o clock at night. All of a sudden, I noticed a moving series of lights (red, green and blue) dropping out of the clouds just to the left of the gap. Suddenly a spacecraft of immense size burst out the bottom of the clouds. It levelled out just under the opening in the clouds taking a slight turn to the left a few degrees, then it suddenly powered up and lifted back up through the clouds on the other side, I would say that it was visible was no more than 10 seconds. It had a power system in the shape of an = sign on

the back of it of which two banks of like ultraviolet light were emitting, (same colour as a banknote checker) The main body of the craft was white, and it didn't have any wings so I'm thinking this has to be antigravity. I also think this craft is manmade and not extraterrestrial in origin. I actually think this is one of NASA's craft that the hacker Gary McKinnon, said he uncovered on his sojourn into their database. I got a new iPhone 12 in 2020, and noticed I had a compass app on it, so I measured the position the object was in from my door and cross referenced that data with Google maps, and found that it was in the direction of Dechmont Hill in East Kilbride. While I can't tell how far off in the distance that it was, I'm pretty sure Dechmont Hill was in the general area. There was no sound and no smell. This spacecraft was huge and was probably about 10 miles away. I'd say you could have landed an airplane on top of it due to its size".

Regards. Tim Barry.

Author's Comment. Tim refers to Dechmont Hill, which was the scene of one of Scotland's most famous UFO events, the Robert Taylor Incident. I wouldn't put too much stock on the fact that this sighting was in that direction, if indeed it was! Tim's word play using words like, 'Spacecraft' and 'Anti-Gravity', all make one wonder if his particular observation was either mistaken, or 'something else'!

THE ENTITY IN THE BEDROOM

Author's Comment. Our next case file is one which 'may' have had a different conclusion! There are those who would say it was all but a dream, and others who would say that what this gentleman observed, is consistent with other worldwide observations. It was in the early hours of the 24th of October 2012 (approximately 01:30am) when Jim Kale's perception of reality was changed. Jim lives on the edge of a small village called Elsrickle near Biggar at the foot of Blackmount Hill, (the last of the Pentland Hills) which is around 500 metres from Scotland's, and possibly the UK's, oldest known and recently discovered habitation. Here in his own words is what he recalls about that night.

"I remember going to bed with an unresolved work problem (quite normal) and was trying to figure out how to deal with it. My daughter couldn't sleep and was in our bed, my wife was in our son's bedroom, (she also couldn't sleep). I can't remember the lead up to the event, all I can remember is that thoughts and feelings were becoming quite unusual, irrational and not completely my own, culminating in a vision of Edinburgh Castle (the image I am working on), when suddenly a metallic disc slowly moves into the picture, followed shortly after by another. (I presume) my subconscious said, "Oh my god they're here", a feeling of dread and immediately at this point 'it started'. The immediacy was shocking, something like an electric shock. I was lying on my back quite awake. I was physically paralysed. I remember trying to reach out to my daughter and I couldn't even raise a finger. My body felt like it was vibrating and going through the physical effects of the sound I was hearing which was profound. The sound was somewhere between mechanical and electrical, a fast rotation at various frequencies resulting in a fairly quick pulsating sound. (Imagine a recording of some grass cutters speeded up with a faint whistle noise in the background)"

"During the first 15/20 second occurrence, I was aware of the room. My daughter still asleep next to me, my wife and son next door, and even the particular shadow of a tree on the window blind highlighted by the moon. Whether I broke free from it or I was allowed to, I don't know, but I resumed full body control, and the sound disappeared. I heard a noise at the window which I was sure my wife would have heard (she didn't) and then noticed a figure standing next to the bed, (my daughter's side). I didn't get a great view at all, to be honest, I was too petrified to look. It was a tall skeletal figure, albeit in watery vision. Head close to the ceiling (2.4m), very thin and white. The pulsating and paralysis happened again, this time for perhaps 10 seconds, (although time appeared to have stopped) I felt as if I were being taken somewhere against my will which I resisted. Afterwards I felt a sensation of numbness returning to normal and slight pain on my left big toe. Needless to say, I didn't sleep that night and my daughter had a very restless night and has not wanted to go to bed on her own since. I'm not new to the reality of UFO's, however this event has cast a whole new light on the subject. I can only describe the event as 'pure trauma' and fear which I have never before experienced. On a Google search I have found a number of witness events recalling strange humming, pulsating sounds across the U.K. on this date, but none with a similar experience. Perhaps they're connected? Anyway, I thought I would pass this on to you considering your research".

Best. Jim Kale.

Author's Comment. Well, that was certainly different. It would seem to me that either Jim was sleeping and having some kind of scary lucid dream, or 'something' entered his consciousness then appeared by the side of his bed. What I found interesting, was when Jim described this 'skeletal being' in a 'watery vision'! I recall investigating the Falkland Hill UFO, and whilst interviewing one of the witnesses at her home, she became aware that there were three small 'beings' standing next to her living room window of which were appearing to her in a watery shimmery way of which she stated if she looked any longer, that effect would disappear and she would see them standing there in their entirety. One could say that Jim might have been abducted but only remembers part of his ordeal, the start and the end, but the middle is missing!

UFO OVER A COMBINE HARVESTER

Author's Comment. Our next case file concerns a farmer out working in the field minding his own business. It was either 1974 or 1975, the witness John McStay can't recall what exact year it was. Then, all of a sudden, things began to take a different turn as John now recounts.

Hi Malcolm,

"I used to farm for a well-known East Kilbride family by the surname of Hamilton. The late Jim Hamilton had a small lake named after him near his farm 'Mains Farm East Kilbride'. In the mid 1970's whilst combine harvesting barley late at night, I saw a UFO hovering above me for about 30 odd seconds. It was

a clear evening with no cloud, and the time was around 10:00pm. I was operating the combine harvester when I saw through the side of my left eye, a light above in the sky. I looked up and saw an orange-coloured ball like object. It hovered over me for about say 30 seconds and it was about 100 feet in the air. I was scared and shut down the combine harvester and put out the lights. I just watched this thing. Then all of a sudden, without any noise, it took off at a very high speed like you would see as a special effect in a movie, but it was real. The year was 1974 or 1975. I will never forget the experience. The location was Stewartfield Farm East Kilbride, next to Mains Farm, where Mains Castle is located. Just thought you would like to know the story. I now live in Harare Zimbabwe Africa. I now believe in these UFOs".
Sincerely John McStay.

Author's Comment. I've said many times before, that it's not always strange, structured objects that people report seeing, more often than not, it's balls of light which still puzzle the watching observer. Are these just a natural earth-based phenomenon, like ball lightning, or are they something different? One thing's for sure; they sure are a lot of them!

THE STRANGE LIGHT IN THE FARMHOUSE

Fran Barnbrook informed me of two strange UFO incidents in her life. The first, concerns a strange light that penetrated a friend's farmhouse in the middle of the night. Here is what she had to say.

"My UFO sighting happened 30 years ago, would make it 1995 and concerns my weekend away at a friend's cottage on her farm near Biggar in Scotland which was well off the main road. Behind the cottage is just fields down to the river. My husband was with me but went away overnight to visit his elderly mother. I was with two of our Irish Wolfhounds, Abbie and Bentley. The cottage had an entrance hall, to the right was the bathroom, ahead was the kitchen, and from the kitchen there was a door on the left that took you into a bedroom/lounge. There was a window at each end of this long room, two single beds to the left, and a couple of armchairs to the right. My friend's 14-year-old daughter Cathrine asked to stay with me that night and we settled down to read in bed with a wolfhound up beside us on each bed. Around midnight I said to Catherine, *"It's time to sleep we will be up early"*. I put off the lamp and closed my eyes. Within minutes I could see what I first thought was lighting, flashing in the kitchen (but not in the bedroom)! I watched for a minute and realised this was NOT lighting. Both dogs were standing on our bed's, heads tilting side to one side listening to a strange wooo wooo noise that matched the flashing light. Our bedroom glowed with a strange green light. I thought maybe it's poachers, but then suddenly, a bar of brilliant white light came in the window and started to scan the room".

"It went up the wall, over the ceiling, then down behind us. As it came over us, I put my hand into it, and it disappeared in the brightness. I kept thinking what the hell is this. I said to Cathrine, *"Can you see this"*. *"Yyyes"*, she replied in a terrified voice. As the beam reached the bottom of the beds (the dogs were still standing on them, watching too) The beam suddenly stood on its end and went into the kitchen to scan it. I switched a lamp on and everything stopped. Cathrine was sat up in bed terrified, I said don't worry, the dogs will not let anyone hurt us. Strange, but I wasn't in the least afraid, just really curious. I said I'm just going to switch the light off again, and as I did, it all started up again. The light went straight back on all night! We both got up and looked out the windows. There was nothing but fields out there. I could see a light on in the farmhouse but no sign of anything that would cause this. In the morning, we told my friend Julia what had happened, and she said she saw and heard nothing. Next thing I know she's on the phone to a local newspaper asking if anyone had reported anything to them. 'No' was the reply. Fortunately, she didn't say much and got off the phone. This happened about 30 years ago, but it's still so fresh in my mind like it was yesterday. I've never seen anything like it since, but I know it happened. I have another one for you".

"I was driving between Kirkcaldy and Kinghorn in 1995ish. My son's friend, Emma was with me. As we drove along the road, Eleanor said, *"What's that?"* I looked over and stopped the car! We were above the River Forth and looking down from the hill onto a large grey ship thing, it was triangular at both ends but long in the middle. It was kind of that gun metal grey with no shine. It was sitting above the cloud hiding from anything on the ground. There was nothing in the water below it and it just sat there. Lots of cars stopped behind us and people got out to look at it. I have no idea what it was, but it made no noise".

Author's Comment. As for the first account of the strange light that entered the farmhouse and went from room to room. There are those that will say that this could have been a helicopter's search light more so as the witness said that there was a strange 'woo woo' sound that accompanied the light. Certainly, that's the first thing that came to my mind. But then we have to consider that the witness would surely have known this. Plus, she describes a strange green light followed by a white light. As for her second sighting of the gun metal triangular object in the clouds, well, that too looks strange.

THE SILENT TRIANGLE

Author's Comment. The witness, Ron Carr and his three friends had left the Weavers pub in Condorrat, where they admit they had been drinking but were not drunk. As they drove along the road, they witnessed something strange as Ron now describes.

"It was September 1997, and my friends and I had left the Weavers pub at 12.40am on a Saturday night (early Sunday morning) and walked to a swing park at Pollock Hall on Maree Drive Condorrat and chatted. We had only been there maybe half an hour or so when I noticed a red light which seemed to be floating towards the north. I said to my three friends, *"Hey look at that"*, and fully expected it to become clearer and that it would be an aircraft. Within ten seconds or so it became clearer. It had more than one light on it, and then we could see three red lights in a perfect equilateral triangle. But I really tried to see what was between the lights but just found it to be the exact colour of the night sky behind it, although my mate Paul, claimed he could see a shiny black metal between the lights I couldn't. I would say it was travelling about 30mph roughly and drifted past us silently. If this object was a helicopter, it wouldn't have been more than 600 metres away although it was very hard to judge. We watched it leave towards the northwest of Glasgow from us in a straight line over the next five to ten minutes. It didn't seem to change speed or direction it just got smaller until it was one red light and was almost impossible to see. I will add that the triangle was upright as in the two lights were at the bottom sort of parallel to the ground and the top light was the point, a bit like a flying pyramid. So, on the face of it not that much happened."

The dream!

"However, about six weeks later I had a dream (and I will only give a quick summary here) This is about the craft coming down closer and us getting excited wondering about running away and a voice in my head saying, *"You won't be harmed"* which was coming from the craft. The craft landed then we were taken aboard. We were terrified. The craft completely stank. It was the worst smell ever. The smell made you scared it was that bad. Once inside, an alien asked us which one of us was the in charge of our group and I said me (don't know why) and it said, *"Can you calm him down"*, I looked across to see my other three mates standing staring blankly, but my third friend who was standing on the far right, was standing in the same position, however his head was shaking and seemed hysterical with fear, so I started saying things like, *"It's OK Alan they said they won't hurt us"*, but was stopped by the alien who said, *"You can't do it, you are not in charge we will do it ourselves"*. It is sketchy now, but I was shown pictures of space and of their planet and of Earth. I was also shown nuclear explosions and that made me upset. I asked them to tell me where they came from, but he said there is no point as you wouldn't understand. I asked again saying, *"I am clever. I will, I will, I'm clever"*. He eventually said OK, and something came into my brain, but I couldn't understand it. I asked if any human could understand it, and he said there are some, but not many. Then, another type of being appeared, a lot more scary looking and black coloured. I was then put on a table, and some things were done to me. Seamen was taken from me by 'him'. I remember it was like a rush of pornography that was injected into my mind. They also said our planet was in danger. I think they meant the atmosphere, and I was asked why we treat the animals so badly, which upset me, as I love animals, and felt shame that they didn't distinguish between me and farmers or abattoir workers or hunters or whatever. Anyway, it came time to send us back and they told me I wouldn't remember what happened. I was begging, pleading with them to let me remember it. I was saying this is far too important to be erased, please let me remember, and he said, *"It will come back to you"*.

"I also have the impression that I was shown around the ship, and we were all taken into space, though I don't remember floating. I also have a memory (though I'm not sure where I got it from) of being in a room with all these glass doored little cubicles on the wall, top to bottom, and the whole length held growing babies or embryos, 'all mine'! And at the end of the room there was one incubator type thing on a stand on the floor. I was told to go over and pick up the baby which was 'mine', and as I picked up the baby and held it, it was like I felt all the love I could ever produce flowing from me. I have never felt anything remotely like it in my life. I was asking to keep the baby but wasn't allowed".

"So, I don't know what to make of this dream or dreams. I just don't know. But when I had the dream, I remember how it wasn't like a normal dream, it seemed real. I watched a programme about ten years ago and it shook me cold to see so many similarities with other people who have witnessed something. I would also add that I barely tell anyone about seeing the craft never mind my dream".

THE BLACK TRIANGLE CRAFT

Author's Comment. In a series of e-mails from Ron, he told me about other UFO sightings that he has had. Take for instance this one which features a large triangular shaped object. Ron now takes up the story.

Hi Malcolm,

"It was the 30th of March 2019 around 9:00pm. I was in Crathie Drive, Denny. not far from Bonnybridge heading north, then everything stopped, and it went dark. I found myself spinning around for about one minute. Then the lights came back on, and heading towards me roughly northeast over my house, was a massive craft 2,000 feet in the sky. This craft was massive, bigger than the biggest airliner by five to ten times. There were lit areas on the craft, and the effect actually looked like if you had white smoked glass illuminated from behind. The 'glass' area had a semi-circle edge to the inside and went to the corner of the craft. The corners were rounded and softened. It was a very strange thing to look at. It was like I was looking through night vision goggles at it. This light had a slight green hue. It almost looked like it was a projection on the sky made of black light. It looked like it was having darkness shone upon it. which is impossible".

Author's Comment. Well, the UFO that Ron saw with his three friends must have been a sight to behold. But then there is this so-called dream that Ron had six weeks after the initial sighting. Was it just an overactive imagination after the sighting, or did something else happen that night, in other words, a UFO abduction? We can but wonder. In his e-mail correspondence to me, Ron stated that he has seen a total of four UFOs, two of which he has managed to capture on video. His first sighting was of a fluorescent green object hovering above the runway at RAF Leuchars in Fife, of which he claims two Harrier jets were scrambled to investigate this object. His second sighting was of an orb which he managed to view in binoculars as it headed north over the North Sea off the coast of Fife. Ron's massive smoked glass shaped craft which he saw in Denny (near the UFO Hot Spot of Bonnybridge) well, if we go with his testimony, it does not resemble any known normal man-made aircraft.

WHEN IS A PICNIC NOT A PICNIC?

Author's Comment. Our next case file is yet another strange one. More so due to the very nature of how it made the witness, Paul Hanton feel. This astonishing event was witnessed in Paul's previous home, which was in Ivanhoe, in Calderwood, East Kilbride, South Lanarkshire. Paul now explains what happened.

"It was a weekend, I think in September of 2005. The sky was a clear blue colour, and the sun was still warm. My 5-year-old son and I were heading out for some lunch at a local fast-food restaurant at the retail centre, it has a kid's soft play area which he loves, but on that day, it was really busy, so we decided instead we'd eat our takeout lunch al 'a picnic style in the garden. We arrived home and parked up. As we exited the car to walk toward the flat, I felt a sudden sense, 'notable euphoria'. I happily embraced this random feeling making everything seem just right. The sense grew until I had to stop for a moment. With my feet together, I took a deep breath and went with it. The wave travelled from my head down my body, I remember thinking how strange it was, as I'd never had that before. At home, I prepared the picnic feast while my son was playing with our border collie".

"We moved outside into the front garden. It was about 1:00pm in the afternoon. As we sat outside, the wind blew some of the paper bags around. Securing the rest of the light paper, I heard my son ask me what that was, and as I turned to him, he was looking directly at me. I asked him *"What was what?"* and he pointed to the sky. I looked up, and to my surprise, there was a large square metallic object with deep blue windows on each face, just floating there in the sky, stationary and silent directly above us, maybe 400 or so feet away. My eyes were transfixed on this amazing object. I noticed a black cable coming from the underneath, it seemed to be moving towards us, snake like in the sky. It was extending out and to the right of the craft. I watched as the cable reached closer. I could then see two larger features, with two smaller round features in the middle in a rectangular casing of some kind. It looked to me, like an array of camera lenses or something. I was staring directly into it for a while, and glancing at the object, allowing the images to burn into my retina and mind. I had that euphoric feeling again, but it was more intense now, something changed, something has happened. I can't tell you what it is, but I can feel it. I can feel them in my mind now. I glance back at the object and feel this connection become crystal clear with the beings; I can hear them in my mind now. A sense of panic starts to grip me; this was potent and powerful. I can hear voices louder than my own inner voice, too loud. I can't seem to stop them. Looking at the object I can see shadows in the windows, are these the occupants? I glanced back to the cable, which was much closer now, too close, so I moved to gesture my son to come and sit next to me on the picnic blanket. I was filling with fear now. My rational self is in full panic mode. How could I be seeing this? How could this be real? How can I hear them? Everything we've been told about UFOs is false, everything I knew about this subject is a lie, because here they are interacting with me in this intimate way, this is not supposed to be possible".

"When I look back on that time, I now realize it was the fear of being unable to shift my rational mind into this new reality, but still in this altered dual state of euphoria and fear, I looked at my son who seemed to need some re-assurance. I was calm and told him not to worry, that they'd be gone in a minute, but inside I was sure that this was it, it was all going to end here and now. That seems crazy to me now, because I knew they weren't malevolent, but my mind was racing a hundred miles an hour. After a few more seconds, I quickly looked up again and to my surprise, relief and disappointment the object had gone. Standing up, I looked in all directions to see it travelling away, but the sky was empty, not even a cloud as far as my eyes could see. I sat back down in complete silence. I noticed I was trembling a little, doing everything I could to keep calm with an external appearance of control. I picked up the blankets and papers and we finished our meal inside. It was then I noticed it was 4:00pm, and a few hours seem to have vanished because the incident only seemed to last about 10 to 15 minutes. This event has completely changed my life for the better, because I now realize we are not alone in the Universe. The questions are whether they travel here with interstellar or inter-dimensional craft, whether they hang out locally on the moon, or are just more advanced indigenous races right here on Earth, either way they're here and I can still hear them".

Sincerely, Paul Hanton.

KIRKY HERALD 17/2/10

UFOs spotted over Kirkintilloch

THE UFO phenomena in East Dunbartonshire has taken another twist, with a mum and her young son reporting another sighting in the area.

Kathleen Scanlan and nine-year-old son Peter saw two orange balls hovering over Kirkintilloch as they unpacked their car at their home in Milton of Campsie on the night of Wednesday, January 27.

Kathleen said the two balls, which were slightly apart, were the size of footballs and moving together diagonally. They then became smaller and disappeared.

The mum-of-three is now desperate to find out what the orbs were and insists, because of their shape, she does not think they were chinese lanterns.

Kathleen said: "I have never seen anything like it before.

"It was a bit strange. I did not want to move away and stop watching them.

"I didn't know what it was, I was just kind of mesmerised. I know it was definitely not a plane. I could see it as it got smaller.

"My wee boy Peter was so excited to see it. When my other kids, John and Erin, came out there was only one ball left and then it disappeared completely.

"I am not sure if I believe in UFOs, but surely other people would have seen it – especially when it was over Kirkintilloch. I'm quite intrigued as to what it was.

"There have been a few sightings in the area. I had not thought anything was going on until I saw that. It was very unusual whatever it was."

Kirkintilloch Herald 17th February 2010

CHAPTER FIVE

Edinburgh and Lothian Region

Not quite what we expected on an SPI sky watch!
(Cairnpapple Hill Sky Watch. Saturday 22nd June 2024)

What you are about to read, was initially featured on my Facebook site, written the morning after a SPI sky watch at Cairnpapple Hill. As you will see, the night was not quite what I expected!

(SPI stands for Strange Phenomena Investigations, which the author set up in 1979. SPI are Scotland's oldest UFO and Paranormal society).

Well, what an astonishing SPI sky watch we had at Cairnpapple Hill near Bathgate Central Scotland last night (22nd June 2024). However, not for the reasons you would imagine! More of that in a moment. Twelve lovely souls gathered at this 4,000-year-old Neolithic burial hill which featured numerous satellite burial graves in the ground surrounding it. The views from Cairnpapple hill are simply stunning, and, as far as views go for sky watching, well you would be hard pushed to find anything better. It affords one a complete 360-degree vista of the sky and landscape. I hadn't visited this site since the 1990's when SPI were there to film a piece for some now forgotten television programme. I recall that the TV people hired a helicopter to film SPI members at the hill (yes, the days before drones) But back to this sky watch. Whilst the views were kind, the sky wasn't, and although there was a slight breeze, it wasn't really cold, although it did get a bit nippy around 11:30pm or so. I asked SPI's Mark Anderson to bring all those assembled up to speed by telling us of the many UFO and paranormal events that had happened near the hill over the years, and boy, let me tell you, there were more than a few. Gavin Dow then spoke about his mystical experiences at the hill, which for him, was like a second home, another great talk.

And then we had the unexpected!

Now dear reader, are you sitting comfortably? You are! good. For what I'm about to inform you, may prove incredible to those of a sceptical nature, but fascinating to those that believe! What am I on about? Well, as we were all scanning the skies in hopes of a celestial visitor, there were two, close at hand!

SPI's psychic medium Steven Bird broke the silence by stating to me and those assembled, that he felt that he was being pulled upwards. Furthermore, he stated that the energies surrounding the hill were incredible (something that others, including Mark Anderson, Jackie Gillies and Gavin Dow had also commented on) Steven stated that around 300 yards or so away from us, he saw through his third eye, two silver white beings standing beside some form of white craft. The beings were around three to four feet tall with very large heads, bigger than a Grey's.

Author's Comment. I refer to the oft described small 'beings' seen in association with UFOs.

Now let me tell you this. I have seen Steven's mediumship at various Spiritualist churches across Central Scotland, and he has had people in tears with his clairvoyant accuracy, and whilst what he was saying now was totally unexpected, I knew it to be true. If he said he was seeing this, then he was bloody well seeing this. Now all this was unseen by the rest of us, but this in itself is no big surprise, for as we know, not all have this wonderful clairvoyant gift.

The Channelling begins!

About 10 minutes later, I was speaking with fellow sky watcher Margaret Tollan away from the rest of the group. Steven Bird then joined us, and I asked him if he could still see these two 'beings' and their craft. He said he could and described to

Margaret and I what he was looking at. Now here is where things get interesting. Steven's demeanour then changed, and he unexpectantly, (certainly to Margaret and I) started to channel one of these 'beings'. Now it's true to say that Steven has never ever channelled an alien before. His life has been providing life after death communication from loved ones to family members, and here he was, atop of a lonely Scottish hill, providing some astonishing revelations, revelations coming from 'someone' not of this Earth! I looked at Margaret, and she looked at me, and we both had faces of awe.

What happened next!

I now had the task of listening back to the audio tape and transcribing it. Sadly, on playback, one can hear the wind howling across Cairnpapple Hill, and in part, it was difficult to make out what Steven was saying. However, Steven came over to my house a few days later where we listened again to the tape and inserted the missing words which were hard to hear on the tape, although some parts we couldn't hear and couldn't put down) Here is the transcript from the recording that I did with Steven Bird on Cairnpapple Hill. It starts off by Steven talking about what he saw about 300 yards away, then suddenly things took a different turn!

Malcolm Robinson: *"I'm here with Steven Bird and we are on a sky watch at Cairnpapple Hill near Bathgate. Steven has just surprised me, and I just want to get this down on tape for posterity as its very important. Steven, whilst I was speaking to the sky watchers about the area that we are in, you said you physically saw something. Would you like to explain?"*

Steven Bird: *"Physically no. What I saw was with my third eye. It was a small space craft over there* (Steven points in the direction) *with two, silvery white, four foot tall, what you would class as alien beings. One was named Aktor, and the other one, Ilieus, and they are from the planet called Agneta, which is a water-based planet. They also told me that they had been here for 300 years, and they were here to try and help the human race* *not to destroy itself and the planet. There are many of their kind on the planet all doing the same job, and their civilisation is based on love and trust. They are very peaceful beings. They are scientists. They are looking around the universe to see what is there, and how they can help. I'll try and get them to channel them through me".*

(NB) At this point Steven closed his eyes for a moment. All was quiet and it was just Margaret Tollan and I standing beside Steven. The rest of the skywatchers were around 25 to 35 feet away doing their own thing. Then Steven spoke.

Steven Bird/Aktor: *"We are of one species. We live to love; we love to study. We are everywhere. We gather in groups; we share knowledge from everywhere we visit. We have been here many centuries, but we live many thousands of years. Our utmost gratitude is with the human race, for they have taught us, where they have gone wrong, where we can teach others and we find it difficult to speak to the people in charge. They are very greedy. They live for money; they live for asset. They don't live to love. We cannot speak to the right people. Your planet needs love. Your planet needs care. Your planet is dying. It's not too late to save it, but we need to speak to the right people. We find that maybe, this is an impossible task. We try, we try, we try. We will try and make ourselves visible as the light dims".*

(NB) Steven, or the being who was speaking through Steven, was implying that they might show themselves at this sky watch).

Steven Bird/Aktor: *"We will try and communicate if you stay here. Please understand that we are only here to help, that no harm will ever come to you from us".*

Malcolm Robinson: *"Thank you for imparting that information. Am I speaking to the person that is coming through Steven Bird, and if so, can I speak to you"?*

Steven Bird/Aktor: *"I will talk."*

Malcolm Robinson: *"Will you be able to show yourself to the people in this area tonight at Cairnpapple Hill, can you do that"?*

Steven Bird/Aktor: *"We will try, there are many that will see. We cannot guarantee that we will be visible to many".*

Malcolm Robinson: *"What is your main purpose for being here on planet Earth? Do you have a purpose"?*

Steven Bird/Aktor: *"Science".*

Malcolm Robinson: *"Science"!*

Steven Bird/Aktor: *"Science and creativity. Care. Protection. We are here to try and help".*

Margaret Tollan: *"Who do you want to speak to, to help the planet. Who are the right people that you need to be in touch with"?*

Steven Bird/Aktor: *"Most people would not be able to see us. They are surrounded by all they love. They love power, they do not love people".* (inaudible)

Malcolm Robinson: *"How long have you been with humankind"?*

Steven Bird/Aktor: *"We have been here for 300 odd years. We have been here before".*

Malcolm Robinson: *"Have you assisted mankind with the building of any structures on this planet"?*

Steven Bird/Aktor: *"We are unable to connect in a way that is meaningful. Your structure does not allow it..."*

Malcolm Robinson: *"To your knowledge, are there any other species working with you"?*

Steven Bird/Aktor: *"We work alone. There are many species not from this planet that are here".*

Malcolm Robinson: *"How long is your lifetime"?*

Steven Bird/Aktor: *"We live for thousands of years in the physical".*

Margaret Tollan*: "Have you helped the planet in other ways instead of just visiting".*

Steven Bird/Aktor: *"Study".*

Margaret Tollan*: "Study*

Steven Bird/Aktor: *"We have studied as we come amongst you. We won't be heard".* (inaudible)

Malcolm Robinson: *"Do you see a change in mankind in the next 50 years, or will things be much the same, or will there be vast differences. In other words, changes to the eco system, deforestation".*

Steven Bird/Aktor: *"We see a downward spiral. We do not see positivity. We see the death of your planet".*

Malcolm Robinson: *"Can you intervene and stop these cataclysmic events, this death knell of planet Earth"?*

Steven Bird/Aktor: *"We are scientists, we cannot speak. We have no access".*

Margaret Tollan: *"Who do you report back to with your findings that you get"?*

Steven Bird/Aktor: *"Our love. We are one".*

(NB) At this point Steven was swaying backwards and forwards and looked to be coming out of what appeared to be a 'trance like state' and as much as Margaret and I hoped to ask many more questions, I felt it best to end it there. I continued.

Malcolm Robinson: *"Well I'd like to thank you very much for parting with your knowledge, and we do hope that perhaps you can show yourselves this evening to these people here on Cairnpapple Hill. Have you any final words that you would like to say"?*

Steven Bird/Aktor: *"Take care and know that not everything is what it seems".* (inaudible) *"Know that things may heal you. Be aware of the energy"*

Margaret Tollan: *"Is that on Cairnpapple Hill. Is that in this area alone"?*

Steven Bird/Aktor: *"We speak for everyone. Doors are open. If you know not what to do, do not step through them".*

Margaret Tollan: *"Thank you".*

Steven Bird/Aktor: *"My host is tired".*

Margaret Tollan: *"Thank you".*

Malcolm Robinson: *"Thank you sir. Thank you for joining with us this evening."*

Steven Bird/Aktor: *"Bless".*

(NB) At this point I walked away for a few yards and spoke into the microphone. This is what I said.

Malcolm Robinson: *"Well that was quite astonishing. Steven Bird went into some form of trance and was communicating these beings through him.* (NB. Steven told me later that it was only Aktor who communicated through him) *He is now being supported by Margaret Tollan as he almost stumbled there and fell. Astonishing. Absolutely astonishing. There are so many* *questions that I would love to have asked, but it's just one of those instances where you are put on the spot. Wow, that was incredible".*

End of tape.

(NB) This conversation lasted on tape for 10 minutes and 32 seconds. I asked Steven the following day, if he could now recall anything about that communication, because at the time he couldn't. This is what he said in an e-mail to me.

Sunday, 23 June 2024 at 10:34

Hi Malcolm.

"As we approached the site, I did not feel a great deal in energy terms, it was only when I sat down that I felt that I was being pulled upwards. My temples were throbbing, and at that point I became aware of two humanoid figures and a craft of sorts some 100 yards away in front of me at the base of the mound".

"The 'beings' and craft were a silvery white in colour, and they all seemed to have a protection bubble surrounding them. One of them spoke to me and introduced himself as Aktor and the other Ilieus. They said they were from the planet they call Agneta. Their words I saw clearly in my third eye. Aktor went on to say that they and many others, had visited Earth over Millenia. They had been here for some 300 Earth years themselves. They told me that their planet was a water planet, and that they were scientists that travelled the Universe. They were here to try and help Earth live better and educate the populace how to keep her in good condition, but that we were failing in this task and on a downward spiral. They were frustrated that the leaders in charge of the earth would not listen to them, even though they were aware of their presence. I asked if they could reveal their presence, and they replied that they would try, but most people would not see them. One of the people present however had an app on his cell phone that took special pictures that were remarkably similar to the vision of them I saw".

(NB). I'll come to that soon.

"They warned me of a Demonic entity that appears occasionally and asked me to put a ring of projection around the whole site which I did immediately. They also mentioned that the area contains many portals from time to time, and just to be careful. I personally felt that above the hill was a wormhole from the pulling sensation I had throughout the visit. The next morning, I drew what I saw and also wonder whether the strange lights in the sky from my house my wife and I had seen recently, was this craft! During the night they asked me if I could channel them and present this for Malcolm and Margaret. Upon leaving the area they wished me well".

Two days later, (25th June 2024) I received the following e-mail from Steven Bird. It read.

"Further to Saturday night, I have not been feeling right. A sense of foreboding and not being myself hit me on Tuesday. I was advised to meditate by my guide Howard. During his session I was visited by a spirit surgeon whose name was Dr Chakrabourty. This surgeon was gobsmacked to see that my energy centres known as chakras were covered in slime. He asked what had occurred to cause this, and I told him that I had channelled two alien beings who were from a water planet and that they were probably the cause after I had channelled them. Baffled and amazed, he set about clearing the slime away from me, only to find my chakras were in better condition than before. He had never seen the like of which and took samples from me to study".

"He said he would come back to me with the result in a couple of days. Before he left me, he urged caution in the future with this idea of channelling nonhuman lifeforms, but he knows that I was secretly fascinated by the outcome. I now, after a few more hours, feel as normal as I can, and await the results from my surgeon".
Steven Bird.

Further recollections

On the 25th of June 2024, I had Steven Bird come over to my house where we sat down and listened to the recording that I did with him on Cairnpapple Hill. This was to ensure that I had transcribed everything correctly, and which might allow Steven to recall anything else upon listening to the tape. I asked Steven if he would be happy to discuss with me more about that night, and anything else that he recalled. Here is what he said.

Malcolm: *"Hi Steven, it's been a few days now since our sky watch at Cairnpapple Hill and you have had time to reflect on what occurred that night. But I believe that something happened last night or in the early hours of this morning which was a communication from your guides in regard to what happened at Cairnpapple Hill. Tell us about that".*

Steven: *"Well I could tell you what happened with the communication from my guide, but first I must reiterate about these two beings. I don't really want to call them aliens because the way that they made me feel. It was like as if we were brothers across the universe. Everything in the universe is connected that I am aware of, and we all have some potential to communicate with not just people here, but people in the next dimension, and people who have crossed over to spirit and, for want of a better phrase, alien spirits as well. These people, I physically saw them through my third eye, and I could describe them quite vividly. And when I drew them, there were what appeared to be ribs running down the torso. But they weren't ribs at all, they were like folds. I'm going to say something like shark or dolphin skin. They initially told me that they came from a planet called Agneta, and Aktor and Ilieus were very visible to me. They looked as if they came from under water in appearance, and they said Agneta was a water planet. So, the craft was the same look as them, it was like a sort of silvery shimmery white. The craft looked remarkably small considering the two beings that were standing next to it, but the craft may have been a few yards behind them. They just looked together in my mind's eye".*

"So, the important thing about the beings themselves, was the make-up of the beings. They said that as we are made from bone, they are made totally from cartilage, and they live for, in their own words, thousands of years. They have been at Cairnpapple Hill for 300 plus years, and they were basically sent here by what I recall as their 'kind'. They don't have leaders, they are all one, and they report back to, 'the one', how they report back, I've no idea. They got here whether they used a worm hole, whether they used propulsion, whether they used bending time and space, whatever method it is, I don't know. As I say, they did say that they were from a water-based planet, so I'm going to say that they are not from here, but the potential is that other beings are within us in different dimensions. I didn't feel quite right for a couple of days afterwards, and last night, which was Tuesday, I felt really out of sorts. When I was channelling them, it felt very much like channelling spirit. It was the same feeling and the same process. Because at the end of the day, it's the same function, it's the same process and its soul to a soul. But I didn't feel right. When I've been channelling spirit, I've sometimes felt sick and dizzy but, in this case, I just didn't feel myself at all. So my guide said that I am going to have to get someone to help you. So, in spirit, we have surgeons, doctors, we have philosophers and scientists. And one of the doctors in spirit has helped me with healing for many many years and he came through, and I asked him his name, and he said that he was doctor Chakrabourty".

"He looked at me and said, "What have you been doing"? And I told him what I had been doing, and he had a look at my soul, and he said, "Right, you have blockages in your chakras". And I said 'right, that sounds interesting'. And then he went further, and he said, "It's slime". So, I thought, well that makes sense, it's a water-based planet, dolphin-like skin, so it's going to be like some kind of slime, so I took it for granted that that's what it was. He said that he should be able to clean it off. And he started a process where he did one or two things in spirit, and he said, "In two or three minutes we will be finished". He also said to me that it looks like we've left your chakras in a better state than what they were before 'they' channelled you. But I do advise you to be careful, if you do this anytime in the future, I *believe you got lucky this time. I did say that I didn't feel any threat from them at all. All I found was love from these beings, these souls, or spirits, I just found love from them. I allowed them to do what they needed to do. But I felt the frustration that they weren't able to do what they ideally would like to do, which is to 'educate'. They are not really meant to change the way we work with free will, but they are allowed to educate the people who are actually making the big decisions on the planet. And I'm not just talking about the politicians, but the people who run the politicians, which maybe is controversial but sorry, that's just the way I think it is. So, they find it so frustrating. But I do get the impression that they are working with not just me, and it's not just me that's seeing them. Also, there are other species doing a similar thing, or trying to impress the need to save the planet, and not just flora and fauna, but civilisation as we know it. As mad as it sounds, it happened as I said it did".*

Malcolm: *"Steven, if I could take you back to that Saturday night. I want to ask you, when did you start to feel different when we got to the location. I was sitting with you in the car, then we went out the car and met some friends and then we started to walk up that staircase on the hill. So, the question is, 'when did you start to feel something. Was it at the bottom of the hill, or the top of the hill, where was it?"*

Steven: *"I was assuming on the way over that I would feel something at Cairnpapple Hill. I didn't feel a thing until I was sat down on the hill, and yourself and Mark were talking. After you finished talking, I felt the need to 'tune it' because I felt that there was something to be seen up there. So, at that point I tuned in. I mentioned to everybody that I felt my body being pulled upwards as if there was an energy above me. I wasn't going anywhere. I was holding onto the arms of the chair* (NB. Steven had taken with him to Cairnpapple Hill, two-fold down chairs) *but I felt as if I was being drawn to something. Then all of a sudden, the tuning in process started".*

Malcolm: *"Do you think that it ends here, do you think that 'they' will be back in touch. I'm sure that even you don't know* *for sure. I mean, would you be happy if they made a further communication with you"?*

Steven: *"I would be OK with it. However, it would be on my basis, on my say so, rather than what happened before. I would say that I am pretty sure that they have been in touch with me before. Me and my wife both saw, two bright white, silver lights in the sky which we photographed not more than a few weeks ago. We both physically saw them, and we blew the photograph up, and you can see a light in the middle of the sky, just above Grangemouth which is on a direct line to Cairnpapple Hill. And we saw another one, which was just over towards Bonnybridge very similar. And even on the night, the very same night as Cairnpapple Hill sky watch, I took a photograph, and when I blew that photograph up, the same light was there in the sky at roughly the same height. So, it's either a message for me, or not just me, but for let's say other energy sensitive people that are out there. Because there are thousands of us, maybe millions".*

Malcolm: *"One final question. We are here in 2024, UFO sightings, the alien presence has always been with us throughout time immemorial. Do you think UFO disclosure will happen say, in the next 10,15,20, years' time where everything will be revealed. In other words, will there be a time when the veil will be lifted, where everything will be out in the open and we will know what these 'creatures' are"?*

Steven: *"I personally think that the people at the bottom, the like of myself, my fellow mediums, my fellow UFO researchers, my fellow experiencers, I think that these strong voices are going to get too strong to hide. I think there is also going to be more sightings, more of the first, second and third, maybe even fourth kind of UFO sightings. I think they will slowly integrate themselves and be visible. And they are going to be visible, in the majority of times through people who are able to connect on a telepathic nature. And I think if not all, but a lot of it will be apparent. And I think that a lot of it has been hidden for maybe two or three hundred years. I think things have been known for a substantially long time. Ever since business took over, the* *industrial revolution and money got involved, I think that's the control mechanism over the population which is money".*

Malcolm: *"Well Steven, thank you very much for sharing with me some further information about what you experienced at Cairnpapple Hill, and also your thoughts on UFOlogy as a whole. Thank you".*

Steven: *"Thank you Malcolm".*

MALCOLM'S SUMMING UP

Again, there will be those who will think that this is all rubbish and is made up, but I would like to inform the reader that Steven Bird is a first-class medium who has this incredible ability to channel through loved ones from spirit. This time however, it was something entirely different. Steven just says it *'as it is'*. If it was made up, he could have come away with more incredible statements, similar to what has been reported world-wide today, but that was not the case here. There was no change of voice when Steven was channelling, he was speaking in his own voice, slow and steady. To be perfectly honest, I was caught on the hop, I just didn't expect that. It was amazing that he psychically saw the two beings and their craft, but I was even more astonished when he channelled through one of the 'beings'. So, here was I, someone heavily into UFOlogy with a chance to ask any question I liked of 'someone' not of this Earth, and all I could ask were a few pitiful questions. That said, I was letting Steven/Aktor speak, I didn't want to interrupt, if I did that, I may have missed something. Whilst he was speaking, many questions were indeed filtering into my head, all ready to be asked, so it was a bit of a disappointment when I heard the words...." *My host is tired".*

At the end of the day, I deal with what is in front of me. I work with people close to me, and whilst I try never to suffer fools gladly, there are people who I respect and have faith in. Steven Bird is one of those. Steven mentioned above that there was a chap at the Cairnpapple Hill sky watch, namely Jackie Gillies who had with him a ghost device, who, during the sky watch, was using this device to see if he could capture any strange and bizarre images. Well, he did. One of the images caught by Jackie, showed an image which Steven Bird said, looked a little like one of the 'beings' that he saw.

Now, let me say here that I am not a big fan of these free ghost apps that you can easily download from the internet. They may be pre-programmed with fuzzy facial images etc. I don't know that for sure of course, but none the less, I would not really trust them at this stage. That said, Jackie used his ghost app and managed to 'capture' strange images. Make of them what you will. Now let us for a moment, think about the make up of these 'beings' which as stated, were made of cartilage.

Wikipedia tells us, and I quote,

'Human skeletons are made of bone, but we also have **cartilage** *in our ears and noses and as padding in our joints. In fact, much of our skeleton is cartilage when we are babies, but as we grow, it is replaced by bone'.*

I mention the above in regard to what Aktor stated when he came through Steven, stating that their bodily make up was of cartilage. Is it possible then, that a humanoid figure can be made purely out of cartilage? Probably not, as the human frame would not be able to support such a structure. If 'they' are from a water-based planet with no land mass, then clearly their physiology has evolved under water. Steven mentioned that they had skin either like a shark or a dolphin. I learned from Wikipedia that scientists from the Stanford University School of medicine, discovered a way to 'regenerate' articular cartilage in mice and human tissue, whether anything will come out of that and where they want to go with this, is anybody's guess. I found an interesting few paragraphs relating to cartilage and sea creatures from the internet. I'd like to present this as it was written.

'Quote: *'Cartilage is too rubbery to support the weight of a person. If our skeletons were made of cartilage, we would collapse under the weight of gravity. Our bodies need the* *unbending strength of bone to support their weight on land. In the water, however, sharks' cartilaginous skeletons have helped them survive and thrive. Since cartilage is lighter than bone, sharks don't have to work as hard to swim. This is very important, because they sink if they stop swimming. If they had heavier skeletons, they would have to work harder and spend more energy just to keep moving. Cartilage is strong but flexible, so it helps sharks be fast and manoeuvrable swimmers. That helps them catch prey and avoid predators'.* **Unquote'.**

Again, if Steven's channelling was fake, then one would assume that he should be going down the normal route of the much sighted grey or reptilian aliens and not talking about some water-based creatures. Yes, some will say that by saying he saw water-based creatures is a 'get out clause', I guess sometimes you just can't win. You either believe it, or you don't.

I firmly believe that humankind is and has been dealing with some form of non-human intelligence for thousands of years. Is 'their' agenda to truly help mankind? If that's the case, why the human abductions? Why are 'they' taking people out of the comfort of their own homes or cars and subjecting them to horrendous medical procedures? Ah, but others will say, they are not all like that. That there are many species 'out there' who have humanity's best interests at heart. Again, it's one of those questions that you pick and choose your winner. There may well be different species of aliens 'out there', who are we to truly say they are not! What happened at Cairnpapple Hill that night was truly mind-blowing, and I present it here in this book for your attention, but ultimately to let you know that things of this nature must be recorded. If they happen, let's talk about them. They say that we live in strange times, ain't that the truth. The night of Saturday 22nd of June 2024 was a night when the veil was lifted, albeit for a brief moment, in which 'beings' from another world showed that their thoughts are with planet Earth and that humanity should 'wake up' and realise that the fate of our planet, is in our own hands.

On the 11th of July 2025, we again held another sky watch at Cairnpapple Hill where Steven again channelled through Aktor.

Unfortunately, my iPhone didn't record that conversation properly as it was quite windy that night, and the recording is hard to hear due to the wind. However, Billy Devlin filmed part of this communication, and this (in part) was what was said.

Aktor comes through again!
(SPI Cairnpapple Hill sky watch, 11th July 2025

Steven Bird/Aktor: *"You need to see love back from yourselves. We struggle to see the good in many, but we see that you all have good hearts. We try to be visible, but we are not allowed. It takes time to affect the way you live your lives. We rely on the few to pass on the message, but they will never listen. All we ask is for the love on everyone on Earth. You have an incredible planet, one of the few we've seen that can sustain anything. Yet you destroy it with much disdain. We point the fingers at people who have nothing but money and asset. We have no power here. We try; we try. We are here, we speak through Steven, we know Steven, he has a good heart. He finds it difficult sometimes for people to listen. The more they hear, the more they will listen. You must know that you are never alone. This planet has never been alone. This planet is far bigger and far greater, than anyone knows. This planet can sustain anything, yet she bleeds, she bleeds, she bleeds. We cannot help, because we cannot be heard, we just study. We hope you see sense. Would anyone like to ask me some questions? You must have knowledge. You must ask questions".*

Malcolm Robinson: *"Who am I speaking to"?*

Steven Bird/Aktor: *"I am Aktor".*

Malcolm Robinson: *"How long have you been here Aktor"?*

Steven Bird/Aktor: *"Many centuries".*

Jon SPI Member: *"What planet are you from"?*

Steven Bird/Aktor: *"We are from Agneta. Agneta is a twin planet system. We are from the water side",*

Jon SPI Member: *"What is the main way that you have contact with people"?*

Steven Bird/Aktor: *"We can be seen. We can speak. We have spoken to many leaders, many times, for many years. They refuse to accept us. They blind us with their hate".*

Margaret Tollan: *"Do you feel sad"?*

Steven Bird/Aktor: *We don't feel sadness; we just feel love".*

Female SPI Member: *"Will there ever be a disclosure"?*

Steven Bird/Aktor: *"We hope, we hope. But that disclosure will never be fully understood".*

Jon SPI Member: *"Why do you pick specific people to get in touch with"?*

Steven Bird/Aktor: *"We do not pick specific people. We absorb people that can absorb. We are attracted to love. We understand that many people can see beyond what is normal. We therefore have the possibility we can work with it. We have worked with Steven before. Steven has many things to say. We would like to help. We need to help".*

Malcolm Robinson: *"What about abductions. Does your race conduct abductions or is that a different race".*

Steven Bird/Aktor: *"We would never abduct anybody. We would never abduct".*

Malcolm Robinson: *"Are you aware of other races doing abductions"?*

Steven Bird/Aktor: *"We are aware. We find this throughout the world. It is cruel. It is immoral. It is for no other purpose. It is a bad thought indeed".*

Margaret Tollan: *"Would you like to be more integrated with the good people of this Earth"?*

Steven Bird/Aktor: *"We cannot. We do not live within this realm. We cannot breathe your air. We cannot live your life. We cannot live with you. We can only interact with the absorption".*

Margaret Tollan: *"Does that go for all extraterrestrial life that you can't live with us"?*

Steven Bird/Aktor: *"We don't know. There are so many. We don't know everything".*

Margaret Tollan: *"And Steven is a good friend of yours now"?*

Steven Bird/Aktor: *"Steven is our friend".*

Margaret Tollan: *"That's nice. That's nice to know".*

Steven Bird/Aktor: *"Steven is tired".*

Malcolm Robinson: *"Thank you for speaking with us".*

Steven Bird/Aktor: *"I'd like to send our love from Agneta. The love we have given you for many centuries. We wish you well".*

Margaret Tollan: *"Thank you".*

Steven Bird/Aktor: *"You are welcome".*

Margaret Tollan: *"And we send our love back to you".*

Steven Bird/Aktor: *"We accept that gratefully".*

Margaret Tollan: *"Thank you".*

Author's Comment. At this point I reached out to Steven asking him if he was OK, as Steven at this point was moving backwards and forwards. I then asked him if he was aware of what had just happened, he replied that he was. I asked him again how he felt, his reply drew several laughs from those assembled as he said, *"F*****g knackered".*

Again, I would state that some may find the above fanciful and somewhat 'airy fairy', but we have to consider that this type of channelling has occurred for many years across the World. Who are we truly to say that this type of communication is false. Steven is a very good medium who has brought comfort and joy to many in his clairvoyant demonstrations across Scotland. He is just as amazed that this happened to him as anyone else. I firmly believe that Steven Bird was in communication with this person who calls himself Aktor.

SPI A70 SKY WATCH 27th July 2024

Staying with sky watches, here is another sky watch, this time near the A70 road which was near the location where Garry Wood and his friend Colin Wright had their strange abduction experience back in 1992. Here is what I wrote about that night.

Well, what can I say, where do you start? Any person who puts on a sky watch is always hoping that they get a perfect clear sky with no cloud, and boy, did we have that last night! A spectacular sky with a multitude of bright shining stars stretched across the heavens as far as the eye could see, simply wonderful.

Prior to arriving at the sky watch location, I was joined at the start of the night in Edinburgh, by Kerry Smith and her mother, both big UFO and Paranormal fans. Our driver was seasoned English UFO and Paranormal researcher and storm chaser, Liz Cormell. Liz had specifically come up to Scotland for the A70 sky watch, and whilst here, took advantage of her trip, by visiting a number of Scottish landmarks, like the Kelpies, Clackmannan Tower, Rosslyn Chapel and other Scottish places of interest.

Travelling down the A70, Liz, myself, and our two passengers, all shared a number of spooky tales, this set the scene for our upcoming sky watch. Prior to actually pulling up at the sky watch location, we drove over the exact location where the A70 Incident occurred. This allowed Liz, Kerry and her mother, to see exactly where the incident occurred. Sadly, as the location was on a blind bend with high grass verges on either side, there was no way that we could have stopped for a look around as our car would have been blocking the road, this was also the reason why we didn't hold our sky watch there, there just wasn't any room or layby at that area, hence we held it less than a quarter of a mile away at Harperrig Reservoir.

We arrived at the beautiful Harperrigg Reservoir in plenty time, and, as it was still light, this allowed us to view the lovely countryside with its rolling hills to our right, and the reservoir stretching away to the distance in front of us. After a short while, people started to arrive, and Alan Brown put his drone up into the clear night sky to take some aerial shots of a few of us who were standing around in the car park. The sound of the drone was like a multitude of buzzing bees above our head, and what with its red and green lights, looked spectacular as it traversed the sky. The sky watch itself was due to start at 10:15pm but we were waiting on the arrival of some people from a Russian You Tube Channel who were in Scotland to film some of our famous Scottish UFO cases, they eventually turned up late and made their apologies to our group, which on the last count was 19 people.

I then spoke to those assembled about the A70 UFO incident itself, detailing all the gruesome details of the abduction, and how there were many similarities between this case and other cases worldwide. On conclusion of my talk, SPI member, Mark Anderson stepped forward and informed those assembled about some of the history of this area, and some of its spooky tales. We were then asked to walk down a small road next to the reservoir, so that the Russians could film our group and interview some of our sky watchers. As we walked along this darkened narrow path, in front of us, in the distance, was an orange glow, which slowly rose above the reservoir. It was a quarter moon, which later, as it arced across the sky, turned white. The orange glow of course was the setting sun striking off the Moon as it slowly disappeared, quite a spectacular sight. The sky remained resplendent in its spectacular starry glory, and all the different constellations could be seen spread throughout the sky, from the Plough, to Cassiopeia, to name but a few. Needless to say, quite a few satellites were seen slowly traversing the night sky, along with a number of shooting stars.

Around 01:15am I wound it up. I was conscious of the fact that our two passengers that had travelled down to the sky watch in our car were feeling the cold, plus one of them had work in the morning. And so, with fond farewells, we bade our happy band of skywatchers goodbye and headed back up the infamous A70 road to Stirling to drop off our lovely passengers. After dropping our passengers off, Liz turned round to me, and with a smile said, *"let's go back",* to which I said, *"yes why not, it would be rude not to".* So, we turned the car around and headed back down the A70. We turned into the car park around 02:15am where only one car remained, the rest had gone. I jumped out of the car and looked skywards, only to be met with a total change of sky. Solid cloud cover and mist stretched across the sky and covered the end of the reservoir and hills to our right. Well, whilst that wasn't expected, I'm glad it happened now, and not at the start.

The quietness was unreal, and a cold breeze blew across my body as I looked around in the darkness. I used my torch to flash into the night sky, which is a common practice in UFO sky watches, by doing this, it sometimes elicits a light response from the sky, however, on this occasion it did not. After a while, I joined Liz in the car where we talked the hind legs off each other sharing ghostly tales. Now, Liz is also a psychic, and long story short, as we sat in silence (yes, there were times when we both shut up) Liz could hear one foot stomp on the gravel near the car which she stated was spirit. Both Liz and I also could see, some pin pricks of light on the shoreline in the distance, some of which, appeared in the water. I only saw a few, but Liz saw more. Admittedly, we both agreed that it might have been our eyes playing tricks on us. Behind the car park, there was a small road that leads off to goodness knows where. Well, we decided to slowly drive down that road, and as we did so, all of a sudden Liz stopped the car and put her hands on her chest. I asked her what was wrong, to which she said that she had felt a sudden thud, across the top of her chest on both collar bones, as if either a falling tree had hit her, or 'something else' (!) She also got a psychic impression of a man herding geese down this track on his way to a market in Stirling, this, she said, was either a 17th or 18th century psychic impression.

As we drove back to the car park having travelled further down the track, Liz got the exact same feeling again. We then pulled back into the car park and sat for a while, where Liz psychically picked up the name of Emily. I did a quick EVP asking if there was an Emily around and if she could step forward and leave her name on my device (i-Phone) having checked the recording after the test, sadly nothing could be heard, other than the sound of the wind. Liz also stated that she psychically got the impression of a body that was disposed of into the Harperrig Reservoir. Now we can only speculate if this was this Emily that she picked up earlier, who knows, it obviously needs some checking, more so on the possibility of a murdered body being disposed of! We then sat discussing more aspects of UFOs and the paranormal until the sun came up. I eventually got home at quarter to six in the morning. It had been some night, and whilst admittedly we didn't see anything strange, it is always a great exercise to take SPI members and interested individuals to these sky watches.

A 1959 UFO OVER EDINBURGH!

Author's Comment. Our next case file concerns a sighting of a strange object by a young schoolgirl. Here is what she had to inform me.

Hello Malcolm.

"I'd like to tell you about a strange sighting I had sixty years ago, (1959) We lived in Edinburgh in the Newington district. At the time I was a fourteen-year-old schoolgirl. I travelled to and from school by bus. One afternoon about 4:00pm, I got off the bus at the usual stop, Newington Station. I had to cross the main road to get home and stood looking northwards up the hill (Newington Road) towards Salisbury for a break in the traffic.

As I did so, my eye was caught by a movement in the sky. It was a clear blue sky, and I am sorry I do not remember the month. It must have been late spring or summer. There was a strange object moving slowly across the sky from east to west. In shape it was oval, a perfect oval (not the shape of a hen's egg) with two lines of symmetry. In colour it was a slightly pale metallic gold, the colour of the moon at moonrise. It appeared to be 3-dimensional, and the surface was perfectly smooth. There were no markings, lines or projections on it anywhere. It progressed at a steady even pace, and in a straight line right across the sky until it went out of sight behind distant buildings. I was able to watch it for perhaps a minute and a half. There was no noise from it, and it was not emitting light. It did not appear to be revolving, although it was perfectly smooth and left no vapour trail or anything like that. I am not sure about the elevation, but I should say it was probably around 60 degrees above horizontal. It was in the northern sky, perhaps above south-central Edinburgh".

"When I arrived home, I told my mother who was ironing at the time. I remember taking her fountain pen and drawing the shape of it. She didn't say anything, and I don't know what she thought. We were a very truthful family and as a daughter of the manse I would have regarded it as immoral (and pointless) to tell a lie. About a week or ten days later, my mother spoke to me about it again. She said she had seen something in The Scotsman newspaper about a man in Edinburgh who had seen a 'flying saucer' the previous week. My mother had not kept the newspaper, but she had read the report. The report went on to say that they thought it must be a part of a satellite which had broken off. This was after all the Sputnik era! It was such a perfectly smooth shape. I don't believe a part could break off without leaving a jagged edge or projection or some irregularity on the surface. Of course, I didn't see the north side of it, but it looked complete and balanced".

With all good wishes, Hattie Stewart.

THE CYLINDER OBJECT

UFOs come in all shapes and sizes, and there are a number of reports of cylinder-shaped objects. Such a sighting was observed by 38-year-old Lorna Gower from Winchburgh West Lothian. It was the 9th of December 2024, and Miss Gower was walking her dog near a playpark in Winchburgh when she happened to glance up into the clear morning sky. She was stunned to observe what she described as a sixty-foot cylindrical shaped object which was white in the middle, but red at both ends. It remained stationary in the sky for around thirty seconds before it was lost to view. Fortunately, Lorna had her camera phone with her where she quickly snapped three photographs of this object. I was sent one of the photographs (see photographic section) where she estimates that the object was only around 300 to 400 feet high. The object in the photograph sent to me, looks slender and bright white, and the sky instead of showing bright blue, has come out a dull pink. Like most close proximity witnesses, this has left its mark on Lorna. However, it would seem that UFO sightings run in the family, as Lorna's father James Gower, has had two UFO sightings of his own. The first was in 1990. Here is what he had to say about his sighting.

THE RAILWAY CARRIAGE UFO

"At the time of the sighting I was aged 35. I was travelling back home in the car from Livingston. It was a weekday evening approximately. 5:15pm. The year was 1990, however I can't recall the month. I had our three children in the car, aged three, six and eight) When I was on the Blackburn Road heading towards the brow of the hill, we could see an oblong 'thing' in the sky resembling a railway carriage. As we turned left into the village of Stoneyburn it dropped suddenly and moved forward and went under the pylon wires. We then lost sight of it, but it reappeared behind us, moving very fast about 100 feet above a field towards Livingstone. It was out of sight in seconds. It was dark coloured with rows of square windows".

Author's Comment. James states that he was on the road in-between the towns of Addiewell and Stoneyburn and that the whole sighting took less than one minute. To see something like a railway carriage in the sky was bizarre, coupled with the fuzzy yellow glow coming from the four windows on its side made the whole scene like something out of the Twilight Zone T.V. series. For the author, what strikes me the most about this sighting, is the fact that this object, whatever it was, flew underneath some of the standing electricity pylons that cross the land. That would make it around less that forty feet from the ground! No light aircraft would even attempt to do a manoeuvre like this. Prior to this sighting, James had another encounter with a UFO, this one was in 1994, he can't recall the month but remembers that it was around 6:00pm. James was driving on the A71 road towards West Calder, accompanying him in his car, were his three children and another adult (name not given) when all five of them were stunned to see a very large dark grey triangle object in the sky which had three red lights at each point. Knowing that this was something out of the ordinary, he stopped his car and got out, as he did so, another car which had been driving behind him, also stopped and that driver got out as well. They all stood transfixed looking at this strange sight. Then, in the blink of an eye, the object disappeared. James reckons that the object was in full view for at least 45 seconds. When the children got home, they all independently drew this object, all of which showed its triangular composition with the red lights at each apex.

THE ENTITY IN THE TREE!

Author's Comment. OK. Seeing UFOs is one thing, but witnessing a strange creature sitting in a tree is another. This is what happened to five young girls back in July 1978. The area in question is in the Newtongrange area in Midlothian, Suttieslea to be precise, which is sandwiched between the towns of Mayfield, and Newtongrange. Anne Calder, one of the witnesses to this incredible event sent me a number of e-mails informing me of this strange event. She states.

"On the day that the encounter happened, there was myself, Anne Calder, my sister Jill, my friends Mary Birrell and Pamela Orr and one other kid from the neighbourhood. We were all aged between 8 and 10 years old. We were all walking my dog Tanya down at the old disused railway track that sat at the bottom of Suttieslea Park. What started as a normal day very quickly became the most terrifying traumatic day of all our lives. We were walking along the old railway track when suddenly Tanya my dog started going crazy, barking like mad (she was always the most placid dog, and we had never seen this reaction from her before) I clearly remember we looked up at this tree and saw a sight that none of us can ever unsee. There was a 'being' with very bright yellow glowing eyes with no pupil and pointed ears looking back at us. I remember being frozen in fear at what we were seeing, then it spoke in what I can only describe as a synthesised vibrating voice (I don't remember its mouth moving but we all clearly heard what it said) *"DO NOT BE AFRAID I WILL NOT HARM YOU"*. We all were frozen with fear. The 'being' was small in size, perhaps three feet. It was not a shadow. My next memory was of us all standing in a field, which was two fields away from where we originally were, opposite Mary and I's house. Even as young innocent kids we somehow instinctively knew never speak of what we had witnessed and we never did until recently, when I reached out to a couple of the girls that I hadn't seen since childhood and I simply asked *"Do you remember what happened at the old railway track"?* their replies were instant, and they said *"Yes we will never forget those eyes"*

"A couple of years after the encounter, I started having night terrors (always the exact same terror) where I'm in a room with no doors or windows and I'm screaming for help because I can't get out. My mother when she was alive, witnessed this going on, and said that I was pulling the curtains down and pushing at walls. My daughters have also witnessed me doing the exact same thing, me screaming for help and saying that there's no doors or windows, and I can't get out. It's all very clear to me. I've had many years of simply not sleeping or going into a deep sleep because I'm frightened to keep having these terrifying terrors. I am not saying this 'being' abducted me/us that day, but

I have no recollection of how we ended up two fields away after hearing what it said? Maybe it's my brain's way of trying to process what happened? I doubt I will ever know, but I can tell you in all sincerity, that the 'being' we witnessed that day was not human, or animal, and it was most definitely not from our world! Real fear never fades from the memory, and the truth of what happened that day stays in our minds forever, I'm 55 now and my biggest question is why did it choose us to see and hear it? Malcolm, you asked me before if it was an owl, but most definitely it was not. The closest thing I've ever seen to what it looked like, was the Kelly Hopkinsville goblin, but the eyes on the one we saw were much bigger and not so spread out. I have a mark which is dead centre on my forehead that I didn't have till after that day and it's still there today".

Author's Comment. Well, what are we to make of that? I initially came across this report on Facebook and quickly got in touch with Anne Calder who kindly sent me a combination of Facebook messages and e-mails of which the above is comprised of. What could possibly this little 'creature' be? Moreover, what was it doing sitting in a tree? Why did all the girls find themselves five minutes away from where they originally stood. Questions, questions, questions. But no answers! This is why I love this subject so much, it's so downright crazy and off the wall. How can I, as a researcher of strange phenomena, come up with a 'conclusive answer' as to what Anne and her friends saw that day? I can't. Anne mentions that the closest thing she has seen to what she saw that day, was the Kelly Hopkinsville Goblin. For those readers that are not aware of this case. Here are the basic facts.

'The Kelly Hopkinsville encounter occurred in 1955 in Kentucky, United States and is probably one of the most bizarre cases in the history of alien creature encounters. On the evening of August 21st, 1955, five adults and seven children, arrived at the Hopkinsville police station claiming that small alien creatures were attacking their farmhouse which they held off with gunfire 'for nearly four hours'. Two of the adults, Elmer Sutton and Billy Ray Taylor, claimed they had been shooting at 'twelve to fifteen' short, dark figures who repeatedly popped up at the doorway or peered into the windows. The creatures were described as 'goblin like', small, with large, pointed ears and yellow eyes at each side of their head. When the police arrived at the farmhouse, they found numerous gunshot holes and shells around the farmhouse'.

Author's Comment. At the end of the day, we must accept that sightings of not just what we call the 'greys' who are described as between three and four feet tall, with grey/bluish skin, large pear-shaped heads with black inky almond shaped eyes, but we seem to be dealing with a whole range of different shaped 'entities'. The obvious question is, 'are they from the same place, (wherever that place may be!) or are they from a whole range of different places.'! Whilst I was checking with Anne that what I wrote above for this book was factual and correct, which she admitted it was, she informed me that she was on a paranormal forum where she came across a similar account to hers (after informing the forum about her own encounter) I can't divulge the name of the forum participant sadly but here is that account.

"Just to steer it ever so gently back to the issue of this type of entity. I remember in the early 70's I was 6 or 7. I was a pupil of Jordans school in Crawley, Sussex, which was an infant to junior (5-11 years), and there was a camping trip either to Ashdown Forest, or possibly The New Forest for I think a week, Friday to the following Thursday. At the time there was a lot of excitement, as it was one of the first, or longest trips away for the 10–11-year-olds for the school. Now as it transpired, they came home early, either the Monday or Tuesday, and there was a lot of kerfuffle, about why, with rumours abounding until I overheard from a bit of chat between my Mum and a couple of others around the school gates. And it turned out that a couple of the girls on the trip had encountered on the first weekend, whilst going to the toilet, what was described as a 'Goblin', up in a tree, close to the camping area; it too had glowing eyes, was a greenish/grey colour, also with a weird way of speaking- and they were so spooked by it. One girl becoming so hysterical, starting a wave of fear throughout the whole class to the degree that despite the teacher's best efforts for calm, they had to come home. I seem to

remember that one of the girls was so upset by the incident that she was out of school for some time and apparently had to be put on medication".

Author's Comment. I could provide the reader with numerous other accounts of similar 'goblin' like creatures the world over, but I feel that may be tiresome and the reader is requested to do their own search of the internet for such cases. As for Anne, her sister and friends, well even now that she is a grown adult, she tells me that the vision of this 'goblin' like creature in the tree will never leave her, that's its imprinted into her very soul.

From a scary sighting of a creature in a tree, we move onto an interesting sighting of a strange object which was seen very close to the location of the A70 UFO Incident where Garry Wood and his friend Colin Wright observed a shiny black two-tiered object hovering silently above the A70 Road. This particular UFO sighting was above the A71 road which is only a few miles away from the A70 road. This case came to me through Phil Fenton. The witness Ronald Hall was driving back from a cinema in Edinburgh along the A71 road near Kirknewton Airfield. As he was driving along the road, he was aware of another car behind him. The area around him, was just farmers' fields for miles. Here in his own words is what transpired.

THE A71 UFO

Hi Malcolm,

"It was 1999, and my wife and I were in our car driving back from the cinema where we had been to see the Pierce Brosnan film, 'The World Is Not Enough'. It was dark outside, and we were on a high talking about the movie and about general life stuff. We were driving past Edinburgh Airport on the A71 parallel to the Airfield where an aircraft was tacking off. We could see the lights as normal and this lit up the side of the normal aeroplane, which was clearly seen, but I also noticed a craft between us and the obvious aeroplane. Weirdly though, this second craft had three red lights only. The three red lights were all on, and there were no white lights at all. Between the lights was just darkness (but this may be down to the fact that I was driving and trying not to crash, so my vision was on the object then looking ahead, then looking back). The two craft took off at the same time in line with each other. I said to Mary".

"Look at that. Something's not right!" Mary replied, *"What do you mean?"*

To which I replied, *"Red lights, that's closer to the road, there's two aircraft there".*

"Needless to say, we were both looking out at the craft as it sped forward and out of sight at an aeroplane speed. As we drove along the winding A71, we saw the red lights zoom from right to left and then from left to right a few times. We were gobsmacked with what was happening. Then the craft came directly toward us through the cloud where the clouds lit up red, and then the lights got sharper as it came closer out of the cloud. I shouted out".

"It's coming straight for us! Whooh!"

"The craft came down to almost touch the silhouette of the trees and then it shot directly vertical at an obscene speed and was gone! We slowly drove along, totally freaked out and discussing what had just happened. We passed 'Linburn' which is a residential area for the War Blind. We were looking everywhere to see if we could see it again. As a field came close to us to our left, there it was. Totally static just above ground, no engine noise, no movement from it at all! It was fixed in the air solid. There were no landing gear, and it was at lamp post top level in the far corner of the field beside a telephone pole and line of trees. This was right beside a railway track. I could see the shape of the craft, the colours, patterns, panel shut lines, and the lights. There were no clear visible markings of any kind in so far as letters and numbers. All three lights were now only white and stuck on. It had a pale blue underside. I panicked as I realised, I was driving at just under 30 mph on the A71 which was a 60-

mph road at that time. I looked in my rear-view mirror to see another car looking over to the object too! They were also driving the same speed as us at a safe distance. We could see their silhouettes in the car. It was a large equilateral triangle with melted down ends, a large top central canopy area. The wings were thick and rounded which weirdly reminded me of the Vulcan bomber because of the curve on the wing edges. This object was larger than a RAF Tornado jet. I would say at a guess, that the sighting lasted around ten minutes. Just to let you know, I was an Air Cadet. I had been around aircraft a lot either by attending ATC Camp on RAF bases or also by attending Leuchars airshows. I was a qualified Glider Pilot (Kirknewton Airfield). I think this is relevant and hope it helps give a little credibility to our account".

Author's Comment. By the sound of this report, it certainly looks like it doesn't conform to what we would term a normal aircraft. (However, in this day and age, what is a 'normal aircraft'?) Let us bear in mind that the object was initially sighted (If I'm not mistaken) from a vantage point 'near' Edinburgh Airport before it again came into view further down the A71 road. Fellow researcher Phil Fenton who spoke to the witness and passed this case onto me, had his own views of what the witnessed observed, he stated.

Hi Malcolm,

"The witness described the object as an extremely large triangular shape but curvy. Much bigger than an aircraft such as the Vulcan bomber. It was duck egg blue underneath (which is a military aircraft camouflage colour) but this object was not flying like any conventional aircraft he knew about. It seemed to be hovering and moving very slowly (about 25 - 30 mph) and he could see what would appear to be riveted panels making up the hull of the craft. On the top was a large bubble canopy as seen on fighter aircraft, but much larger. The three corners of the craft had lights that were white when it was stationary, and glowed red when it moved away".

"My own thoughts on this are that it must be a military flying machine. Most likely a rigid airship but incorporating stealth technology. This would explain its ability to hover and move very slowly as well as the strange shape. I put this to the witness, and he agreed that this could be the case, but he went on to explain that when it left, it accelerated away very quickly, much quicker than a cumbersome airship could hope to achieve. It also manoeuvred and changed direction very rapidly in ways that are well beyond any aircraft's capabilities. What also interests me, is that there is an old RAF station (RAF Kirknewton) near where this occurred, it's now used as a base for gliders and the ATC (Air training corp). It's also very near the A70 and the Harperrig Reservoir where another incident took place which you have written about in your book UFO Case Files of Scotland. And I wonder if the cases are related. A secret RAF Stealth Airship would be a very useful device. It could hide in the clouds and take off and land undetected in foggy conditions. And (assuming it was stealthy and undetectable to radar) it could creep up on the enemy undetected and land in any open space without the need for runaways allowing troops and armaments to be deployed. When you think about it, if the military don't already operate such craft, then they really should develop one for the reasons just described? What puzzles me though are the rapid speeds and changes in direction also described by the witness that are beyond our current understanding of technology".

Regards Phil Fenton.

Author's Comment. Well, whether this was indeed some kind of new stealth aircraft or something else, I guess we'll never know. One thing is for sure; our witness and his wife will never forget that night and the strange object they saw. Our next case file concerns the observation of a silver sphere by Rosemary Waters and her brother. Here is what she had to say about it.

THE SILVER SPHERE

Hi Malcolm,

"I had a UFO experience which happened in 1996 near Edinburgh? I was travelling with my brother (he was driving, I was front seat passenger) on the A90 from Fife to Edinburgh. Just as we were approaching the city and in the vicinity of the Edinburgh airport flight path, I saw a UFO. I can only describe it as what looked like some sort of dull silver metal sphere. I would roughly estimate it as 3 to 5 metres in circumference. It was sitting deadly still about 100 feet up in the sky, not moving at all. I must have looked at it without saying anything, for maybe 10 seconds trying to come up with an explanation, but I couldn't. I pointed up to it to show my brother, but as I did, we went under a fly over bridge and to my complete disbelief it disappeared when we passed under it! Gone in two seconds, completely vanished! (The fly over bridge we passed under is the bridge to the village of Craigiehall which was on our right, the UFO was above the road in front of the bridge)".

"I was baffled but relieved when a car of people overtook us, they too were all looking up and pointing excitedly, so they definitely saw it as well! My poor brother didn't have a clue. I wish I'd reported it at the time and can't believe we didn't stop and speak to the other car about what we had witnessed. I haven't encountered anything since. But so delighted to have had a UFO experience. It was not a weather balloon as some friends have speculated. It was a definite solid metal sphere as you could tell by the way the daylight hit it, and yes, this happened in broad daylight, early afternoon. Unfortunately, I don't remember which month in 1996 it was".

"I'd also like to add, that around this time, (1996) I had some peculiar experiences. One in particular happened in Edinburgh involving some sort of telepathy! I have to say when I saw the UFO I remember feeling very calm and almost 'in tune' with it. I felt I had been chosen to see it, and it was having a little fun with me when it disappeared as I went under the bridge. I hope this doesn't sound farfetched, I'm just reporting the facts".

Author's Comment. The witness in our next case file, Mark Bailey was another person just going about his daily business, never expecting for one minute to encounter something out of the ordinary, but back in a summer's evening in June 1993, his day was changed by seeing something which was out of the norm.

THE BALL OF FIRE

42-year-old Mark Bailey had just left his job at Wallyford in East Lothian, the time was around 7:15pm. As he drove west to join the A1 heading homewards, he noticed what looked like a large fire on the eastern slopes of the Penland Hills. He kept this in sight for most of his journey puzzling over what it might be, but as he got closer, he realised that this orange glare which he initially thought was a fire on the hill, was not in fact on the hill at all, but airbourne at some distance from the hill. From his vantage point, he said that it looked like a large orange balloon which was stationary, roughly about twenty to thirty feet in diameter and at a height of between 400 to 500 feet. Looking for a tether, still thinking it was a balloon, he couldn't see one. He then thought, 'could it be one of the Chinese Lanterns', but no, it wasn't that. It appeared to be near the Army Ranges at Castlelaw. Here is what Mark had to say to me in an e-mail regarding his sighting.

"I set off down the A702 to see if I could see it closer or find where it was hovering over. By doing so, because the road moves close into the hills, I lost sight of it. I carried on to West Linton but I could no longer see it. When I got back to Lothianburn Junction, I went to the same layby where I had seen it earlier, but it had gone. What I can be absolutely certain of, is that it was not anything astronomical, nor a Chinese Lantern nor a conventional aircraft or Hot Air Balloon. This was a spherical object, most likely some sort of illuminated balloon. It was not reflecting sunlight because it was lower than the hills. If it was military then I cannot understand why the army would want to draw attention to themselves, since they do their best trying not to be seen most of the time. I had thought of a flare, but I described it to a retired Royal Navy Captain I know, and he

confirmed that even a parachute flare would not have remained airborne all that time. Unfortunately, this being the early 90's camera phones were not around, or I would have taken photographs of it".
Regards. Mark Bailey.

Author's Comment. I learned through research that the Castlelaw and Dreghorn training area (CDTA) is a Military Training area in the Penland Hills which includes live gun firing ranges. There is also an area for simulated combat. Could this bright 20 to 30 feet sphere of white light just have been a flare? The witness doesn't think so. But by being so close to an army training area, one has to speculate that this might have been the answer, even although, many UFO sightings have been seen around Military establishments. One other interesting fact about the area where this large light was seen, is that the area is known for its historical significance, this includes a hill fort dating back to the iron age.

Our next case file again brings to light, another one of those strange triangle craft, this one was fortunately filmed by the driver's dash cam. Here is the story.

BLACK TRIANGLE SIGHTED AND FILMED NEAR THE A89

An interesting black triangle UFO sighting was mentioned to me on Thursday the 14th of May 2020. Basically, what transpired was this.

On the evening of Thursday January 9th, 2020, Mr Martin Morrison was driving East in his Mitsubishi Outlander. He had just left the town of Broxburn West Lothian and was heading East along the A89 towards the town of Newbridge to collect his wife from her work. It was around 7:31pm when he was surprised to observe a strange looking stationary aerial object about 300 feet above a farmer's field next to the Almond Valley Viaduct. Mr Morrison initially thought that it was an aircraft 'of sorts' as Edinburgh Airport is only around three miles from this location. However, the hovering object was well below the normal height that aircraft fly in and out of Edinburgh Airport.

As Mr Morrison got closer to the object, he could clearly see that this was something that he had never seen before and could not equate it to any known aircraft currently flying. Mr Morrison stated.

"When I approached the viaduct in the car and was passing under the viaduct, I craned my neck to look backwards only to see a black triangular object just hovering silently there. It was quite apparent that I was looking at a strange aircraft which had what looked like strobing lights on each corner of its triangular shape. It also had solid white lights on each corner. At the time I never gave it much thought, that was until the following Sunday when I thought that perhaps my car's dashcam had some footage. I got lucky, it did have. As you will see when you look at the footage, you will see from the date stamp on the dashcam footage, that I arrived at the viaduct at 7.31pm. I have no idea what this could be, and I'm sure that there 'MUST' be a number of other motorists on the A89 that night who must surely have seen it as well"

Author's Comment. Having viewed the footage, (see still from the footage in the photographic section) one can clearly see this black triangular shaped object sitting in the sky above a farmer's field. This triangular shaped image is similar it must be said, in appearance to many other worldwide descriptions, and has also been seen in the Scottish skies for many years now. One may ask the question, 'why'? What was it doing sitting above a farmer's field in full view of a busy road giving good views to its watching observers? Was it our own technology? Of course, we have to bear in mind that this observation was only around three miles from the busy Edinburgh Airport, and as such, there should be evidence of this object on its radar scopes.
Needless to say, I just had to look into this sighting, and I contacted the various agencies in search of an answer.

1) Letter sent to Edinburgh Airport Air Traffic Control.
2) Letter sent to Glasgow Airport Air Traffic Control.
3) Letter sent to Cumbernauld Airport Air Traffic Control
4) Letter sent to Broxburn Police.

5) Letter sent to Police Scotland.
6) Letter sent to the West Lothian Courier Newspaper.
7) Letter sent to the Ministry of Defence in London.
8) Facebook post on the Uphall and Broxburn Legends.

As for the Various airports, my request letter went like this.

Dear Sir Madam,

"I wonder if you would be able to assist me with the following enquiry".

"I am investigating a UFO sighting made by a gentleman from Uphall who inadvertently captured a large black triangular shaped object in the sky on his car's dashboard camera. The object appeared off to the right-hand side of the road as he was approaching the Almond Valley Viaduct which is placed just outside Broxburn. It appeared to be stationary in the sky. The date and time of the sighting is as follows".

Date: 9th January 2020.
Time: 19:31pm.
Location: On the A89 road (going East) approaching the Almond Valley Viaduct, near Broxburn, West Lothian, Central Scotland.

"I would be indebted to you if you could check you records and let me know if any air traffic was in the vicinity of the Broxburn area at 19:31 hours on Thursday January 9th. Was anything picked up on your radar scopes? I have attached the footage for you to view for yourself, where you will see the time and date stamp on the car's dashboard camera. So clearly there was something there, and I'm pretty sure that your air traffic controllers simply must have recorded this. Please note, it was below normal entry flight height, and it appeared stationary above a farmer's field. Please also note the strange lighting characteristics".

In an e-mail to me, the witness Martin Morrison stated that,

"This object was next to a railway line Viaduct; do they use some special lifting craft for Railway works? If they do, why do such dangerous things at night in the dark without safety lighting as none was there as verified in the footage? Just trying to get a logical explanation. bearing in mind that its right in the main flightpath to the Airport at Edinburgh. Personally, I think it's some craft of ours, experimental or otherwise, but look forward to you telling me what it really is. put my mind at rest".
Regards. Martin.

Just for the record, the Almond Valley Viaduct is the longest Railway Viaduct in Scotland. This viaduct is close to the village of Newbridge in West Lothian. It has 36 arches, 15 more arches than the better-known Viaduct at Glenfillan, which has only 21 arches!)

SO, WHAT WAS THE OUTCOME?

Well, I guess I shouldn't have been surprised. The MoD did not reply to my letters. I heard nothing from either Glasgow, Edinburgh or Cumbernauld Airports. I sent e-mails to both Police Scotland and the Broxburn police. The following is a reply that I received from Police Scotland, it read.

OFFICIAL

Good Afternoon,

"Thank you for your email".
"Unfortunately, I cannot see any reports made to the police in relation to the information you have given me from the 09/01/2020".

Regards, Service Advisor 20954.

Police Scotland Tel:101. Email: C3 Division Service CentreGlasgow@scotland.pnn.police.uk
Website: www.scotland.police.uk

I also never had a great response from a couple of social media sites, namely the Broxburn and Uphall Community Centres and also their Facebook sites. There were quite a few comments as to what it might be, but no corroboration as far as further witnesses went.

All this is to be expected. Whilst we UFOlogists treat this wonderful subject with the respect it deserves; other agencies may well poo poo it, and one can wait forever to hear back from your request. I got nowhere with the letters and e-mails. It was the same with my phone calls to the agencies involved. Of course, let us not forget, this UFO sighting may well have had a natural explanation, most, if not all of them do. But what makes this one so different, even although it was three miles away from a major Scottish airport, was the size of the thing, and that it appeared to be hovering, or at least stationary. Admittedly the witness only saw it for a few moments, and thankfully with the advent of the car's dash cam we have the footage to back up his testimony.

I SEE UFOS REGULARLY!

Author's Comment. I've said before, social media is a great vehicle for people to get in touch with me regarding their UFO sightings. One such man, Lewis Thornhill, provided me with a number of UFO sightings that he has seen in the sky above Edinburgh. Here are some of his sightings, and his thoughts as to what they could be.

First Sighting

Wednesday January 29th, 2025, I was outside St. Mary's Catholic Cathedral in Edinburgh. I was making my way to meet a friend for coffee. It was 12:21 in the afternoon, the sky was clear as it was a hot day. Upon walking towards my destination heading to the top of Boughton Street, I felt the inclination to look up, and when I looked up, I saw a silver object glimmering and moving across the sky. Due to its unrecognisable appearance, that being a lack of wings and shape, I took out my phone to take photos of this anomaly. The craft was roughly six to seven thousand feet from ground level, and between sixty to seventy-five degrees above the horizon, heading east northeast, overlooking the top of Leith Walk. The craft was heading in the direction of Fife.

Second Sighting

It was Saturday March the 15th 2025, I was waiting on a number 3 bus at Calder Drive, Main Road to head into work. It was a clear day, and I was looking towards the Sight Hill area. I spotted a crow flapping around a spherical object stationary in the sky above the houses in broad daylight. At first glance, I thought it was a balloon but then realised that it was stationary and rotating. Taking out my phone, I snapped a few photographs. Then the bus pulled up. I headed to the top floor, sitting three seats away from the stairs on the right-hand side. I was able to take more pictures and video footage of this object as we approached the next stop outside Sight Hill College. Upstairs there was one Indian man who was sat two seats behind me and who took no notice of my frantic filming and picture taking, he must have thought I was a tourist. At the Napier University stop, I was able to catch clear footage of the object stationary and spinning. Then suddenly, a second sphere appeared above it, both were stationary yet rotating with blinking lights. These lights were not from the suns reflection but the objects producing their own light source. Intrigued, I continued to film these objects as the bus moved onto its next stop at Sight Hill Green. Upon observation I came to speculate that the blinking was possibly similar to Morse code or some form of communication between the two spheres. Sadly, due to work obligations, I did not get off the bus which I now regret, as I believed I could have possibly stood under them to get even closer.

Third Sighting

Thursday April 17th, 2025, at 5:55pm. I spotted another sphere in view 80 degrees above the horizon moving across the sky. This time the sphere was not stationary but heading north easterly. I was sitting on the right hand side of the 30 bus at

Hailesland Grove in the direction of Wester Hailes Plaza. As the bus was driving slowly, I was able to film the sphere passing by onto its destination.

Fourth Sighting

Saturday May 17th, 2025. Again, I was on the number 3 bus heading to work when at 3:30pm, I spotted which I presume are the same spheres above the Sight Hill Gardens area. This was a little further along from last sighting on March the 15th, but only by one bus stop. They were stationary, only a few feet above the roof tops of a few houses between Calder Road and Sighthill Loan, before the Sighthill roundabout. The bus made its usual stop, and I quickly took out my phone and filmed the two spheres stationary in mid-air along with photographs. After showing family and friends the footage, we were intrigued and left to wonder why these highly advanced spheres would been situated over the Sighthill area as it is a residential area.

Fifth Sighting

It was Thursday May 22nd, 2025. On returning from the city centre at 6:07pm, I was sitting upstairs on the left-hand side of the number 3 bus looking at the sky in the Sighthill area at 70 to 80 degrees above the houses. Then, as we were heading up Calder Road towards the Wester Hailes Plaza, I spotted another sphere flying in the direction of the Pentlands. Again, taking out my phone, I recorded the mysterious sphere fly through the atmosphere. Upon studying my pictures and footage, I am convinced that anti-gravity is already a reality.

Sixth Sighting

Thursday May 29th, 2025, across from Calder Road looking towards gate 55 Community Centre in the Sighthill area, I was able to capture images of a single sphere for a few moments above the houses until it vanished or turned on its cloaking capabilities.

Seventh and Eighth Sightings

On Saturday the 21st at 7:14 pm and Sunday 22nd of June 2025 at 11:49, I filmed on both days, a similar craft flying across the sky towards Fife. Because of its long shape and movement, it resembled the craft spotted earlier this year on January 29th, 2025. I showed my findings to those around me, leaving me curious to research into the phenomenon.

Personal research and opinion of these events

Upon my own investigation into the subject based on my own personal observations, I came across the works of Dr. Eamonn Ansbro and his spherical probe theory which proposes that Earth is under continuous observation by a network of autonomous, orbiting UAPs, many of them appearing as glowing spheres that follow fixed, low-inclination orbital paths synchronized with the planet's rotation. Dr Ansbro's analysis of global sighting databases led him to identify a recurring 66–67-minute cycle, and inclinations of roughly 0–25°, suggesting a structured system rather than random phenomena.

He estimates there could be around 660 probes arranged in grid-like or shell formations, providing near-total planetary coverage. These spheres might travel in coordinated groups, forming geometric patterns, triangles, arcs, or concentric rings as they sweep over cities, rural areas, and oceans. The model implies that over locations like Edinburgh, the network could create temporary surveillance clusters, with orbs spaced in a patterned perimeter a few kilometres apart, before moving on to the next segment of their orbital track. Ansbro's work frames these objects not as isolated curiosities, but as components of a persistent, organized monitoring infrastructure, possibly extra-terrestrial in origin that has been active for decades, or longer, and in correlation to my own experiences due to dates and repeated sightings in same locations, I feel his theory holds weight in regard to this topic of public interest.

In speaking with family and friends we felt the comparison between the film *First Contact (1983),* directed by Bob Connolly and Robin Anderson, was applicable as this documentary recounted the remarkable meeting between gold-prospecting Australians and the uncontacted highland peoples of Papua New Guinea in 1930. Told largely through archival footage and first-hand accounts, it captured the shock, confusion, and fascination on both sides. The highlanders, who had never seen outsiders, suddenly confronted pale-skinned strangers with strange clothes, power of flight, and firearms, and the Australians, who entered an untouched world with its own complex culture, language, and social order. The film explored how each group tried to interpret the other through its own worldview, highlanders sometimes viewing the newcomers as spirits or supernatural beings, and the prospectors struggling to communicate and assert control in an unfamiliar environment. This initial meeting became a turning point, forever altering the highlanders' isolation and reshaping the cultural landscape of the region.

Personally, this film gave me a better, less fantastical perspective on our current phenomenon being documented all over the world, including my own experiences, as an allegory for a potential encounter between off planet terrestrials and present-day humanity. In my own version, the Australian gold prospectors are the extra-terrestrials, technologically advanced explorers, while the highland peoples of Papua New Guinea represent 'us' modern humans, living within the bounds of our familiar planet and understanding of the universe. The shock, confusion, and fascination depicted in the film, mirror what humanity might be feeling, as we are confronted by dazzling craft, wielding technologies beyond our comprehension. Just as the highlanders saw pale-skinned strangers with unfamiliar clothing, tools, and weapons, it will not be long before we see visitors with energy-based devices, advanced materials, or methods of travel that defy our physics. It's evident our initial attempts to interpret them through our existing frameworks, scientific, cultural, and even mythological, would parallel the highlanders' struggle to explain their unexpected guests.

Such a meeting would be a turning point for our species, granting an upgrade, from technological, psychological, economical, and cultural, while ending our nonsensical cosmic isolation and forcing a profound rethinking of our place in the universe and I welcome this with an open heart and mind as we make way for another jump in our evolution.

Author's Comment. It would be hard to argue with Lewis's thoughts above. But if planet Earth is being observed by these spheres, then surely, they have enough data by now? Why are they still observing us, if indeed that is what these spheres are doing? Let us not forget dear reader, that these types of spheres have been seen from all corners of the Globe. From Mexico, to Peru, from the United States, France, and Europe.

THE MANCHESTER SPHERE

And then there was that silver sphere that actually landed on the tarmac at Manchester Airport in June 2024, which was eventually scared off by an airport vehicle despatched by Air Traffic Control. The story goes that an individual by the name of Captain Bigelow claimed that he received a number of images by a colleague that was part of a flight crew that observed and filmed the object in June of 2024. It initially appeared as a transparent sphere which was hovering a few inches above the ground. Captain Bigalow stated that in size, he would compare it to the size of a small car. He further stated that this object descended vertically in 15kts [27.8 km/h or 17.3 mph] of wind. As the airport vehicle approached the sphere, the object took off vertically. In a post featured on the social media site Reddit, Captain Bigalow was quoted as saying,

> "I have been an airline pilot for a [UK] operator for several decades and we know what is normal and what isn't. We know what we are looking at in the skies. This is not a balloon or a drone and has been a hot topic of conversation in our community for quite a while."

As for the airport authorities, well a spokesman stated to the Independent Newspaper online (5th December 2024) that they believed the images to be fake, and that they saw nothing that proved the images were genuine. A spokesman (you always get the spokesman don't you!) said.

"We have systems that pick up anything that could be a threat to aviation. Anything that gives off a signal we would know about. If there was anything on the airfield at the airport, as is depicted in the imagery, it would be treated as a major incident, and no such disruption event has occurred".

At the end of the day, aerial spheres have been witnessed all over the world, for one to land however at a major British Airport, well that took it to a different level (if of course we believe the witnesses and the photographs) As for Lewis Thornhill who I mentioned above, well such was his desire to get to the truth regarding what he had witnessed in the Edinburgh skies, his UFO sightings were mentioned in the Edinburgh Evening News (online) 27th June 2025. It read.

EDINBURGH RESIDENT DEMANDS UFO DISCLOSURE HEARING, AFTER SPOTTING SILVER SPHERES OVER SCOTLAND'S CAPITAL

'An Edinburgh resident is calling for a formal parliamentary hearing on Unidentified Aerial Phenomena (UAPs), often referred to as UFOs, after witnessing and documenting multiple silver spherical objects displaying extraordinary characteristics over the Sighthill area. The sighting, which was said to have occurred on Saturday 14th June at approximately 11:33am, has prompted the witness to provide photographic and video evidence to Members of the Scottish Parliament (MSPs) and the local media. Lewis Thornhill, a resident of Edinburgh, recently described the experience as 'life changing.' According to Mr Thornhill, the silent, reflective silver spheres floated effortlessly above the Sighthill skyline'.

"They were perfectly spherical and remained absolutely still for a significant period. Then, they transformed, turning into pure light before either becoming completely invisible or shooting off at speeds no known drone could achieve".

'Mr Thornhill captured clear photographic images and video footage of the objects, which have been shared with MSPs and are now being made public to support the call for greater transparency'.

"The footage speaks for itself. This wasn't a drone, a plane, or a balloon. This sighting adds to a growing number of UAP reports worldwide, including recent disclosures and discussions by governmental bodies in the United States".

'The NLP practitioner believes it is time for the Scottish Parliament to seriously address these phenomena'.

"The implications of these unidentified objects flying in our airspace are profound. It raises serious questions about national security, air traffic safety, and what exactly is operating in our skies. We need a public hearing where evidence can be presented, experts can provide testimony, and the Scottish public can finally get answers".

'Lewis has formally written to MSPs, urging them to initiate a parliamentary inquiry into UAPs. The witness hopes that sharing this evidence publicly will encourage other witnesses to come forward and put pressure on elected officials to act'.

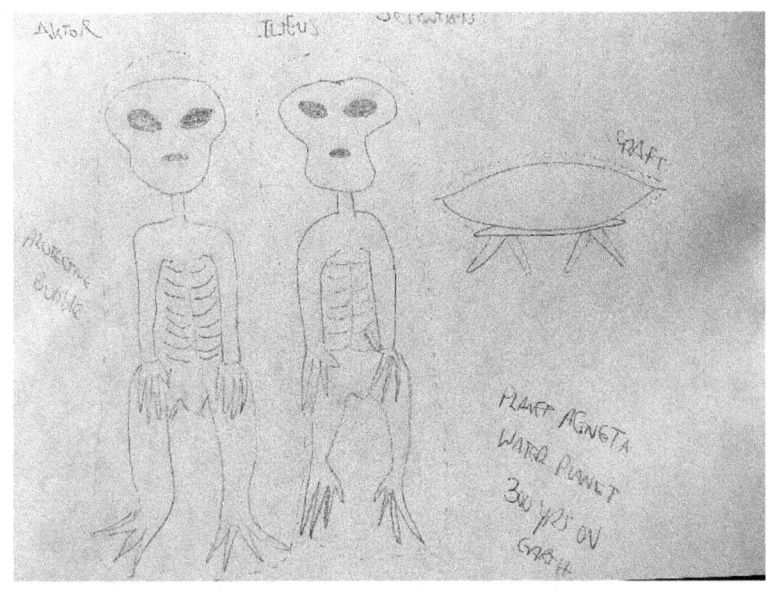

Sketch of Aktor and Illeus drawn by Steven Bird

Cairnpapple Hill Sky Watch 22nd June 2024

Sky watchers at Cairnpapple Hill 22nd June 2024

Steven Bird on the right, channelling Aktor at Cairnpapple Hill 11th July 2025

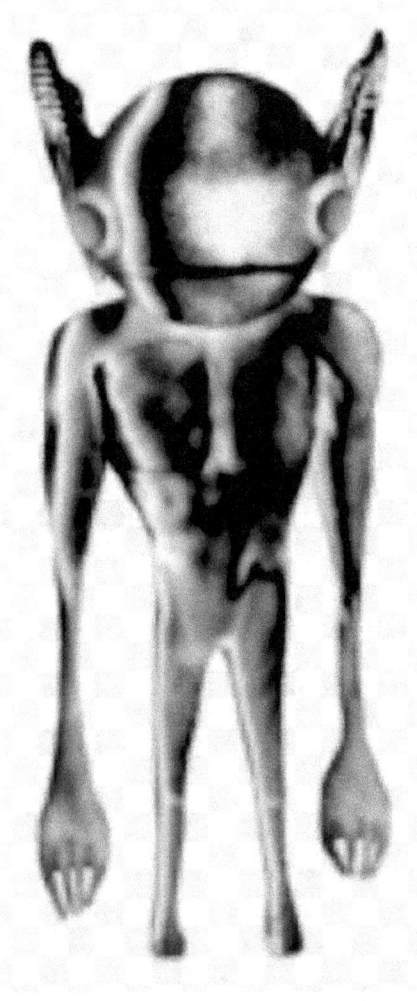

Hopkinsville Alien. Similar to Newtongrange creature

Mock up of the Newtongrange creature in the tree.

At original location July 1978

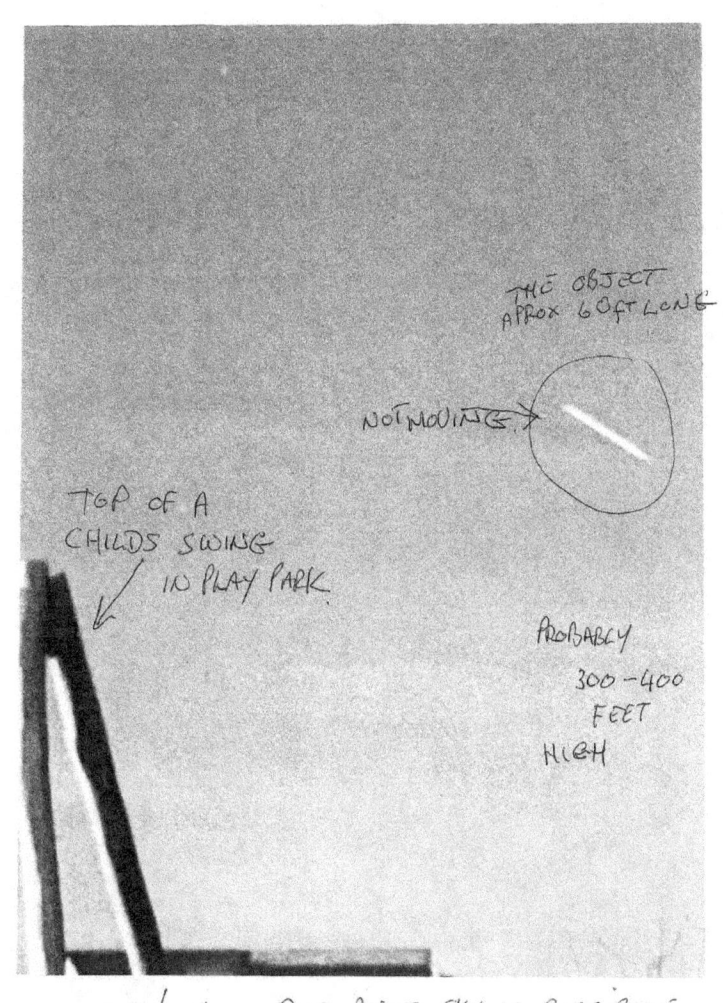

Lorna Gower's UFO photograph 9th December 2024

**Martin Morrison dash cam grab of his A89 UFO
January 9th 2020**

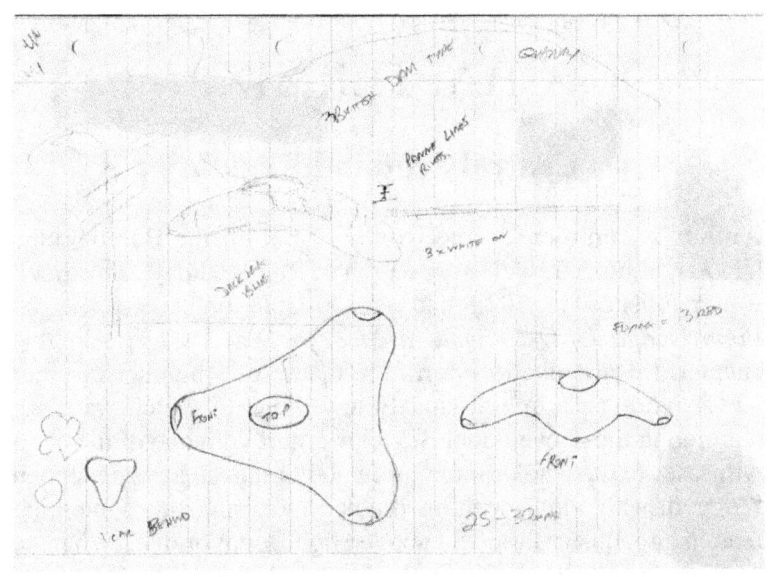

Ronald Hall drawing of his A71 UFO sighting 1999

CHAPTER SIX

Central Scotland Region

Author's Comment. I co-wrote a book on the Bonnybridge UFO sightings with fellow researcher, Ron Halliday. This book was published in 2025 and is available on Amazon. *'The Bonnybridge UFO Enigma, a Modern Day Mystery'*. In this chapter, I'd just like to inform the reader of a number of other UFO sightings in and around Bonnybridge of which were not featured in the above book. But let me start with one of the main witnesses to the whole Bonnybridge UFO saga, that was Stephen Sloggett, who, along with his mother and sister, saw something land in a road near farmland above High Bonnybridge. When he read my account in the book, he decided to give me more information on his family's sighting that night. Here is what he had to say.

STEPHEN SLOGGETT ACCOUNT

Hi again Malcolm,

"Myself and my mum (Isa) and sister (Carole) were walking home from my sister (Carole's) house in Hallglen. We took the backroads from Falkirk to Bonnybridge as this is the fastest way back. We must have got halfway back home, as we got to the forest area of the moorland and still walking along the road. I had a feeling to look up which I did, and when I did, I saw a large black object with lights on it going over my head and just missing the top of the forest trees. There was no noise at all. You could hear a cow mooing from a field nearby, that was how silent it was. I then asked my sister and mum did they see that. Which they did, as it was flying over. We carried on home as we thought nothing of it. We then got about five to ten minutes along the road when we saw another object parked on the road, also with lights on it. We stood staring at this object, then we suddenly heard a mechanical noise from the object. The best way to describe this

noise, would be like a bus door opening and the air brakes from a lorry. Then there was this scary howling cry that we heard just after the mechanical noise (like from the horror film werewolf) then without warning, this object shot up towards the sky and moved to the left of us where we saw two more of the objects just hovering over a field in the distance which looked like they were pulsating in the night sky. We were running along the road now, my mum in front and me, and my sister and I together behind her. We got to an opening in a field, where, to the left-hand side of us, this light appeared from the field entrance and stopped at us. Then, without warning, it flashed at us, as if your picture was being taken. Then it left as fast as it arrived. My sister and I looked at each other wondering what had just happened, then we just ran faster to catch up with my mum and eventually got home".

"I hope this is OK for you Malcolm. I find it weird that I can still remember what happened in detail, but over the years there is certain points that are blank as I can't remember getting past the lights in the sky to the light at the entrance. It's like that bit is blank to me. So, I'm not sure if we have missing time on this or not. I'm still not certain".

Author's Comment. Well, some of the above is certainly different from what I was told at the time. Could it be as time has gone on, that Stephen's recall has come back, or has he added to it? What I will say, is that I thank Stephen for getting in touch and giving me his recollection of events many years after his March 1992 encounter. We stay in Stirlingshire where Les Selby witnessed something that he will never forget.

THE STRANGE TRIANGLE!

It was around ten minutes to eight on a cold October night in 2022 when Les Selby was walking home in the dark to his house in Bainsford near Falkirk. Staring up into the night sky, he had a good look at the planet Jupiter shining bright amongst the millions of other stars spread out across the sky when all of a sudden, his attention was drawn to a large black triangular object coming into view which had an array of flashing red and white lights. He watched in stunned silence as it made its way slowly across the sky and disappeared behind an old birch tree. It was more the size of this object that stunned Les, way bigger than a commercial airliner. To this day, Les still ponders over that incredible sight and wonders what could it have been!

Author's Comment. Our next case file comes to us from East Mains, East Kilbride in Central Scotland. Linda Davenpot was walking back towards her house when she witnessed something strange. Linda now takes up the story.

Hi Malcolm.

"I had a strange sighting around 2006 when I was approaching my house after walking my dogs. Above my neighbour's house, was a huge silent black triangle object with a red laser type light in the shape of a triangle underneath it. As it flew over, I ran into the house to shout for my parents. I went back outside, managed to take a picture, and when I ran into the living room, the picture wasn't on my phone, and my mobile went weird with squares and triangle shape symbols on the screen which freaked me out. I've also seen loads of orb like lights moving around when I have been walking home at three in the morning from a friend's house".

Author's Comment. I'd now like to inform you about a few sky watches that my society, Strange Phenomena Investigations (SPI) have put on in the Bonnybridge area. Bonnybridge is know the world over, as a 'UFO Hot Spot', or 'Window Area'. Our society held a sky watch at Bonnybridge in June 2021. Here is what happened.

Bonnybridge World UFO Day Skywatch July 3rd, 2021

Well, I'm pleased to say that SPI's part in the World UFO Day where we held a sky watch went off well. Over 20 people turned up to participate in the event, and, after initially meeting up in the car park adjacent to the Bonnybridge Community Centre, we all headed up in a convoy of cars to the designated meeting place that Provost Billy Buchanan had arranged for us all to meet. Billy had provided some plastic chairs for people to sit on and also provided a box full of crisps and cans of iron bru and bottles of water for those who liked to nibble whilst watching the skies. Not only that, but Billy was also on hand with his trusty midge spray to ensure that those pesky wee blighters didn't annoy those assembled too much.

The location was perfect, and one had a commanding view downwards looking over the Stirlingshire countryside. A rolling mist could be seen lying over parts of the ground which eventually dissipated as the night wore on. When we arrived, the sky was 95% clear, but eventually cloud cover came over later in the evening. It was around 11:10pm when I assembled all the sky watchers together to brief them on what to expect of the night. I also spoke about some of the UFO sightings in the Bonnybridge area, and how it all started for me. I then turned it over to Provost Billy Buchanan who informed everyone about his role in the Bonnybridge UFO sightings and how this small Scottish town was at one point, dubbed the UFO Capital of the world. Billy is a wonderful speaker, and at times had the assembled crowd in giggles with his patter. Psychic Ian Shanes, also spoke about what his views were on these so-called alien entities, and how mankind should interact with them. All good stuff and very thoughtful. I then asked other people to bring forward their own stories all whilst our eyes were continually scanning the skies. By now the cloud cover had covered most of the sky, but the good thing was, it didn't rain. Indeed, the night was quite cool, so much so, that I was out there without a jacket!

I then mentioned to those assembled about a gentleman by the name of Arthur Shuttlewood, who was a former newspaper correspondent at the Warminster Journal in Warminster (The town of Warminster in Wiltshire England, was, for a time, the English equivalent to Bonnybridge in so far as UFO sightings) What Arthur Shuttlewood used to do, was to shine a torch (flashlight for our American readers) up into the night sky and was surprised when he received strange lights coming back at him. So, needless to say, when in Rome and all that! we just had to do the same. There were a few attendees who had brought with them, some very powerful lasers, and boy, were they powerful! Within seconds the Stirlingshire sky was awash with dancing green lasers lights, one of which produced a stunning square box of circular lights. Someone pipped up and said that people miles away would be surprised to see this, and would no doubt think that the UFOs were back in Bonnybridge! Sadly, our desired attempt to draw forth any possible UFOs didn't work. But in the crowd was a lady well known to me, she asked me to call her Wooshwa, her real name is Tress Blair.

Wooshwa

Now please understand, that there are many people who deal with the subject of UFOs in their own way. This lady claims to be from another planet and is here on planet Earth to help people come to terms with the visitors. I spoke to the assembled crowd saying that Wooshwa would attempt to bring forth her 'space friends' by what she called her 'calling'. Her 'calling', in point of fact, comprised of her singing in a strange language towards the sky. Yes, it looked and sounded kind of strange, but that's the thing folks, we were here on a sky watch, and I was prepared to allow anyone to show their wares 'so to speak'. Wooshwa followed that by speaking out in a strange language, again hoping to entice her 'sky friends' to appear. Although none of us assembled could see anything, Wooshwa did say that they were near, and that there was a strong presence, a heavy presence around. I've no problems with people doing their own thing. We are well aware that Steven Greer and his friends have tried something called the CE5 Protocols to try and contact UFOs. At this point we then tried another attempt to bring forth UFOs. Wooshwa had everyone join in a circle and lock arms, where we all sent out loving and positive thoughts, again hoping that we could bring forth these Bonnybridge UFOs. All but one, saw nothing. One chap said he saw a bright white light move from one part of the sky to another very quickly. That could of course have been anything, but then again! The sky watch was being filmed for a documentary on Scottish UFOs, and prior to arriving at the sky watch area, the lady who was doing the filming, had us all filling out disclosure forms. It was great to have one of my daughters at the sky watch, Karen, she brought along her boyfriend Garry. My other half Carole was also in attendance.

Provost Billy Buchanan then made a statement to the crowd about taking me and some others to Roswell New Mexico where he hoped to get Bonnybridge Twinned with Roswell. Billy has already been to Roswell and met the mayor of the town, and I believe discussions are still ongoing. Billy then presented me with a large bag regarding the twinning of both towns.

At the end of the day, it had been a great night. Yes, some might see the singing to the stars part a bit off the wall, but I was happy to try it. Some may also say that it wasn't scientific, but advances in science come in many ways! So, whilst many parts of England were getting rain, here in Stirlingshire it had been a dry night and thankfully not cold. It was great to meet old and new faces, some of whom it took me a while longer to register, as I hadn't seen them for many years. So, we never saw any UFOs, but it had been a great night, where like-minded people came together to share and enjoy their passion that is UFOlogy.

Author's Comment. The following is yet another sky watch that the author and fellow enthusiasts held on the outskirts of Bonnybridge.

BONNYBRIDGE SKY WATCH.
SATURDAY 18TH MAY 2024

Around 15+ like-minded souls met up outside the Bonnybridge post office on the evening of Saturday 18th of May 2024 to take part in our SPI sky watch. Our sky watches are set up to inform not just our own SPI members, but the general public as well in regard to what one can expect to see in the sky and what 'not' to expect. In other words, strange aerial objects flitting around the sky. And as we were in a so called 'UFO Hot Spot', we had high hopes that perhaps we would see something which many others have witnessed in the skies above Bonnybridge over the years. After a brief chat, it was time to head off in convoy to our new sky watch site, that of the Wheel Camp and Caravan Park which sits just a few miles away from Bonnybridge. Once all the cars had parked up, I then invited our merry band of sky watchers into the Ceilidh House. This was a wooden building set up on the camp site specifically for those campers and caravaners who have travelled from all over the U.K. to chill out. We had the full use of the Ceilidh House for our sky watch base. After we all had assembled inside, I gave a short talk about what to expect at a sky watch. Also attending our sky watch that night, were a few, mums and dads with their children who were staying over at the camp site. These people were told of our sky watch by the camp site owner, Ian Hogg. When I asked if anyone had any questions, one wee boy who was staying over with his parents at the caravan site, spoke up and told us that he had a ghost in his house that kept knocking over chairs. Nice one son. After that brief chat inside, I then assembled all the sky watchers outside, where we then walked up and over a pile of solid, (but in part, a crumbly shale like mound of earth which ran for a good 50 or so yards) this led you up to a track that continued to the sky watch site. There were a few falls over this earthen hurdle, but thankfully no one was hurt. The owner of the camp site told me that he aims to clear all this earthen mound away so that a clear, and uninterrupted walk can be made to the site.

After a beautiful warm sunny day all over Scotland, our night time sky was obliterated with a hazy misty cloud. There was not one single patch of clear sky to be seen. This for me, was the worst sky watching conditions that I have faced anywhere in the British Isles. Thankfully it wasn't cold, although the temperature did drop a few hours later. Once we all had walked up to the sky watch site, and had placed our fold down chairs, I then proceeded to inform those assembled about some of the Bonnybridge UFO story. This included the sightings, the media, and the British Government's role in what was going on. After which some people broke off into little groups to do their own thing.

With us on this night, was Tress Blair (Wooshwa, mentioned earlier) who is in contact with 'beings' not of this Earth. Tress, states that her real home is on the planet Sucruma. She was here at the sky watch, to try and bring forward her 'light beings' and their energies. Before we tried this experiment, SPI's medium Steven Bird opened up with a protective prayer which ensured that no harm would come to the group. Around 14 of us, formed a circle and raised our hands skywards where Tress then spoke out into the night air, asking that her 'light being friends' come forward. She then proceeded to speak out in a strange language, followed by her singing in this strange language. A language which she states is from her home planet of Sucruma. Yes, all this does sound bizarre, but who are we, to judge others? Who are we, who chase ghosts and UFOs, to decry anyone else about what they do? I think that it's a disgrace when people attack other people simply because they are different. It will never happen on my watch. Whilst Tress could see small beings standing around us, we couldn't. That said, there were a few people who did pick up strange 'energies' that surrounded our circle. One lady in our group, could not close her open outstretched hands. (She did eventually, but it took a while) In a photograph that I took as I stepped away from the group, you can see a thin light coming down from the sky to our group. Also, if you squeeze up on the photograph, you will see two small orbs in the sky. Moisture in the air or something else?

SPI's Steven Bird also felt bizarre energies a few hundred yards away from our main sky watch location. Whilst the sky didn't clear on the night, this was still a successful night, for it provided a great opportunity for people to get to know one another, share stories, and build lasting friendships. I particularly enjoyed watching a bizarre Ring Bell door cam footage shown to me by Margaret Tollan of a strange light next to her house. This small light got larger, then shot away to the left and was gone from sight. And whilst I suggested a few possible explanations that could account for this strange footage, even I was floored by this, and my feeble attempts to explain away this footage didn't even sit right with me! I'd like to thank the following people who turned up on the night. Steven Bird, Mark Anderson, Paul John Grey, Gavin Dow, Mark Wilson, Mike Porter, Ian Abbott, Margaret Tollan, Emma Pear, Tress Blair, Andrew Hyde, Anna Bell, Stuart Bell, Stevie Bell, Elisha Bell, Gordon Stuart, Angela McDade, Janette Gillespie, Marie Adens, and a few others whose names I didn't get. Then there were at least another 7 people, those mums and dads with their kids who came up to the sky watch site. So, whilst the sky wasn't great on the night, a good time was still had by all.

Author's Comment. Another sky watch we held, was this time at a location just a few miles away. This was to be the very first time ever, that my society, Strange Phenomena Investigations (SPI) undertook Steven Greer's CE5 Protocols. Here is what happened.

BONNYBRIDGE UFO SKY WATCH 28th JUNE 2025

SPI members and members of the public attended our sky watch at the Wheel Camp and Caravan Park near Bonnybridge. For the first time, SPI decided to try Steven Greer's CE5 Protocols in an attempt to see, if we too, could hopefully attract some strange aero forms in the sky to appear. Like anything else in life, if you don't give a try, then you will never know! But what are the CE5 Protocols?

CE-5 is a term describing a fifth category of close encounters with Extraterrestrial Intelligence (ETI), characterised by mutual, bilateral communication rather than unilateral contact.

The CE-5 Initiative endeavours to establish a cooperative, peaceful and sustainable relationship between humans and any and all ET 'peoples' which may visit Earth.

CE-5 Initiative protocols are used to 'vector' UFOs into an area and then engage them in a peaceful, cooperative exchange using lights, sounds, thought, intentions, other modalities.

OUR CE5 SKY WATCH

Billy Devlin drove me over to the meet up point which was outside the Scot Mid Co-op on Bonnybridge High Street. Thereafter, and along with some others, we all drove off in convoy to the sky watch location, that of the Wheel Camp and Caravan Park. Park owner Ian Hogg once again had given SPI permission to use his site which we thanked him for. Arriving at the site, I met up with Ian Hogg who told me that he had removed tons of shale which once blocked the pathway up to the UFO sky watch site. Some SPI members will no doubt remember scrambling over those 5-foot-tall shale mounds on our last sky watch there. Not only was it slightly dangerous in the dark that last time, but it was a test of endurance to those who did not have such agility to scale those mounds. If I recall, there were a few slips and slides from people on that last visit. Well, no such problems this time around, it was all gone, and it was an enjoyable 10-minute walk to the top of the hill where we had our base camp.

But prior to that walk up the hill, we all settled down on chairs in the ceilidh House which was on site. A lovely wooden log type cabin which we have used before. I gave a short speech about why we hold these sky watches, I then spoke about some of the UFO incidents that had occurred in the skies above our heads, after which, I then proceeded to talk to everyone about our plans to do the CE5 Protocols and explained that this was the very first time, that we at SPI had ever used them. I started SPI up in 1979, and here I was in 2025 using something for the very first time. I explained that there were no guarantees, and that it's the old adage, *'no cheek. no chance'*. In other words, you don't get nothing by sitting on your backside reading about it! It was nice to see that four other people who were on holiday at Ian's camp site had joined us. Two were up from England, (husband and wife) they had no interest in UFOs whatsoever but were more than happy to take time out and join us.

After my talk, we all started the slow walk up the pathway, up past the UFO Landing Site signage, and made camp at the top of the hill. After some more information by myself about sky watches in general, I asked that they all join hands in a circle where I proceeded to read out the CE5 Protocols of which, playing in the background, were the sound tones which Steven Greer states helps facilitate any 'craft' to appear.

Prior to the sky watch, and for the past few days, the weather had been dreadful with driving rain, but tonight the skies were clear with a few scattered clouds. The temperature was also comfortable, in that it was not cold. So all in all, perfect conditions for a sky watch. As Billy Devlin and I were standing outside the circle monitoring the event, taking pictures and taking notes etc, I continually scanned the clear skies for anything that looked out of place, but all was quiet. Other than the Scottish midges that is, who were out in abundance. And how did I know that they were Scottish midges? Well, because they had kilts on, didn't they! After a period of time, I concluded the CE5 Protocols and asked all those assembled to keep watching the skies. We all saw a number of satellites, and a few flashes in the sky, but nothing that I would say was out of the ordinary. No matter, it had to be tried. Again, if you don't try, you don't get. And whilst we tried and still didn't get anything, it won't put us off from trying this procedure at further SPI sky watches. It's like the paranormal, you can't expect ghosts to appear at the drop of a hat, they will appear when they want to.

All in all then, it still was a very productive night. Some people who attended had brought along with them, those thin tiny green laser lights, this was something to behold, as were their night vision goggles. Talk about turning night into day! Meeting new friends and sharing stories at these events is also a plus. Getting 'out there' instead of sitting at home reading about it is something that more people should do. Engage with others, enjoy the comradery. So, whilst no UFOs were seen, it had been a successful night.

DID THE CE5 TONES BRING FORWARD THIS OBJECT?

Whilst writing the above in August 2025, I received a text from Marc McLean who told me the following.

Hi Malcolm,

"I was out trying see some Perseid meteors. I knew I was going to be out for a few hours, so got myself all chilled out and fired up the CE5 app. I followed all the steps, and after 15 minutes of playing the CE5 tones through my car stereo, this piercing white orb came out of nowhere. Before this photo was taken, I was taking photos above the horizon, when this amazing pure white ball appeared out of nowhere. It just appeared like someone switched a light on extremely bright. It moved left to right three times rapidly. I quickly panned my camera down to take a photo".

"I went to take a second photo but it flickered and vanished, I immediately checked my Flight Radar App, there was no aircraft in that area, no noise, nothing, my mind was blown. Every hair on my arms and back of my neck were on edge. I am out on a regular basis photographing aurora, star constellations and meteor showers, I've seen all sorts of planes and helicopters, drones, starlink, ISS and other satellites in the night skies all year round, I have NEVER seen anything like this before! Quite shook by it to be honest".

13sec exposure - F4 - ISO100 - 18mm Nikon.
Location: top of Eaglesham Moor looking East.
Date/Time: 14 August 2025 @ 0:52hrs.

Author's Comment. One of Marc's photographs can be seen in the photographic section of this book.

THE BRIGHT SPEEDING LIGHT

The beauty of today's technology provides one the opportunity to get in touch with anyone across the world in the blink of an eye. The internet has brought a great opportunity for people like the author to get in touch with fellow UFO investigators, or in this case, UFO witnesses. Whilst the following case may not necessarily have been UFOs, we have to bear in mind that the light forms witnessed in this case, are part and parcel of the whole makeup of the UFO phenomenon. The following is the testimony as given to me by the witness. someone who most certainly is a 'pillar of our community', and someone who has served in the armed forces. This, as far as I am concerned, makes him a trained observer. Here is what Alec Lowe had to say.

Hi Malcolm,

"My name is Alex Lowe. A brief bit of my personal history before I reveal my sightings. I lived in Bonnybridge in Stirlingshire and attended school at Bonnybridge Primary then Denny High. I did nearly two years of apprenticeship in Denny

as a carpenter with a company named A. B. Hornall & Sons before beginning my 23-year, 52-day journey in the Armed Forces, a decision I took for several reasons. Mother passed away when I was five years old, and in 1965 I left Bonnybridge in search of a new family, where I found hundreds or Armed Forces Brothers in many places. On completion of my service, I found employment in Glasgow with the Territorial Army and Volunteer Reserves Association, till my retrial at the age of 65".

"As you are probably aware, Bonnybridge was a busy hub for many industries as were other towns like Denny and other Falkirk area towns and villages. From my knowledge and understanding, UFOs were not something that put Bonnybridge on the map as Spaceship City. Well, not until some serious opencast mining developed in the area where the old Fish Works used to be sited in the area between High Bonnybridge, and what is now the site of the Falkirk Wheel. To my knowledge this was the period that sightings all began".

"Some years ago, when I returned to the area and set up home, I was visited by an armed forces veteran and his wife. With them and my wife, I drove them on a journey which was on the road from Denny, Fankerton area that leads to Fintry. At some point during the journey, a very bright light appeared in the sky, that penetrated the cloud base above the Carron Valley Reservoir area, it accelerated towards the Glasgow direction at a speed which meant that it could not possibly have been car headlights or a low flying aircraft, the speed was phenomenal. Moreover, there was no sound from the sky or surrounding area. The four of us could think of no possible reason for it, and where one single person may possibly think it as something they imagined, it was in fact something we all saw and a subject we all discussed at the time. Some years later, whilst travelling from Denny in the direction of Stirling on the part of the journey that forms a straight stretch of road near to the rock quarry near Denny, there was a very bright light that appeared above and to my right, which then sped off at speed in the direction of Stirling. Again, the speed of this sighting was well beyond any aircraft even military jet aircraft, or reflection of vehicle headlights. Yet again no noise to support the aircraft theory. I have discussed these sightings with only people in my immediate family. There was one other report of the last sighting that I witnessed, and it was reported in a local newspaper that a girl had also witnessed the speeding light in the sky above a town called Cowie, in the Stirling area, this would tie in with my own sighting that would be visible from the Cowie direction".

"I always show a keen interest in anything above me in the sky at any time as a result of a military awareness of something that might be a threat or something of value or pure interest. I am glad now that I can report what I have seen to a person who has some genuine take on the matter and putting this information onto record where it can be shared with others who have an interest in what we have in our area that is unique. I hope this information might possibly be of some value in connection with other events reported to you on the subject".

"All the very best with your pursuits on the matter".

Best regards, Alex Lowe.

Author's Comment. I thanked Alec in an e-mail, and he replied by saying.

Hi Malcolm,

"Thanks for your email, it's good to hear that research has been getting carried out in the background when the sightings are being reported. People probably talk about the sightings a lot less than maybe they should. I spoke about the things that I witnessed with some friends out of the area, but not with locals I know. You always get the feeling that there has been so many sightings and what you witnessed might be viewed as just another person getting on the band wagon. I am glad now that I can report what I have seen to a person who has some genuine take on the matter and putting this information onto record where it can be shared with others who have an interest in what we have in our area that is unique. I am not so sure about what Area 51 has to boast about, Bonnybridge area has witnessed so much activity that has not came about from the reports of scientists or boffins in the United States. I get the feeling that Area 51 is more a part of Hollywood rather than a desert area. By all means use anything you wish to from my email, if it contributes to a much

larger picture of what we are experiencing it can only explain everything individuals have witnessed and how it ties in with another sighting about the same time not too far away".
Regards, Alec Lowe.

STRANGE LIGHT ENTERED OUR BEDROOM!

Hi Malcolm,

"I have two incidents to tell you about when I lived in Bonnybridge. First In around 2003 (ish) I was waiting at traffic lights in Denny and saw a bright stationary light low in the night sky over Bonnybridge. As I watched it for around 10 seconds or so, it rushed upwards at a speed that was hard to comprehend and shot up through the cloud base. The second sighting, me and my wife were woken by a brilliant white light filling the bedroom. It was silent outside. My wife rushed outside only for the light to blink out as she stepped out onto the back garden. The light was from directly above our house. There were no cars that could have affected the light etc. I know for certain that UFOs are real. I am also frustrated that the common man keeps on awaiting disclosure. We need to stop seeking disclosure and move the narrative on now and talk with certainty and clarity about the phenomenon".
Regards. James Fisher.

Author's Comment. The following case file was brought to my attention when I spoke at a UFO Conference in Falkirk in 2017.

Hi Malcolm,

"Just to let you know we thoroughly enjoyed the Conference on Saturday at the Falkirk Town Hall, your presentation on UFOs being of particular interest". "Near the end of the conference, my wife Kerry spoke to you briefly to describe an incident we witnessed back in 1992. The following gives some details of what was observed"

Date: Monday 16th November 1992.
Time: Approx. 19:50 hrs.
Place: Greenhill Bonnybridge.
Present: Myself, my wife Kerry, our daughter Elaine.

"Travelling eastwards along targets road, Greenhill moor, about halfway between Bonnybridge and Camelon, we noticed a small bright light travelling towards us. This light gradually got bigger until it stopped and 'hovered' almost straight above us at a height of approximately 200 feet. I stopped the car and Kerry got out to get a better look. Since it was dark, we could not describe the colour of the object, but from the lights, I would estimate it to be approximately 60 feet wide, with a classical 'flying saucer' shape and domed roof. The lights were orange/red. No sound was heard at any time. All the lights seemed to be underneath the object. We don't recall any lights on the sides or top of this object. The lights were static and not flashing or blinking".

"After approximately 30 seconds, the object started to travel in a northerly direction, disappearing over the Ochil hills in approximately three seconds, again there was no sound. We were in a 'state of shock', and, for the remainder of that evening, we never spoke about this, either to each other, or anybody else. Only in the past few years have we been able to discuss the incident. Hopefully our sighting can be added to your SPI library".

Best Regards, Jim Marsden.

A STRANGE TALE OF MIB'S AND A BLACK CADILLAC

Hi Malcolm,

"After listening to a recent podcast, you were guest-speaking on, the host asked if you had a 'Men in Black' story you could personally account for. This is my recollection of that night back in 1992 on the outskirts of Bonnybridge. As I had previously mentioned on the phone about four years ago, the sighting of this object wasn't that spectacular, it was the incident shortly thereafter that really had us in a panic, and to this day a sobering account when we were nearly wiped out by a car in the dead of night. I have to mention that at that time I had no concept about what the 'Men in Black' were. I only became aware of the 'Men in Black concept many years after the event".

"I was 22 years of age when this occurred and lived in Glen Village, which was only 3.8 miles away from the incident. Typically, during weekends, three of my friends and I would head out into the surrounding area of Falkirk on our mountain bikes, which often turned into late night-time cycle jaunts. We were just average Falkirk boys hanging out late at weekends and enjoying each other's company. On one clear Saturday evening, during the summer, myself, John, Simon, and David, cycled out to two dirt binges, which were mountainous piles of dirt, that were the spoils from a nearby quarry. These binges were on the boundary between Bonnybridge (B816 b-road) and the council estate called Tamfourhill. We sat at the top of one of the binges, smoking cheap hash and chilling out into the wee small hours. (Note-When I say cheap hash, I mean cheap hash that was known as "Soap Bar Cooncil". Just to be clear, you don't hallucinate on this rank hash!"

"I estimate that the time was approximately about 12.00 at night. Looking west towards Jawcraig and Old Shields. I was the first person to notice this silent stationary object, which we estimated to be roughly 600 feet above the ground. The object was blinking three different colours, in a repeated pattern of red, orange, and white. This repeated pattern of continuous sequenced flashing, lasted for about 20 minutes. It was at this point; we must have felt conscious of what we were seeing didn't make sense. We knew of the reported local UFO sightings at the time, and didn't pay much attention, thinking that the whole deal was just a joke. I had once lived close to Edinburgh Airport, so I was used to seeing commercial aircraft, and remember having that discussion with the other three, and then ruling out every known conventional airborne craft out of the equation. (My farther worked for the British MOD, so I spent my childhood on military bases, so I knew just about every British helicopter and military plane at the time) We decided that we should start making our way back down the binge. The sighting wasn't that remarkable per say. It's what happened after it, that had us all petrified, and cycling for our lives".

A black Cadillac in industrial Falkirk during the 90's was just unheard of!

"We headed along the B816 towards Tamfourhill, which is where I grew up in my teens, and at that time of the incident John was living there. About a quarter of a mile before the roundabout that turns into Lime Road, a car appeared out of nowhere, and at great speed, came roaring up behind us, purposely trying to knock us all down, or at best trying to scare us! It was the old-style dark Cadillac! We absolutely freaked out! At the time I knew extraordinarily little about the UFO topic, and absolutely nothing about 'Men in Black', and their association with UFO sightings. A black Cadillac in industrial Falkirk during the 90's was just unheard of. It drove further down the road across the roundabout, at which point we turned into Lime Road heading for Kilbrennan Drive where John lived. Outside Johns flat, we decided to separate, leaving John and David to head into John's flat. Simon and I both lived close by, so decided to head home, making our way through the council estate towards the south end of Tamfourhill, and then using the Union canal cycle path, knowing, that if they had decided to follow us, they wouldn't be able to chase us by car along the canal path. What I distinctly remember about that night was the absolute fear in Simon's face. He was the trailing bike in our group of four, and his back tyre must have only been inches away from the car bumper. Our journey along the canal cycle path was uneventful, although Simon who was a serious churchgoer was really shaken up. I've lost touch with Simon and David but still keep in touch with John. We met for a curry night just before the first Covid lockdown. I brought up the incident during the meal and he clearly remembers that night and can offer no explanation to the sighting or the dark Cadillac".

"Before this incident, I had never seen a Cadillac car before in Falkirk. These cars are for the TV, and movie theatres. A rare car by all accounts, especially for an industrial area like Falkirk. To this day I now consider that this incident was a warning! We shouldn't have seen what we saw. But what we saw we can be certain that it was otherworldly".

Best wishes, Straiph Wilson.

THE ORB OF LIGHT ABOVE A HOUSE

Another e-mail that I received from a witness regarding a UFO, came from Peter Whitehead. He explained that it was the summer of 1993 when Peter's sister rushed into the family home shouting out that there was a large bright white light above next door's house. Knowing that something was amiss, all the family rushed out to see what this light was. Sure enough, there was this large light in the sky which Peter states, "Was not too high up". Apparently, this strange light did not hang about for long, as it soon sped off towards Bonnybridge and was lost to view within seconds.

A CYLINDRICAL UFO

Another e-mail that I received from a UFO witness, (Jack Cole) came about after he read an article about me in a Scottish newspaper. He told me that along with his wife and friends they saw something in the sky that they just couldn't explain. It was around 9:30pm on Saturday the 21st of March 2021 when looking up into the night sky from Jack's back garden, one of Jack's friend's Stewart, saw a strange cylindrical shape. A few seconds later after shouting for his friends to look, they all turned around to see this strange cylinder-shaped light, which, then got really bright and suddenly changed shape into a circular light. This appeared in the direction of Stirling. It then, according to Jack, just 'pinged away' and was gone in seconds. The only way I can describe it, and I know this sounds crazy he said, was like the back end of the Star Wars Millennium Falcon. I always keep looking up to see if it comes back.

FAUGHLIN RESERVOIR UFO

Hi Malcolm,

"I'd like to inform you about a UFO that I saw last night, (15th August 2021) I was out fishing and was walking down Tak Ma Doon Road near Faughlin Reservoir. Me and my friend saw some very strange, quick moving white oval lights flying around overhead about the hight of a two-story house. Absolutely silent, and most definitely not any sort of thing that has been man made. There was around eight of them. The lights were not an intense sort of light, and they did not even disturb the dark clouds as they passed through them. Two of them landed in the trees nearby. We left the area immediately. I have witnessed things before, but certainly not like this. I'm a big fan of your research and also Steven Greer s work".

Author's Comment. There are a number of UFO sightings that are brought to my attention, many of which are only told to me many years after the event, and as such, it can be quite difficult to gather any further facts. That said, I still feel that they should be told, for one never knows who might come forward and say that they too, saw something near Faughlin Reservoir!

THE M9-M80 BLACK TRIANGLE

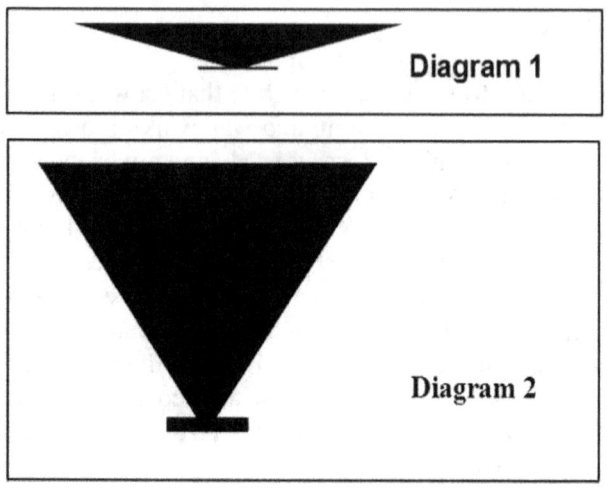

Sighting Time: 6:00pm
Day/Night: Daytime
No. of Witnesses: 4
Duration: 1 min

Appearance and Description of Objects

Completely black and completely triangular except for a small rectangular 'bar' at one apex.

Size of Object(s)

"The object was an equilateral (or very close) triangle. The object's relative size became bigger as we approached it and drove underneath, but holding my hand at arm's length, my fingers would never have been more than a few inches apart even at the closest point".

Description of Surroundings

"The sighting took place on the M9 (M80) motorway near Stirling in Scotland. This is a very rural area of Scotland with only small towns dotted either side of the motorway I am unsure whether there are any military bases nearby, but the oil refinery at Grangemouth would have been fairly close".

Full Description And Details

"On Sunday 6th July 1997 at about 18:30hrs, we were driving back from a volleyball tournament in Perth. It was a beautiful clear summer evening, there were four of us in the car (I was sitting in the front passenger seat), and I think we had just passed Stirling when I noticed a strange object directly above the motorway in front of us. I asked the driver if he could see it and he said he could. I then asked him if he'd ever seen anything like it and he said he hadn't. It was hard to tell exactly how big the craft was or how far away. My best guess is that it was a bit wider than the wingspan of a small two-seater aeroplane, and that it was flying at no more than a few hundred feet above us. It certainly wasn't anything like as high as a passenger jet, more like the height you see helicopters flying at when you can still see the pilot inside. Because it seemed fairly close, we were able to get a very good look at the craft as we approached it and then passed underneath it. It appeared to be very flat, as we couldn't see any height to it at all. All we ever really saw was the triangular underside of the craft (The diagram shown here, shows how the object looked as we approached it from 'behind'.) It must have been either hovering or travelling very slowly since we appeared to catch up with it and pass underneath it in much the same time we would have if it had been standing still (we were probably travelling at about 80mph). I remember actually asking the driver if he knew which way it was moving, and he said no. (Diagram 2 (shown above) shows how the object looked from directly underneath.)

I remember the shape very clearly and apart from the 'T-bar' at the 'front', the rest of the craft was completely uniform and triangular. The craft was totally black, there were no markings of any kind that we could make out, there appeared to be no source of propulsion, and we couldn't hear any noise at all as we passed below (although being in the car it's not clear whether we would have been able to hear anything anyway). All four people in the car saw the craft, although the driver and I probably got the best view as we were sitting in the front. The whole sighting would have taken no more than minute or so from the moment we first saw the craft until we had driven so far past it, we couldn't really make it out anymore. There was a fair amount of traffic on the motorway at the time so I would guess that many others must have seen it as well".

Can this sighting be explained as a conventional man-made object?

"The object was certainly not a natural phenomenon of any kind. I suppose it could have been some sort of stealth aircraft; the black colour and triangular shape are probably the best evidence for this. However, the stealth aircraft I have seen still look a bit like conventional aircraft. This was, or appeared to be, completely flat and completely triangular. We couldn't even really tell which end was the front. It had no visible source of propulsion, it had nothing, not even joins, underneath suggesting anywhere that landing gear could be stowed, and it appeared to be hovering or travelling very slowly. I heard somewhere that current stealth aircraft have a minimum air speed of around 100 mph".

Witness Background

"At the time of the sighting described above, I was just about to start my final year at university I would have been 31 at the time. The occupations of the other witnesses in the car at the time were a policeman, a teacher (I think) and the other I don't know".

Views on UFOs, before and after sighting

"I had an open mind before but didn't think too much about them, although I still probably knew more about them than the average person. I have always had an interest in 'fringe-scientific' topics, but UFOs were nowhere near top of the list. Since this sighting my interest has grown considerably, and I have become an avid watcher of the skies. I have also had four subsequent sightings (two daytime, one dusk, and one night-time), all with other witnesses, and three in the same place. Which oddly enough were above the Oval Cricket ground in London. And while each was a bit odd in its own way, none were anything like the clear sighting of an obviously structured craft seen at close quarters described above.

Author's Comment. I would say that this sighting, is probably one of the best triangular UFO sightings in Scotland, and whilst there is that possibility that the object might have been some kind of super stealth technology, we can't be sure. The above was written up for me by witness David Luther Flint.

We now move over to Fife, a part of the central region of Scotland that has also seen its fair share of UFO sightings, the most notable of which is the 'Falkland Hill UFO Incident' which concerned a family who not only witnessed large black triangular shaped craft in the sky near the small village of Newton of Falkland, but they also claimed to have seen numerous small grey 'beings' in a field near the village. All this was written up in my book, *'The Falkland Hill UFO Incident'* available on Amazon. Since that book was published there have been a few people who have come forward with UFO sightings in and around the date of the Falkland Hill UFO Incident, namely, the 23rd of September 1996 as the following case files now relate.

THE SAME NIGHT AS THE FALKLAND HILL UFO INCIDENT!

Our next case was sent to me by 35-year-old Samantha Skelly; however, at the time of her sighting, she was only seven years old. She also witnessed this with some other school children. Here, in her own words, is what Samantha had to say about this incident.

"On the night of Monday 23rd September 1996, I was seven years old. Myself and my mother and two other neighbours, along with my sister and a few other children, including the neighbours' children, were waiting for a junior session to end at the local Baptist Church in Collydean North Glenrothes. The time was either. 6:25pm or 7:25pm. One of the adults said something about something in the sky and remarking. *'What is that'?* At this point the object grabbed my attention, and I excitedly ran into the church a few times. The minister was just looking at me in confusion, guitar in hand and nursery aged children, too young to understand, were staring blankly. *"There's a UFO outside, There's aliens. You all have to come out and see this"*, or words to that effect, but nobody did. I must have entered an exited the building a number of times in around a minute and it was still there. A massive black triangular object in size, gliding silently with an air of authority over the church. I cannot recall if it vanished, glided off, or it went away elsewhere"

Author's Comment. In her UFO sighting account form to me, Samantha stated that even although she was seven years old at the time, she still, to this day remembers what effect this object had on her. She said that it had a combination of a calming effect on her, coupled with bewilderment. She said that there were around seven children, aged between five and eight, along with three adults. Her mother aged thirty, and two neighbours aged thirty-two and twenty-eight respectively. The sighting only lasted for around two minutes, but in those two minutes the vision that she had that day, still remains with her. But what makes this case so interesting to the author, is that it fell on the same exact day as one of Scotland's most controversial UFO cases, 'The Falkland Hill UFO Incident' which also occurred on September 23rd, 1996. With the Falkland case however, that occurred just under two hours later. Only a matter of a few miles separates the town of Glenrothes from Newton of Falkland. Was the object that Samantha saw along with school friends and a few adults, the same object that was witnessed by four other people that same night? Well, I guess we will never truly know. But for me, in all likelihood, it's a strong possibility. For more information on the Falkland Hill UFO Incident, see my book of the same name available on Amazon. I should point out however, that the big difference with the Glenrothes sighting and the Falkland Hill sighting, is that the Falkland sighting involved small grey 'beings'!

ARE YOU THE SUSAN FROM THE ORIGINAL FALKLAND HILL CASE?

Back in 2014, I received an e-mail which I received from someone who I believe to be Susan, the daughter of Mary Morrison in the main Falkland Hill UFO Incident. I've written to her since that original e-mail, but sadly I've not had a reply. In a reply to my original e-mail to her, she responded with.

Hi Malcolm.

"I don't have anything noted down. As for the times and dates, you pretty much have them right anyway. I can remember clearly what happened that night though unfortunately it's not something easily forgotten. It is also not the end of my experiences if you like. I'm not sure what's relevant to what actually happened that night, but it does seem to have opened some kind of door into strange happenings. At the time I was told not to say much or give much information, I can only imagine this was because I was just a teenager, not sure not talking about it helped though. I think

my mother just wanted things to return to normal again. As for Mary and Peter, I don't see them anymore. I was in a relationship with her older son for a while, we all stayed close for a long time. I started to notice things about her later though, things I felt uncomfortable with, and since then we have not stayed in touch".

Author's Comment. I do hope that Susan gets back in touch with me, as she was a leading witness to the events of that September night back in 1996. I'd now like to present some more UFO sightings coming from the Fife region. We start with Fiona Williamson's testimony.

TRIANGLES, ORBS, AND ALIENS

"My first 'sighting' was in March or April 1996. I was driving northwards up the B920 between Lochgelly and Lochore. It was between 10.00am and 11.00 am, and it was very dull and cloudy. To my right I saw a black triangular shape that appeared to be bobbing in and out of the clouds, with hindsight, it probably wasn't, it was probably the clouds that were moving rather than it, but it was hanging in the air, with the cloud cover coming and going. I told myself it was maybe a kite, but it was very high up for a kite, and actually far too large to have been a kite but I never really told anyone about it, pretty much dismissing it with it only coming to mind occasionally over the years".

"My second sighting, which I can't remember if I mentioned when I contacted you all those years ago, so apologies if I did! I dismissed as some sort of natural phenomena, until I read about so many similar stories in your book. In April 1997, living in the same flat that we were in when we had the black triangle experience in September 1997, I was getting out of bed approximately 6.15/30 one morning, and looked out the window, where we could see right across the Forth. In the sky, I couldn't judge how far away though, were three dancing balls of light. Two of them were only moving slightly (almost like balls bobbing along on water), but the one in the middle, was, what I could only describe as dancing, up and down and around the other two. My husband wondered what I was standing staring at, so he came to look as well. We both stood and watched this for about five minutes, when the 'dancing' light seemed to concentrate on circling the left-hand light, which, after about a minute, disappeared. It then moved to the remaining light, and once again, danced around it until it then disappeared about a minute later. The remaining light continued to 'dance' around for another minute, then completely disappeared. It didn't shoot off, didn't fall into the sea or anything like that, it was like a light had been switched off. It's something we still talk about occasionally, neither of us have a clue about what we were seeing, but after reading your book, I was shocked at the amount of other people who have also seen these lights. The black triangle incident, which you reported on in your book, well there is one other thing I would like to add to it, which I didn't at the time. The next day, I noticed on my forehead, just at the hairline, three small red dots in the shape of a triangle. I dismissed this immediately as just that, spots of some kind, that would disappear in a day or two. Only they have never gone away. When I spoke to you, you asked me if I had any missing time, or had any strange visitors, there was nothing like that, and I didn't mention the 'spots' because even a couple of weeks later, I was still thinking they would disappear. More than 25 years later, I still have them. They have faded slightly in the last couple of years, but they're still visible".

"Reading your book, it's also of interest to me, the question about why some people seem to see UFO's and some don't. I've always had more than a passing interest in the paranormal and UFOs in particular, and in the 90s, I used to buy UFO and Encounters magazines. Over the years (since the early 00s), I joined a private Development Circle and became a 'developing medium' with Scottish Paranormal for a few years. I never really took the mediumship any further though. I have issues with it being tied in with any sort of religion within the Spiritualist Church, and they always seemed to want to try and push me to become a 'platform medium' which I have never wanted to do. I left the Scottish Paranormal team in about 2009, but remain good friends with Ryan O'Neill, who has since taken his investigating to quite a phenomenal level, and I still go to the odd investigation as a normal guest/friend. I think my point being, that I wonder if being able to see such things, is linked with people who have some sort of ability to interact with the paranormal in some way. I've always described being a medium as being like an untuned radio, and we can tune in to different frequencies, and I wonder if being able to see UFO (or UAP now!) phenomena means the person can link in with other frequencies, whether they're aware of it, or not"?

"Over the years, every so often, I dream very vividly of being with aliens in some sort of craft, and I am rarely frightened by it, in fact, I find it exhilarating most of the time, but I have never thought for a second that I am an abductee, and I am openminded when reading about other's experiences. If I am, then they are doing a pretty good job of covering their tracks"!

Sincerely. Fiona Williamson.

FOLLOWED BY STRANGE LIGHTS

Author's Comment. Another strange case file coming from Fife, was the account given to me by Helen Murray. Here is what she had to tell me.

"On driving home from Freuchie in Fife on a Sunday evening about 6.15pm travelling towards Newburgh via Lindores Loch, (I can't recall the year) We were coming down a hill towards the crossroads at Charleston where there was a ball of light hovering up high and almost following us. I can remember my mum saying to my father, *"faster Jim faster"*. We three were in the back seat on our knees looking out the back window. I remember seeing small lights jumping along the road behind us just about a ruler's height off the ground. For years I thought it was a dream, that was until in 2015 at my dad's funeral, we were all chatting away when my mum came out with that story and then we all started talking at once. It had never been talked about before. My mum said she had read about strange lights above the Lomond Hill the next day in the Courier. When I asked my brother about this at the funeral, he replied that he couldn't remember the year, but he was sure he was around five or six years of age which would have made the year around 1973. My sister recalled that it was on the A913. She said that she remembered it vividly and was terrified. She recalled the lights hovering behind the car, and then the car engine died. These lights then passed over towards a hill then the car restarted. She can't recall the year. The surprising thing about her recall was, she said that she didn't remember me being in the car! And yet I was old enough that I was sitting on my knees staring out the back window. *"I wasn't in the car! This was not what I was* asking her about".!

Sincerely. Helen Murray.

Author's Comment. Is it the passage of time that Helen's sister can't recall her being in the car, or did something else happen which as yet, the story is yet to be told?

MY STRANGE UFO EXPERIENCES

Hi Malcolm,

"Just wanted to let you know about a couple of experiences. Unfortunately, I'm really bad with the dates on these. My apologies for this but these are genuine experiences, and I am a person who has a science degree and worked until recently at a university in a responsible position. They have always intrigued me; I am convinced we are not alone".

1) "My major UFO sighting was back in the early 2000s. Sorry sadly I cannot remember the exact year. I used to be an antenatal teacher with the NCT, and my sighting was in November when I was driving back from teaching an evening antenatal class in Dunfermline. It was around 11:00pm or so as I'd stayed behind chatting with the couple hosting the class (in their home) after the class finished at 9:00pm. I was on the A92 approaching the Prestonhall roundabout in Glenrothes. There were no other vehicles on that stretch of road with me at that time. As I approached the roundabout coming down the hill on the dual carriageway towards the roundabout, I caught sight of the front of what I initially thought was a black aircraft. My first thought was it was a plane attempting an emergency landing on the dual carriageway running into Glenrothes town centre (a road called Queensway). Then I realised it wasn't an aircraft. It was skimming the Cypress trees on the roundabout probably about 80

feet up. The trees were about 40 to 60 feet tall (they're now bigger). I thought *"Oh my God, it's like something out of Star Wars, that's not a plane"*. There was no sound at all, no electrical effect on the vehicle. It was black, sort of wedge shaped, wider at front, sort of tapered to the back, no wings, no tail fin, small white lights (more than 10) along the length of the craft on the side (not windows) just little lights. The craft was about the size of a passenger jet (Airbus 320 sort of size) It was travelling at the sort of speed an aircraft lands at, so didn't see it for more than a few seconds as it passed. It seemed to be following the road. I was sitting at the roundabout by now and saw another car at the junction to my right (coming from Woodside). The other car driver had obviously seen it too. He was also sitting staring. We looked at each other and sort of exchanged a look along the lines of *"You saw that too?"* Then I let him go onto the roundabout before me and continued on my way home. I live rurally near Star. It wasn't just a light; it was a craft. I saw it relatively close. My only thought about why it was in that area, is due to the presence of Raytheon factory along that road, they manufacture guided missile systems as far as I understand. I really don't think it's our military craft. A few things struck me about it. It was flying really low, a conventional aircraft would stall at that speed if it wasn't landing. I used to live at the back of Largo and was used to Vulcan bombers coming over our house and the noise from these was huge. There was absolutely zero noise. Not any sound before or after it. Also, if it was something military, why fly so low over a built-up area? It didn't look like any of the stealth planes, and drones were not a thing at the time, it wasn't a small vehicle. Also how was it staying up no wings, no tail fin. A few weeks after I saw this, I was taking my kids to a schools' country dance event in the Glenrothes Sports Institute. A police search was being conducted for a missing old man (dementia sufferer) a helicopter was flying around and around Glenrothes using a thermal heat scan camera to search for hm. You could hear it just about anywhere in the town, usual thud, thud of the helicopter blades. The craft I saw was silent so definitely not a misidentification".

2) "I've had a couple of other experiences, once taking my children home from swimming lessons in the mid1990s. It was about 6:00pm, it was still day light probably end of May. I turned off the road from Kennoway towards Star, and at the T junction, a round orange light started to follow my car. It was difficult to say the size but seemed basketball size but likely bigger and higher up. The cloud base was fairly high though it was a completely overcast sky. The orange light glowed like the colour of an infrared lamp. It kept pace with my car (between 20 and 40mph) following me until I turned into my drive further up the road from Star. It headed off due north. I jumped out my car to see where it went looking in the sky at the back of my house, it had disappeared before I reached the place where I could see, possibly up into the cloud base".

3) "It was June, mid-90s. My family were all asleep around 3:00am. My two girls were in their room, and my son was in his. My husband and I were lying in bed asleep in our bedroom when we were both awakened and became aware, of the sound of someone (something?) creeping, shuffling in our room next to the bed on my husband's side. My first thought was that it was one of the kids (they'd be quite young then). I was lying (unusually) with my arm over my husband with my hand resting on his belly. Neither of us felt able to open our eyes or move. My husband said he initially thought child, then (weirdly) alien. Suddenly there was an extremely loud noise in the room. I can only describe it as a weird tubular wailing noise, but it was screaming pitch. So loud I'd opened my eyes and saw a sort of blue dot of light near the window sort of blink out, almost like someone switching off the noise. This was followed by complete silence and us leaping out of bed wondering what the hell had just happened. Nothing, no one there. We checked the kids, no one was out of bed, all were sound asleep. We checked outside and around the house, in the garden and looked around down the county road we live on. Nothing. Totally baffling. We both know we woke and recognised what we felt was slow shuffling in the bedroom. My husband definitely didn't make the noise; my hand was on his belly, and he would have felt it. We were not both dreaming exactly the same thing. The noise was so loud and the

only thing I can compare it to, was like a child swishing one of those long tubes in the air, those that make a noise around their head, but much, more louder than that. The noise also cut off like a switch very suddenly. An extremely weird and unsettling experience. It was light outside it was around 3:00am in June. The strangest thing about it, was despite the upset and the going outside to check everything, we went back to bed and instantly fell back to sleep. Very odd".

"Thanks for reading my experiences I don't know what you make of them or if anyone has approached you about anything similar".

Yours Truly. Jenny Mailer.

Author's Comment. In regard to that strange noise that awoke them from their sleep, Jenny stated that she and her husband were long time country dwellers and knew all the birds and animals around, and that sound, was nothing like they have ever heard before or since. She further speculated that maybe that noise was not supposed to 'wake them up'. Our next case file again relates to, yet another large black triangular craft seen in the Fife skies, although admittedly, our witness in this case, does not think that it's a UFO, but still ponders what it could be. Here is what she said to me.

IT BLOCKED OUT THE STARS!

Hi Malcolm,

"It was 18:30 on Thursday 18th November 2021. Me and my partner were driving up the dual carriageway from Kirkcaldy to Glenrothes. As we were driving, I noticed a constellation in the sky which I think was the plough. I always notice it as it's the only one I recognise. I then noticed (what I thought) were the stars moving, so I said to my partner, *"Oh there must be a laser show on",* but the 'stars/lights' were moving steadily towards us down the carriageway. We pulled into a layby (this would be on the left side as you head up to Glenrothes) and just watched as this moved slowly and steadily towards us. I thought it might be drones, set in a triangular pattern, and my brain might be filling in the actual black triangle, but on reflection 'it was a solid triangle' because *it blocked out the stars in the sky as it went past.* It made no noise at all that we could hear, although the traffic was quite noisy. But in between vehicles passing by, we didn't hear anything".

"It was flying quite low and had three lights on in a diagonal pattern and a white light on the opposite corner of the triangle. The lights were all white and the middle light on the diagonal, occasionally blinked. It was on the opposite side of the carriageway above the fields. My partner reckoned it was 1000 feet up and travelling between 50 to 80 mph. It was very large, with no noise and the slow speed of travel made it all the more unusual. I had left my phone at home, but my partner took video footage of it. I'll send it, but it's truly dreadful and nothing really to see as the thing was so big it was hard to zoom out. Plus, the lights and noise from traffic obliterate anything useful. We had to watch it on the TV to even see the flashing light. It headed down the dual carriageway roughly in the direction of the Garden Centre in Kirkcaldy. When we got home, I messaged Fife Airport but was told nothing would have come from there out with daylight hours. I messaged someone on Facebook I know who does drone photography and asked if he was aware of any drone action taking place. He said no, and that usually there is some buzz as people want their drone displays noticed".

"I thought about contacting the Police the following day to see if they had any other reports but felt I would be wasting their time. A friend suggested contacting Leuchars Airport, but my partner thinks we shouldn't 'open up a can of worms,'. I do not think this was some extra-terrestrial sighting, but I have wondered if it was a Stealth Plane. But what would it be doing there? I hope this interests you".

Regards. Jane Marshall.

Author's Comment. I viewed Jane's footage, and it was indeed difficult to make out the object on screen. I saw the flashing lights but not the triangle shape.

IT'S TIME TO TALK ABOUT IT!

Author's Comment. As I've said many times before, Facebook can be a wonderful thing in so far as people can share their UFO sightings online. One particular sighting that caught my eye, was shared on a forum by one Steve Arnott. Steve was only 14 years of age when he had these sightings and told me that when he initially told his school friends at the time, he got 'ruthlessly mocked on the school bus', and as such, decided to shut up about it, and get on with adolescence. He stated.

"A few very close friends and family know about this and know my story hasn't changed in 46 years. It's the first time I've ever discussed it in a public forum. I've kept quiet about it initially for fear of ridicule; however, I'm sixty now, decades have passed. I feel that rational people who have seen something anomalous should be prepared to speak about it".

FIRST INCIDENT

"It was either October or November 1976, in the sky near Mossgreen Village. It was late, around 11/11:30pm. I'm taking the dog out for its last walk of the day which took me around the housing scheme where I lived. The skies were fairly clear, and a friend was with me who I will call witness 2. We both saw a bright orange light high in the sky. There was something about its movement. It seemed to be getting bigger, and we realised it was coming lower and in our direction. As quickly as we could, we moved round the corner to where there were some garages and a clear strip of grass next to a field in order to keep the thing in sight. Now this is the bit that people might have difficulty with. I would have difficulty with this myself if I hadn't seen it with my own eyes".

"The object was now hovering directly above the houses on the corner. You could have touched it if you had been sitting on the roof of the house. It was about the size of a small van or people carrier, but you couldn't see the shape or structure because the orange had now resolved itself into two very bright lights, one green, one red which was right at the front of the object. It was completely silent. And it was the most wonderful, amazing thing I have ever seen in my life! Totally silent. No obvious means of propulsion or lift, clearly a manufactured craft and no more than forty or so feet from me. Just then witness two who was behind me, said something, and I turned around. Then, a second object exactly the same as the first was now hovering behind us above the field, maybe ten feet or so higher than the nearby garages. If the first object was at my 12-o clock, then this second one would have been at my 7-o clock. Neither were more than forty or so feet away".

"As you might imagine my mind was churning at this point. They weren't there for very long, maybe forty seconds to a minute? I'm thinking, *"Who are they? what are they doing here? what should I do next?".* At that point, car headlights appeared over a rise on the main road in the distance and both of these objects shot up and away. The first in a kind of curving parabola, in opposite directions, at an unbelievable speed. The second behind us, left a moment later, straight up in a kind of 'Sieg Heil' salute angle. They dwindled to a bright orange point and then nothing in a few seconds. No engine noise. No sonic boom. Incidentally, the village of Mossgreen and Crossgates were just basically small villages surrounded by fields. The area now is built up by the Edinburgh over spill".

SECOND INCIDENT

"It was a clear winter night in February 1977; the time was around 5 or 6 pm. I was walking the dog with next door neighbour and friend, Steve Hynd on a well-known path just outside the village of Mossgreen. We were looking at the Plough constellation which was really big and clear and fairly low in the sky to the north and above one side of a large local hill feature. It happened very quickly. We saw first one, then two, and then another, bright stars which appeared in that area of sky, and then moved very quickly in our direction. Then they were above us, at what I thought was a quite high altitude, jinking and zigzagging, moving quickly between one another, with very sharp turns. Looking back, I think we were quite gobsmacked. I think there were four or five of these pin point bright white objects. But they were moving so quickly in and around each other that it was difficult to count. I'm pretty sure one of us said to the other *"It's like a dogfight"*. Then these objects all sort of wheeled parallel to one another into a line and shot off into the distance over the River Forth and, to my recollection, east of Edinburgh. They traversed half the arc of the sky in no more than a couple of seconds and were gone. At no point was there any sound whatsoever. The duration of the incident was no more than maybe 60 to 90 seconds, but it's burned into my memory. So, there we go. If folk think I need psychiatric assistance, so be it. But this happened and I've sat on it for forty-six years too long".

Sincerely, Steve Arnott.

Author's Comment. We now move over to Clackmannanshire in Central Scotland where our witness, Graham Hutchinson was perplexed by what he saw. This is what he had to tell me.

THE SPLITTING LIGHT!

Hi Malcolm,

"Saw your post on the Bonnybridge UFOs and would like to tell you about my sighting".

"I'm going back to 1996 or 1997. I was with my dad, and we were parked on Branshill Road in Sauchie outside where the college used to be waiting on my mum to finish a course she was on. It was probably around 6:00pm and was dark, as it was the winter months. The sky was generally clear with a few clouds around. We were facing east in the car so looking over to the Ochil Hills in the general direction of Tillicoultry. We saw a very bright, round/spherical light coming from over the Ochils. It looked like a search light on a helicopter and that's what we thought it was. Then, as it got closer, it suddenly split into three lights which shot off in different directions, then flew around the sky before coming back into one light. This light then shot up behind a cloud and wasn't seen again. The initial height was hard to determine but the size looked just like a helicopter spotlight would appear to be from the ground. The lights were white and not blinking or flashing. The whole time we saw it would be no more than three or four minutes. Hope this is of some interest".

Sincerely, Graham Hutchison.

Author's Comment. Staying in Clackmannanshire, we move from Sauchie over to the small village of Cambus where James Madden had quite an unusual sighting. He stated.

THE CAMBUS UFO

Hi Malcolm,

"I worked with your lass Karen for 10 years plus and was always interested to listen when she talked about you and your books. Long story short, about three years ago, myself and my daughter, had what can only be described, as an amazing UFO experience. We witnessed a UFO up close one December night in 2019 on the farm roads between Alloa to Cambus. The reason I'm messaging you, is my curiosity relating to the sound that we both heard during this sighting, it was a deafening deep pulsating base sound which emitted from the UFO. I have searched online since and cannot find another story the same. Also, why, during this experience, was I not scared in the slightest? I was joking and jovial. Why has it taken a few years for me to process what we saw from a star like object to a large craft with multicoloured lights to watching a clear triangular shaped UFO move away. It really amazes me. I remember clearly coming home to tell the wife that we'd seen a UFO and nothing more really".

"During the event I was shouting, *"She's here come and get her"!* essentially having a joke with my then 10-year-old daughter who was not too scared and has her own distinct memories of that night. She also joked that they didn't have a beam strong enough to lift me! (I'm a big bloke) I guess like many Malcolm, I'm now looking for some answers, but the most inexplicable thing was the deep loud all-encompassing pulsing sound which is also strange given what we saw (I guess most reports are silent with no sound). I have to say I have always been open to all things 'paranormal' in my opinion just things we humans can't explain yet".

"Also, another thing that I have thought about so many times, was as I watched this object come closer towards us, I heard a voice in my head telling me not to be scared, that this is a man-made object. It wasn't until I'd really considered this aspect that I've concluded that I was somehow hearing what I needed to hear so as to remain unafraid. Could it be a subconscious defence mechanism? But I personally feel that it was maybe some form of communication to keep me at ease. Who knows. Finally, we have no recollection of missing time, however I do have at one point broken memory, as in one moment the UFO was right in front of us a few hundred feet up, maybe closer, then my next memory is of a triangular shaped ship silhouetted against grey dark sky".

"Thanks for reading this Malcolm. As I said, your lass knows me really well and having supported people with autism for 20 years plus myself, I can genuinely say, she is as beautifully kind- and big-hearted person as I've ever known".
Sincerely, James Madden.

Author's Comment. I know this road very well, as I have cycled it to Cambus many times. It is indeed all farmers' fields. Needless to say, this has left a big impression on James. As for the sound, whilst it is rare to hear a sound like this, it's not that uncommon, as there are instances of strange sounds coming from these objects in reports across the world. We can but ponder, was the sound its downward descent towards the witnesses? Here again, we have yet another one of those large black triangular objects seen at low level.

I had a message from UFO witness Raymond Meyer regarding a few of his UFO sightings. After taking a note of them, I decided that I would give him a call just to find out more, I'm glad I did, as there were some interesting aspects of his sighting in there. But first, here is the gist of a few of his UFO sightings which he told to me about over Facebook Messenger.

R.A.F. LEUCHARS UFO?

Hi Malcolm,

"I've seen four UFO's, two of which I've managed to capture on film and would appreciate your opinion on these. Briefly, my first sighting was a fluorescent green object hovering above the runway at RAF Leuchars, in Fife. Two Harrier jets were scrambled to investigate this object. My second sighting was an orb which I managed to view in binoculars as it headed north over the North Sea off the coast of Fife. The first one I caught on film was in Benalmadena in the south of Spain on the 12th of September 2009. This was filmed using hi8 tape. I watched this object until it turned on its end and went straight up until it disappeared in the atmosphere. Unfortunately, the camcorder couldn't focus on this happening. The other strange thing is the high-pitched noise throughout the footage. The second object I captured, was when I was tracking the ISS as it passed overhead. Suddenly a very bright light appeared in the night sky and by the time I grabbed my camera I could only manage to get a couple of seconds of footage before it suddenly disappeared".

Author's Comment. What follows are some notes that I took from a telephone call to Raymond about his RAF Leuchars UFO sighting. At the time, Raymond worked at RAF Leuchars as an airfield light and electrician, a position that he held there for 31 years before retiring.

Raymond told me that he couldn't remember the actual year of his UFO sighting, but he thinks it was either 1995 or 1996. His office at RAF Leuchars was down at the end of the runway. The Harrier jets he told me, were from Germany who were on detachment doing night time infra-red vision flying, and as such, there was a complete and total black out of the runway to allow these jets to train with their night vision goggles. As there was this total blackout, there was of course no light pollution. Taking advantage of the dark conditions, Raymond decided to go out from his office and look at the night sky. As he scanned the night sky, he saw an object which he described to me as 'sausage shaped' or 'cylinder shaped' but it had some kind of curve on it.

Most peculiar of all, was the colour of the object which was a fluorescent green. The Moon he said, was behind him to the West, whilst Raymond was looking at this object in the East just over the North Sea. Raymond's initial thoughts were that this object could have been a 'cloud-based monitor', which is a light that shines directly up to monitor the cloud base, but that he told me, had been switched off as well for the night exercise. Whilst looking at this strange object, Raymond noticed that a bit of it seemed to 'break away' from the main object and then shot straight back up towards it, but admits, this could have been the way that the clouds were moving, and this might have caused this illusion. The following Sunday he saw an article in the News of the World newspaper which stated that a couple were flying down from Inverness to London, and they had spotted something strange above the clouds of which they drew a sketch of. When Raymond saw this, he said that this was exactly what he had seen. This was on the same night as his sighting. There was also a report of something above Balmoral Castle, of which two Harrier Jets were diverted up to the castle's vicinity to investigate. Raymond said that when he found that out, he went up to speak to the senior air traffic controller at RAF Leuchars, the controller then checked the incident book for that night and confirmed that two Harrier jets were indeed diverted up to the Balmoral area. However, nothing else was reported, they hadn't seen anything, and they returned to base and that was the end of the matter.

Three years after that, Raymond was in the Bowling Alley in the camp at Leuchars having a pint, when he saw a man at the bar wearing a T shirt which had an alien on it. So, he casually struck up a conversation with the man and asked him if he was into aliens and UFOs, at which point the man said that he wasn't, that it was just a T shirt that he bought in Italy. Raymond then proceeded to tell him all about the UFO that he had seen three years before here at RAF Leuchars, at which point the man butted in and said that he remembered that event, as he was working in the air traffic control at RAF Leuchars that night. He further stated that he had diverted two RAF Harriers into the air. In my phone call to Raymond, Raymond said he particularly remembers the man said 'Harriers' and not 'Tornados' as they were normally based there, so he knew that the man was telling the truth. Raymond went on to tell the man that he had spoken to the Senior Air Traffic Controller that night who had told him that they hadn't seen anything that night, and that the Harriers had just returned to base. At this, the man with the alien T shirt on said,

"No, that is not what happened. The Harriers made visual contact with the object at Balmoral, and as they got closer, this object just shot off and then they returned to base".

Author's Comment. I've had a look online to see if I could find anything about any UFO sightings above or near Balmoral Castle but came up empty handed.

In my previous book, The Bonnybridge UFO Enigma, (A Modern Day Mystery) co-authored with Ron Halliday, I mentioned the UFO sighting by Freddy France along with his children back in 1992. Well, I met up with Freddy again on the 20th of August 2025 in the town of Stirling where we sat down and I re-interviewed him about that sighting, and one or two other sightings that he has had in the years that followed. Listening to Freddy's account 33 years later, there were some other details that I didn't have at that time but felt it best to include here. Before we get to those new details. Here is how I wrote up his sighting in my first book, 'UFO Case Files of Scotland (Volume 1) At that time I had given him the pseudonym of Patrick Forsyth.

UFO ABOVE ROAD
(The Patrick Forsyth Case) 27th October 1992

It was around 7:00pm and 37-year-old Patrick Forsyth (pseudonym) had just dropped his wife off in the town of Denny as she was going to the bingo. After dropping his wife off, Patrick then headed off towards the town of St Ninians near Stirling where he was going to get his car washed. He was driving along the A872 doing around 45 miles per hour. In the car with him on this drive to Stirling, were his two young sons aged 11 and 6. It was a cool dark night with scattered cloud and there was a fair sprinkling of stars in the night sky. The road ahead wasn't busy, and he knew that it wouldn't be too long before he reached St Ninians. It was a road that he had travelled many times before which he knew very well. Then, on the outskirts of Dunipace at the side of the road, there was an overhanging tree. At this point, he suddenly became aware of a strange object roughly 100 yards in front of his car which he described as circular, two tiered, and had a row of green lights encircling the bottom rim of its structure. The object's upper tier appeared to be larger than the bottom tier, and it didn't appear to have any windows. It appeared to be hovering above the road's surface at a distance of between 25 to 40 feet. At this point, Patrick turned round to his two young sons sitting in the back and said, *"What the hell is that?"* followed by, *"Can you see this boys?"* Patrick went on to say that the object was completely static and noiseless, and he knew straight away that this was some kind of unidentified object that he had never seen before. Patrick stated in an interview to Malcolm Robinson, that this object clearly was 'not' man-made.

As his car approached ever nearer, Patrick's attention was drawn to a car directly in front of him which had just entered what appeared to be an instantaneous 'fog bank'. This 'fog bank' had suddenly sprung up from nowhere. This 'fog bank' was only on Patrick's side of the road and did not cover all the road. It wasn't wispy he explained, it was like a solid fog like door. Patrick informed me that although it was a cool October evening, there were no signs of any patches of fog on the road that night. Patrick then again cried out to his two young sons, *"Boys, can you see this?"* To which they excitedly replied, *"Yes dad, we see it."* Seconds later, Patrick's car entered this mysterious 'fog bank' and as it did so, he became aware of a strange 'humming sound' coming from above. He described the sound of it as if you were listening to the sound of a washing machine on its final spin, that high pitched screeching sound. Upon coming out the other side of this strange 'misty fog bank', the strange object was nowhere to be seen. He remembers that just before his own car entered the 'fog bank', the car in front of him actually skidded as it entered it. Patrick can't recall seeing this other car when he went through this fog bank. This was quite surprising, as he wasn't that far away from it before they both went through this strange misty effect. And although Patrick didn't see the object again, he recalls his son shouting at him from the back seat that he could see it travelling in the direction of Grangemouth, which is a town a few miles away. In a face-to-face interview with the author, Patrick was insistent that the object he saw that night, was 'not' an aircraft of any shape or design that he was aware of. Moreover, he found it extremely hard to understand where this instant fog bank had come from. When I pushed him on this matter, he said that this fog bank was sharply defined, it was not puffy but had clear cut edges like a tall oblong piece of white card. However, the most interesting point about it, was that it only went up to the white lines in the centre of the road, it did not encroach beyond them. In a sense, he said, it was like a cloudy doorway which they had entered, which stretched from the left-hand side of the road to the middle of the road and was roughly 10 to 12 feet in height. He did not see this fog bank after he went through it, because when looking back, it just wasn't there anymore!

This 'instantaneous' fog bank, put me in mind of a similar case from England which happened to the Avis family on October 27th, 1994. This case was considered at the time, to be Britain's first multiple UFO abduction case. It was a late Sunday evening when the Avis family from Essex were driving along a route between Harold Hill and Aveley. Their journey was to visit relatives and was a journey that they had made many times before. However, on this occasion, things were to be different. The family, which consisted of John Avis, then aged 32, accompanied by his wife, Elaine, 28, and their three children, Kevin, 10, Karen, 11, and Stuart, aged 7, were at a point on Hacton Lane about one mile from the town of Hornchurch when, as they were coming around a bend in the road, they suddenly encountered an instantaneous 'fog bank', similar to the Patrick Forsyth case mentioned above. However, there are some differences. For instance, in the Avis case, the fog bank was green and covered the whole width of the road. This was a massive case researched by Andrew Collins which included the use of hypnosis where a strange abduction scenario unfolded. This case also included weird poltergeist effects at the Avis family home. I think that this instantaneous fog bank effect is something which researchers should not ignore, for it seems to turn up in a number of UFO cases worldwide. We could speculate that this could be some kind of 'smokescreen' or dimensional effect which could render the occupants of vehicles unconscious, and that their vehicle is somehow 'looked after' in so far as it will not crash. No hypnosis was ever conducted on Patrick Forsyth in our Scottish case to see if perhaps 'something else' might have happened that night. As far as we are aware, there was no missing time either. Come what may, there is no denying that this is quite a peculiar case.

FREDDY FRANCE AND HIS 1992 UFO SIGHTING RE-VISITED

Sitting down with Freddy in Stirling 33 years later listening to him recount that 1992 sighting it was pretty much the same account that he gave then. He went on to tell me that it was a few weeks later that he read the Scottish Sunday Mail which featured a number of UFO sightings seen in the skies above Bonnybridge. In that article, was my telephone number to which Freddy called, he went on to say that I came out and interviewed him and his two children (Duncan was his son who was six years old at the time, and Brian his stepson was eleven) and got them all to fill out a questionnaire which included a section where one could draw what they saw. Freddy said that Duncan, his son, drew something very similar to him, but Brian, his stepson, who saw the object head away towards Grangemouth, drew the object as a triangle. Freddy asked Brian *"Why did you draw that son"?* to which Brian said, *"But that's what I saw".* Freddy went on to tell me that he had appeared on a number of television programmes at that time as the Bonnybridge UFO sightings were becoming more well know across the United Kingdom. However, he stopped appearing on them as his six-year-old son Duncan was having nightmares. At this point in our conversation, Freddy began to speak about the possibility of missing time. Here is how that conversation started.

Freddy France: *"Now you Malcolm came back a number of times from your first visit, and one of the things that you said was bothering you, was me saying that when I got home that night, I* *didn't have time for my supper. Now I know that the bingo started at half past seven; after dropping my wife off at the bingo, we then travelled over to St Ninians which only takes ten minutes. All in all, by the time we left the house, dropped my wife off at the bingo, put the car through the car wash at St Ninians, it would have been roughly forty-five minutes, so we should have got back home at quarter to eight, but it was near enough quarter past nine".*

Malcolm Robinson: *"So there appears to be, going by what you have just said, that there might indeed be a period of missing time? What, if anything, do you think happened during this period of missing time?*

Freddy France: *"Well you gave me the possibility of going though hypnotic regression at that time, well it was actually a year down the road in 1993. But my son Duncan was still having nightmares at that time, so I decided not to do it. But not long after that sighting, anytime that I walked into a shop, I set alarms off! This happened all the time. Then, when I met my second wife, she didn't believe in UFOs and had never seen one. Before we married in 2001, I went over to visit her at her farmhouse in Bonnybridge, we were in the sitting room just talking, it was a summer's night, about 7:30pm, when suddenly this 'thing' appeared outside the window. It was like scaffolding poles all joined together in a rectangular shape and it was different colours, and I said to her, "Do you see that" and she said "Aye". It eventually past the window, so the two of us dived outside but it was gone. She had a big loft space in the farmhouse which had been converted into two big bedrooms with big windows, and I was staying one night, I can't remember what time of year it was, but it was pitch black. I went to the Velux window and opened it about six inches to get some fresh air, and I looked out the window where you can see the lights over at Callander Park. There they have big pylons with red lights several feet apart on them. Suddenly I saw a big silver orb coming down parallel with the pylon lights then it shot away in the sky at a fantastic speed. By this time, I was joined by Liz, and as we were sitting talking about what I had seen, another one appeared, she saw it to".*

Malcolm Robinson: *"What size was this light"?*

Freddy France: *"It was the same size as the red lights on this pylon mast. It wasn't any bigger, and it wasn't any smaller".*

Author's Comment. Freddy then went on to discuss a UFO sighting that he and his second wife Liz saw in 2010 when he was on holiday in Gran Canaria. The area where his hotel was, was cut into the mountain side like a V shaped cleft in the valley from the beach inwards. One night between 11 and 12pm as they were looking at the stars, Freddy's wife was looking at the sky with night vision binoculars whilst Freddy was just looking at the stars beside her. Suddenly, Freddy states, this 'thing' came down the valley which he described as white and translucent and was shaped like something out of 'Star Wars' it swooped right down in the valley and at its closest, it would be within 300 to 400 yards away from them. Then this 'thing', just flipped up and shot away in a matter of seconds. He further stated that it was a disc shaped object, two tiered, and that he could see straight through it. The next morning, they decided to go out for a walk. Near the hotel where they stayed, is a man-made bay about eleven hundred yards away, there is also a path that has been cut into the mountain side. As they walked up the mountainside path, Freddy reckons that they were about 100 feet up this mountain side path, they both saw an army helicopter hovering above the crystal-clear sea. They also observed a boat. As they looked down, through the crystal-clear water, they could see underneath the water, sitting on the sea floor, which wasn't so deep at that part, a very large dark circular shape about the size of one and a half buses. So, they saw this army helicopter hovering above this shape, and also a boat just beneath the helicopter. What was going on? At this, Freddy said to his wife Liz, *"That's what we saw last night"*. Both Freddy and Liz, after watching this for a while, went back to their hotel for lunch, all the while they were at lunch, they could see and hear this helicopter hovering above the sea. Freddy reckons it was there for a good four hours.

Freddy went on to tell me that his son Duncan has been over to Gran Canaria a few times and has seen a number of UFOs. Indeed, Freddy showed me a photograph that his son had taken over at Gran Canaria which he believes was a UFO. I must admit, when I looked at this photograph, it sure did not look like any normal flying machine that I've ever seen. What I was looking at on the photograph, was a yellow elongated light in the dark night sky above the sea. To the left was a multitude of houses and hotels. Normally with so many lights in a dark photograph, I would have said that it was lens flare, but not on this occasion, this looked way different. It may of course have a natural explanation, but on this occasion, I couldn't find one. Freddy also told me that he has seen a number of UFOs whilst on holiday overseas and several orbs in the Bonnybridge area.

WHO WERE THOSE TWO STRANGE MEN?
What happened to the video tape?

Probably one of the more interesting stories that Freddy told me that day in Stirling, was that a friend of his knew a farmer in the Bonnybridge area who had taken numerous video footage of strange orb like lights hovering and moving across his farmland near Bonnybridge. But there is a twist to this tale. Here, in part, is the story told to me by Freddy, transcribed from a recording.

Freddy France: *"I had just come back from my holidays, so it would have been around the summer of 1994 and there was a problem on a site up at Livingston that I had to go up to and sort out. When I went up to the site, I was introduced to the site foreman, and, as it turned out, it was a guy that I knew from years before. I guy called Danny. As we were walking around the perimeter fence, we had the usual chit chat, 'how are you getting on', 'what have you been doing' etc. Now Danny told me that he and his mate went out at night time where they shot foxes for the farmers in the Denny – Bonnybridge area, they had done this for the past twenty years. They had all the equipment, they had the shotgun license, they had the jeep with the open sun roof. They had the floodlights in front of the jeep, and this was their hobby, if you like".*

"One night, or in the early hours of the morning, Danny and his mate stopped and had a bite to eat and a cup of tea, and they saw headlights coming up towards them from the populated area

down below. And Danny said to his mate, "Who is this coming up here, it must be a lorry. How is this lorry getting up here, what road is it on". But as the lights drew towards them, these lights suddenly turned into orbs, and they shot right up in front of the jeep, and right over the windscreen and shot up right into the sky above Danny and his mate. And they both could follow them due to the open sun roof. And Danny turned round to his mate and said, "What was that" and all his mate said to him was, "Take me home Danny, take me home". He wouldn't answer him, and Danny tried to speak to him, but his friend was having none of it. His friend never spoke all the way home. He never ever came out with Danny after that. Danny continued to go out and shoot the foxes. And one night, one of the old farmer's said to Danny, "I see your mate's not here Danny", Danny replied "No", to which the farmer said, "What's up"? Danny replied that his friend wouldn't be coming back up. And the farmer said to Danny, "Did you see the lights, is it the lights?" and Danny replied, "Yes". Now when I questioned Danny if it was orbs, Danny referred to them as lights, as did the farmer. The farmer then said to Danny that he had seen these lights for years and years, so much so that he went away and got this cam-corder and had actually videoed them. Not just on one night, but on numerous nights. And he said to Danny that he had a video of them. And when all this came out in the newspaper about the Bonnybridge UFOs, he saw in the newspaper, a name and a telephone number that he could contact if people had any information. So, he had this video of UFOs, or lights as they called them. And he phoned the number".

"Now I never asked him what the number was, I assumed the number, was the same number that I phoned which was for yourself Malcolm. The very next night, two men, in suits, chapped the farmer's door. I don't know how they introduced themselves, I'm pretty sure that they said they were from the Government, and they had heard that he had this video of UFOs. The farmer said that's right, and they said, "Do you mind if we see it"? and the Farmer said "No, I don't mind". So, the farmer invited them in, and they sat down, and they watched this video with the two gentlemen. Their words to the farmer were, "That's amazing. Do you mind if we take it away and copy it and we'll *bring it back to you ASAP". The farmer said, "No problem", and handed them the video".*

Author's Comment. Some weeks later, the farmer received the VHS tape back from one of these two 'gentlemen' and invited Danny to his farmhouse to view the footage. We return back to my interview with Freddy.

"And the farmer said to Danny, "Would you like to see the video Danny"? and Danny said, "Yes". So, the farmer said that once he (Danny) had finished his duties to come back up and see him. So, Danny hurried up with his duties that night and went down to the farmer's house. He chapped his door, was invited in, and the farmer poured Danny and himself a whisky. They then sat down, and the farmer put the video on. And as Danny was sitting down ready to watch the video, it just played, but all it showed was a black screen. And Danny watched it for a few seconds up to a minute and turned to the farmer as if to say, 'what's this', and the farmer said, "Well that's it Danny, this is what I got back from those guys, a blank tape".

"Now Danny later said to me that he didn't know why he was telling me this story as he hadn't told anybody this story other than his wife. He hadn't told his brother, his mother, or his father, but he felt compelled to tell me this story. And I said to Danny that maybe he told me as we both had something in common. And I proceeded to tell him my experience of what I saw in 1992 with my sons, and that put him at ease, because he knew that I would keep it to myself and likewise so would he. Now I never ever found out who the farmer was or where those two guys came from".

In 2008 Freddy was travelling along that same stretch of road where he saw his UFO back in 1992. Now, as he was driving past that very same spot, he noticed in the same farmer's field where he saw the UFO in 1992, several sheep all standing stock still, all staring towards the Stirling area. He thought this was very strange. And whilst he said you can get sheep standing around in a field, what set these sheep apart, was the fact that they were all grouped closely together and standing all facing the one direction. In the off chance that there are any farmers reading this book, let me know if this is a normal facet of sheep behaviour.

All in all then, it had been a great day catching up with Freddy and listening to him recount his 1992 UFO, and also his other UFO sightings in Gran Canaria including his orb sightings in the Bonnybridge area. Needless to say, it was the story about the two men that visited the farmer and took away his video tape of the strange orb like lights that he had filmed in the Bonnybridge area that got my attention the most. Who were these guys? Again, it's just another puzzling aspect to the enigma that is called, 'The Falkirk Triangle'.

Let us now move further up the country to the Perth, Kinross and Tayside region of Scotland.

Marc McClean UFO photograph Eaglesham Moor Renfrewshire. 14th August 2025

CHAPTER SEVEN

Tayside, Perth and Kinross Region

Author's Comment. Our next case file comes from Robert Ferguson, a singer songwriter and author. Here in his own words, is what he had to tell me.

Hi Malcolm,

"I woke up last night (Sunday 16th November 2014) around 02.30. As I walked towards the bedroom window and looked into the garden, a flash like a camera flash but faster, boomed in front of my eyes. This was just to the right of my window and right of the garden near the shed. This was rugby ball shaped and was approximately 12 feet long by 6 feet deep and was facing away from the house. It was an enormous flash. I checked outside and saw nothing that would account for it. I thought at first a power blow out, though the more I thought about that and added it to the mix, that would never add up to what I saw. Even stranger and the more I think about it, was, why I awoke! Anyway, it was a massive camera type flash".

Author's Comment. Robert at that time, lived in a house in the small village of Blairingone (Perth and Kinross District) which is surrounded by countryside. I replied to Robert by saying.

Hi Robert,

"There could be a number of possibilities. As your bedroom looks out onto those back fields, might it have been a farmer or poacher out with a bright torch searching for something. Daft I know, but sometimes out in the countryside you get poachers as well going lamping as they call it".

Robert replied to me saying that this sighting, the one of this white rugby shaped ball object in his garden in the village of

Blairingone, had triggered another memory of a UFO sighting that he had in Alloa many years before. Here is what he had to tell me.

"While watching TV one early evening, something caught my eye, a bird or a bat, as it was beginning to get dark. I walked to the window and saw a neighbour cycling home. When I looked to the left, beyond the main Tullibody road, where the Inglewood Pond sits, there is a red sandstone wall, and above the tree line sat a round silver object which could only be described as a UFO. It had a large, curving window on one side, at the front. It blew my mind. I went outside and stared at it, and it remained static. I wanted to shout from the rooftops, grab a camera, or tell a neighbour what was appearing in our town, in our neighbourhood. I saw several small beings through the window and a larger, human-like being behind them. Then, suddenly, it shot upwards, moving away several hundred feet before becoming static again for about thirty seconds. It then moved at speed and disappeared in a second".

Author's Comment. I asked Robert what year this was and could he tell me more about these small 'beings'. He replied.

"I can't remember the year, Malcolm. It was way back when, the early 80s? They were all the same size, just like what you call little grey aliens. The big one looked human. I honestly believe they looked at me as I looked at them. It was eerie and strange".

WAS IT REAL, OR JUST A DREAM!

Hello Malcolm,

"I don't really know if you are the right person to be contacting regarding a couple of 'experiences' I have had. These experiences aren't something that I've spoken much about. In fact, the second one I haven't told anyone about at all. This would be the first time I've ever mentioned it even occurring to anyone".

"My first experience was of witnessing a black triangular UFO seen cruising (which is the best way I can describe its movement) over the small village of Milnathort in Perth and Kinross. This incident would have been around five years ago (2009) and is something I have told only one or two close friends and work colleagues about, as well as a couple of family members. Basically, I haven't told too many people because I don't particularly like being looked at as if I'm nuts!"

"The second incident happened a couple of months ago and is the one I haven't told anyone at all, not even my closest family members, but it has been playing on my mind ever since, and pertains to what I can only describe as an attempted (or perhaps successful) abduction. It was a strange experience which at the time I told myself it must have been some sort of dream, however if it was, it was extremely vivid. Even now, I don't want to go into too much detail as I'm not sure if this would be the kind of thing to approach you with. But for what it's worth, here is my account".

"This is my full recollection of the abduction experience. I went to bed one-night, early August this year (2014) at around 3 a.m. I fell asleep as usual, but a couple of hours later, I consciously woke up. What I mean by this is, that I woke up, but I hadn't opened my eyes yet. As I lay there, I tried to go straight back to sleep. I realised that I was completely unable to move. The best way I can describe this feeling was that I was either being pressed down on by some sort of invisible force, or that somehow gravity itself was working overtime on me. I just couldn't move at all. It was at this point I opened my eyes as quick and wide as I could, and I was presented with, what I can only describe, as a grey alien standing at the bottom of my bed. The thing that struck me later, was that this alien didn't look entirely like the conventional grey alien that I have seen depictions of, either on T.V. or in movies etc. This guy at the bottom of my bed was smaller than I would have expected. I would say around two and a half to three feet tall, but he was also extremely thin. Far thinner than I've seen these guys depicted, particularly his head, which was very narrow, probably around six inches wide. His body was also roughly the same width but slightly narrower".

"As I opened my eyes, I was looking directly at this guy, but I could also make out the rough form of another one standing a couple of feet to the left of him and I'm not sure why exactly, but I also had the feeling there was also a third further to the left. However, I was completely focused on the first. Although I was unable to move at first, when I took all this in, I got a sudden and strong feeling of anger inside of me and managed to raise my head off my pillow a couple of inches and focused my attention on this first alien. I remember at this point trying to focus my anger, and I shouted in my head at this guy, I have no idea why I didn't just speak out loud, but for some reason it just came naturally to focus all my energies at a point I guess you would call your 'mind's eye'. As I pulled my head up and focused on this guy, I started to shout in my head,

"WHAT THE F**K ARE YOU DOING IN HERE. GET OUT! GET OUT! LEAVE!".

"Although the alien showed no real physical facial change, in as much as if you said that to a person you would expect to see a change or reaction in the facial expression. This guy's face remained as it was. However, I got the feeling inside me, that as I rose my head and started to shout through my mind, that he almost panicked, and was kind of worried. I saw him glance a couple of times quickly towards the other guy to his left and shift around uncomfortably, that's where everything just kind of stopped. I can only recollect after this moment, of sitting up and being alone in my room. It stood out because it was, and is, still so vivid. Of course, I dismissed it as some kind of strange dream, but I have never experienced anything like it before or since, although I have had the paralysed feeling before just without opening my eyes which is usually accompanied by an uncomfortable and intrusive feeling which is hard to describe. A couple of things that have made me question whether this might actually have happened rather than being a dream, was that my room during the experience, was exactly like it was when I woke. What I mean by this is, that the door was ajar by the same amount (I usually sleep with the door closed) and I have a coat hanger by the door which has a few jackets and a dressing gown attached.

The coats were in the same order in both the experience and when I awoke. This may mean nothing, but it was the details like that, as well as the vividness, which have made me remember this moment. Another thing I found strange, was that if this was a dream, why wouldn't I have dreamt the alien in the way I would have expected to see him! This guy was a lot smaller and thinner than I would have thought or have ever seen them depicted. Another point was that the room in the 'experience' was not pitch black as it was when I went to bed but lit to the same extent as when I woke up and looked at the clock (it was just after 6 a.m.) and there was an early morning light in the room".

"I have thought about this experience a lot in the last couple of months, and as I said in my previous email, it is something I have not spoken a word of to anyone else, and I really have no intention to, but I felt I had to say something to someone, if not just for the sheer vividness of it, both then and now. It was a strange experience, and I still don't really know what to make of it all".

Regards, Simon Pollard.

Author's Comment. And there's the rub! People who have these experiences are left wondering if it all was 'just a dream'. They can't believe that something like this could happen to them. I would accept that a fair amount of these types of experiences are indeed just a dream. But can we in all honesty say for certain, that some of these experiences are, for those people who experience them, 'reality', and an intrusion into the comfort of their lives. When will these true UFO abductions cease? What is the purpose of them?

DID I PHOTOGRAPH A UFO!

Hi Malcolm,

"I was walking in a party of 7 hikers on the 25th of October 2014. We were tackling Ben Vorlich at Lochearnhead in treacherous conditions with heavy rain and strong winds. We had set off from the carpark about 11:00am and finally got back down about 2:30pm, the weather had cleared when coming back down from the Mountain. On turning back, I took a photograph from the single-track road looking towards Ben Vorlich the mountain which you can see in the distance of the photograph. I was randomly taking scenery shots with my phone before heading home and not spending too much attention to specific distant objects. It was only when I was back home and uploading photos onto my PC, that I noticed the strange image in the sky. The photograph was taken at 3.30pm".

The phone used was a BlackBerry Q10 camera. Here are its specifications.

Rear camera.
8 megapixel auto-focus camera.
Back Side Illumination for better low-light performance.
5-element F2.2 lens.
Dedicated ISP (image signal processor) with 64MB frame buffer.
Flash, continuous and touch to focus, image stabilisation.
Enhanced Super Resolution Digital Zoom (5x)

Sincerely, William Allison.

Author's Comment. I did speculate to William that it might be a bird frozen in flight by the camera, but that was just speculation on my part. (See the photograph in the photographic section of this book)

THE RANNOCH MOOR UFO PHOTOGRAPH?

Author's Comment. Yet another alleged UFO photograph was brought to my attention. In October 2020, Tony Steen from Stenhousemuir contacted Bonnybridge Councillor, Billy Buchanan regarding a possible UFO photograph that he had taken. Councillor Buchanan immediately got in touch with me and passed on Tony's details of which I soon got in touch with him.

Hi Malcolm,

"Just to give you a heads up on what I photographed and seen the night the photo was taken. The photo was taken at 20:02 hrs on the 17th of September 2020. It was taken from the head of Loch Rannoch at Kinloch Rannoch looking down the loch in the direction of Rannoch Station and the distant Glen Coe mountains. I took several photographs in the space of a few minutes. As you can see from the photo, it was a beautiful sunset. The picture with the object was the second photo I took and was the only one to show any kind of anomaly. The first three photos were taken seconds apart. There was other people present taking photos also, mostly tourists from England going by their accent. There was one other guy there that had a camera set on a tripod and was also taking photos of the beautiful sunset. I only had a brief courteous word with him, saying 'hello and it's a beautiful night' which he acknowledged back. I was with a friend who took some photos also, but his photographs showed nothing unusual. I should point out that I saw nothing unusual when taking the photos, it wasn't until I had a good look at them and zoomed into the photo, that I noticed the anomaly. That particular photo was taken using a bit of a zoom lens".

"After we took our photos, we jumped back in the car and made our way three miles up the North side of the loch to a place that we have camped and fished countless times over the last 40 years. As the last embers of light faded from the sky and darkness started to fall upon us, it signals the time to start fishing. We fish for trout through the night, as it's the best time to catch them as they are largely nocturnal hunters. Anyway, it was a beautiful clear night, and you could see the milky way and millions of stars. There were also the usual satellites and aircraft in the night sky. However, there were also other lights that we noticed, and they were making irregular changes in direction which was pretty unusual. My friend also said that he had seen a light shooting up into the sky or coming down from the sky. He also seen the lights in the sky that I had seen making the irregular changes in direction. But the one thing that really got our attention, was right overhead in the sky, there was an extremely bright brilliant white light which came on for a second or two, then off in an instant.

This was a stationary light, and it did this three times. There was no beam of light which I could see emitting from the source. It was pretty incredible to see, I've never seen anything like it before, and I've spent all of my life outdoors in such environments all over Scotland, and that was a first time seeing such things. We both agreed that it was a pretty strange night with these things going on in the sky. We fished on till after midnight without any other strange things happening, then a mist descended down the loch and we packed up and headed off home. The strange lights that we witnessed in the sky would have been round about 21:30 hrs, though I can't be exact about the time. When we saw the photo with the anomaly in it, and the strange lights in the night sky, we guessed that it was no coincidence, and we both truly believe that they were connected in some way".

My first encounter

"My first encounter with what I regard as a UFO sighting, was a few years ago maybe five years (2015)? but I'm not really sure. I was working with my brother-in-law giving him a hand to do some underwater inspection on a railway viaduct near Elvenfoot close to Sanquhar. We had to wait until the last train that night had passed to commence work, where we then travelled along the railway on a bogey with workmen from Network Rail. Anyway, we got the job done and headed back home. I got dropped off at 03:45 and it was a lovely quiet May morning, can't be exact about the date, but it was probably the beginning of May. I made myself a cup of tea and was sitting down at the kitchen window looking out. It was very quiet, and there wasn't any wind blowing, only the distant sound of a blackbird making an early morning call. It was a mostly clear sky with a distant cloud bank in the west. My eye then caught something coming into my view, and there, right above me, was a large delta shaped craft with a light on each apex. Even though it was high in the sky, I could tell that it was huge in size. I've seen countless aircraft flying overhead before, but this was something different altogether. It looked black in colour from what I could make out, and it was heading in a westerly direction. It was moving very slowly. I watched it all the time until it disappeared into the cloud bank lying in the west. All this time it never made a sound, any aircraft I've ever seen flying overhead makes a noise and you can hear them no problem. This aircraft was huge, slow, and soundless very strange indeed".

"I think, the next strange anomaly that I saw, was when fishing at night again, but this time it was for pike on the union canal near Polmont. This was about three years ago (2017?) but again, I can't be exactly sure when. It was my friend whom I was fishing with, that brought it to my attention when he said to me, *"What is that in the sky"?* I looked up as he pointed it out, and I could see a large brilliant bright orange ball of light travelling very fast and low on a horizontal trajectory. It was first seen in the direction of Bathgate and made its way to the area of Edinburgh Airport or so it appeared. We reckon it travelled at the very least 15 miles in five seconds and appeared to fly directly under an aircraft which had just taken off from Edinburgh Airport as it was still climbing into the air. The anomaly appeared to stop in a split second, then disappeared in an instant. My friend who was a sceptic, is now a believer, and doesn't slag me off anymore when we talk about UFOs, and that concludes my encounters with any kind of UFO phenomenon. If there is any further information you require just let me know".

Author's Comment. Having read Tony's e-mail, I quickly got in touch with him and stated.

Hi Tony,

"Many thanks for your e-mail. It sure looks like you have had some interesting UFO sightings, more so the delta shaped craft which seems to be most prevalent these days. The Rannoch Moor photo is spectacular, that sunset is truly beautiful. It is quite possible the reason that you didn't see anything whilst taking that shot, is 'possibly', and I do say 'possibly', that it might have been a flying insect that just zipped across the frame, being frozen in flight by the camera as it did so. A lot of claimed UFO photographs fall into this category. From a small blob to an elongated blur. It is surprising how common this is. But again, it might 'not' have been that, and this is just pure speculation on my part". With best wishes. Malcolm Robinson.

Author's Comment. Tony replied.

Hi Malcolm,

"We thought the same, that it might be some sort of insect flying past caught in the aperture as I clicked the button. But I have to say, it doesn't look like any insect I've ever seen, but I'm aware of the illusion of such, especially if in flight and could possibly look like something completely different. However, it does look like a long cylindrical shaped object, and one could argue metallic in nature. It's a great photo for the debunker, but I'm happy to stick with my theory".
Sincerely, Tony Steen.

Author's Comment. The following is a report that I wrote for the Outer Limits Magazine edited by Chris Evers of which I am their associate editor. This concerns a lecture that I attended about one of Scotland's strangest UFO encounters. The Calvine UFO.

THE CALVINE UFO - 35 Years of Mystery

Saturday, August 2nd, 2025, from 4:00 PM to 6:00 PM (BST) Blair Atholl Village Hall, Blair Atholl, Perthshire, Scotland, PH18 5SG

(A report by Malcolm Robinson)

Before I give you my report on how the Calvine UFO talk went, it's best that I inform those readers who are not privy to this incredible UFO case about what happened (and if you are not aware of it, where have you been!) So, the following (in part) is the gist of the case, most of which was spoken about at the village hall in Blair Atholl by the various speakers (as recalled by me) Other segments of this report have been briefly taken from Wikipedia, So, what is all the hullabaloo about?

THE CALVINE UFO. WHAT HAPPENED?

The Calvine UFO (also known as the Calvine Sighting) was a reported sighting and the taking of a photograph of an unidentified flying object (UFO) near the hamlet of Calvine in Perthshire, Scotland in August 1990.

It all started when two hikers (Chefs from a Pitlochry Hotel) were out walking on the moors near the small town of Calvine in Perthshire in the Scottish Highlands who claim to have seen an extraordinary sight in the sky of which they managed to take six photographs of. They stated that as they were hiking on the 4th of August in 1990, they saw a 'diamond shaped object' being escorted by what appeared to have been a Harrier Jet. They took shelter underneath some trees to observe this fascinating sight keeping their eyes firmly fixed on this noiseless strange object. The object hovered, then ascended vertically, before finally disappearing from view. Knowing that they had captured something very strange, they handed the prints and the negatives to the Scottish Daily Record newspaper, Scotland's biggest selling newspaper of the day, who then passed them over to the Ministry of Defence (MoD) And surprise surprise, those photographs and prints somehow disappeared. One would have thought that the Daily Record would have published these photographs whether they believed in them or not, but surprisingly they didn't, which, as it would later turn out, they missed out on the scoop of the century!

The main player who brought this astonishing episode to the public, was Dr David Clarke, associate professor at the Sheffield Cultural Industries institute and head of the National Folklore Society. David is also a broadcaster and author. David decided to look into this enigma and try and track down the two witnesses. Looking through the National Archives in 2009 he came across some further information which he published in the Daily Mail on the 13th of August 2022. From there, the story went global. Before we get into the Blair Atholl talk on this case, let me tell you about why I just had to attend this talk.

THE CALVINE UFO LECTURE. BLAIR ATHOLL, AUGUST 2ND 2025

If ever I had to attend a UFO talk, it certainly was this one. I have known Dr Clarke for many years, most notably when I lived in England and when I was in charge of the British UFO Research Society's lecture programme. David and I have had many a chat about British UFO sightings, and whilst we both come from different angles, in that (I believe we are dealing with something 'off Earth') whilst David believes that most, if not all, UFO sightings can be explained away as ordinary mundane events, we both shared a deep held fascination for these sightings.

I travelled up to Blair Atholl with my partner Carole and we settled into our hotel, The Atholl Arms which sits next to the train station. Before the event, I met up with fellow researcher and Calvine UFO enthusiast, Straiph Wilson where we had a pint in the beer garden of this wonderful pub. Needless to say, we talked shop until it was time to get ready and attend the event. As I approached this massive building which looked nothing like a village hall! (I was expecting a small building, this wasn't a small building!) I could see many people already making their way there. At the door, I was met by some of the Calvine research team, namely, Andrew Robinson, Matthew Illsley, and Giles Stevens who said they were expecting me and that two seats had been reserved for Carole and I at the front. I then introduced myself to Dr David Clarke where we both shook hands, hugged and said it had been too long since we had met up. He kindly bought my latest book, 'The Bonnybridge UFO Enigma' co-authored with Ron Halliday, speaking of which, Ron was in the audience with fellow enthusiast Gordon Rutter. Ron and I had a nice catch up, after which it was time to sit down and get into this lecture.

Dr DAVID CLARKE
(The Calvine Event and Search)

First up, was Dr David Clarke himself, who informed the audience how he became involved in this case, and how the case shaped his life with all the twists and turns trying to find some answers. He stated that the very first mention of this case, was in the former Ministry of Defence desk officer, Nick Pope's 1996 book, *'Open Skies, Closed Minds'* which detailed UFO sightings that had been reported to the MOD while he was assigned to Sec (AS)2 effectively known as 'the UFO desk'. Nick worked there from 1991 to 1994. Dr Clarke explained that Nick Pope stated that analysis that was undertaken by the MOD on the Calvine photographs, had concluded that the photographs, (remember, they initially were six) were 'not fakes' and the sighting was put down as a UFO in the truest sense of the word. The case was closed with no further action taken. Dr Clarke uncovered a copy of the photograph of the Calvine UFO through the National Archives in 2009 and informed the large audience of a government briefing from the MoD Secretariat Air Staff, and a handwritten summary of the sighting from a Sec (AS)2 officer both dated September 1990 (DEFE 24/1940/1 – page 113–116). Additionally, two poor-quality photocopies of Vu-Foils (images on transparent plastic) made from cropped versions of the original photographs, were included in records assembled by DI55, a branch of the Directorate of Scientific and Technical Intelligence (DSTI) that dealt with missiles and air defence. (DEFE 31/180/1 – pages 36–7). These files revealed the images were the subject of an investigation by DI55 and a RAF photo analyst agency.

    Dr Clarke went on to discuss how one of the witnesses came to take the photograph, and how the negatives were taken to the Scottish Daily Record. He read out the witness statement of what he saw, and mentioned that the Aurora aircraft, a so-called secret stealth type aircraft which was allegedly stationed at RAF Machrihanish, which is three and a half miles from the town of Campbeltown at the tip of the Kintyre peninsula in Argyll and Bute, was allegedly flying around the Scottish skies, or certainly within the Machrihanish area. He then spoke about other so called secret aircraft which are noiseless and have the triangular aeriform in which he was drawing comparisons to the Calvine object in the sense that could this too, have been a black budget project?

Dr Clarke read from a number of once classified files/memos that he had uncovered, all of which proved 'eye opening'! These memos clearly showed that the British and American Government had been briefed about these new prototype aircraft. David stated that in 2018, his interest was piqued when he came across a Defence Intelligence Officer's claim, that the witness had photographed a classified U.S. black project platform. This black project, he was told, had been flown from RAF Machrihanish, escorted by both U.K. and U.S. aircraft. As David's lecture progressed, he went through various documents which began to build a picture of not only how he became aware of this case, but also of who else were aware of it! In one particular case, David was made aware of a gentleman who said that it was indeed an experimental aircraft than was being escorted by Harriers from Machrihanish Airbase. David then spoke about the copies of the photograph and how they were reprinted and processed in various ways. What Dr David Clarke presented in his part of the afternoon, was nothing short of astonishing. I honestly thought I knew about this case, well, after listening to Dr Clarke, evidently not. So many facts were given, that I wish I had the space to present them all here. David uncovered that a 'copy' of the Calvine photograph (after the MoD had finished with it), was sent to Craig Lindsay who, at the time, was the RAF Press Officer, at Pitreavie MHQ. It was reported that when David spoke to Craig, Craig's first statement was,

"I've been waiting for someone to call me about this for 30 years!".

Craig explained to David, that the Daily Record newspaper had provided him with a print of one of the six images. On the back of the photograph was possibly the name of the photographer, which we'll come to in a moment. Craig Lindsay found out that the witness had been working in a hotel in Pitlochry and proceeded to interview him over the phone. Craig then typed up a short report of his findings which he faxed, along with a photocopy of the image provided by the Daily Record, to the MOD in London at which point he was told to *'leave it to London'.*

Dr Clarke informed the audience that in October 2021 Craig Lindsay had emailed him a copy of a 'photocopy' of the original photograph which had been sent to him by the Daily Record. Unfortunately, Craig, at that time, couldn't find the print itself. It wasn't until many years later when Dr Clarke again asked Craig to look again for the original copy that Craig eventually found it. It was secreted in a book in his loft, entitled, *'Great Aircraft of the World'*. Now the thing is, Craig was going to throw a lot of these old books out to make more room in the loft, just think, if Craig had have thrown all those books away, one of which contained this incredible photograph, we may never have been aware of the significance of the whole story and we wouldn't be where we are today.

The bottom line for Dr David Clarke, is that it is his contention, that the Calvine Object is indeed a black budget aircraft, being test flown in the wilds of Scotland with knowledge of it from both the British and Americans.

ANDREW ROBINSON
(Image Analysis and Missing Evidence)

Next up, was senior lecturer of photography at the Sheffield Hallum University Andrew Robinson, who said that his part in the story was when Dr Clarke sent him a copy of the Calvine UFO Photograph and asked his opinion, to which Andrew submitted a twelve page report to David which, as he states, 'He got sucked up into this UFO story and went down the rabbit hole with him'. This was effectively when David's article appeared in the Daily Mail. Andrew's part in this presentation, was to go through various things about the photograph and how he studied it. He states that his study showed him that there is a landscape in the distance, which, he admits, he has been challenged on, but his analysis clearly shows a background of such. Andrew's work on this photograph was clearly valuable to the Calvine team. His expert knowledge of photography clearly was brought to bear in looking at this photograph. He spoke about the distance, the depth of field, where the photographer must have been when he took the photograph. The measurements of the UFO with the measurements of the wire fence in the foreground, all played a part in deciding a number of factors. The fence was roughly 10 meters from where the cameraman took the photo, this assisted the distance comparison to the object and the Harrier jet. That said, it all depended on what lens the cameraman was using, and that, at this point in time, we don't know. Andrew then went on to show the packed audience some photographs of where he and the Calvine team believe the photograph was taken from. (They had ventured up to the location the previous night) Andrew then broached the subject that the Calvine UFO photograph could have been a hoax, and explained how easily this could have been done, by probably hanging a small model from a very thin line from a tree, or, in one case, a model suspended from a line on a fishing pole. Andrew Robinson provided the Calvine team, high-resolution digital copies and an in-depth analysis of the image and other materials which all combined into his full report of the Calvine case. Andrew believes that the photograph is genuine and is a genuine photograph of a scene before the camera.

Andrew's talk was truly fascinating, a gave a different perspective to this enigma. His deep knowledge of photography, helped enormously by providing further clues about this historic UFOlogical image.

MATTHEW ILLSLEY
(The search for the witnesses)

Next up was Matthew Illsley who spoke about his search to try and track down the two witnesses, and what a search it was! Matthew's first involvement with this case, started in 2001 when he saw an article in a newspaper. One of the big find leads, was tracking down Craig Lindsay who was at the time, the RAF Press Officer, at Pitreavie MHQ. Craig provided Andrew with his copy of the Calvine photo which had the name of Kevin Russell on the back of it, it read…..*'Copyright Kevin Russell c/o Daily Record Glasgow'*. So, if this Kevin Russell held the copyright, was he the photographer? So, a massive search was undertaken to track down this Kevin Russell, and believe me dear reader, it sure was a massive search, way too much to go into here.

A PANEL DEBATE

Following Matthew's presentation, there then followed a panel discussion on the case. This featured, Matthew Illsley, Andrew Robinson, Dr David Clarke, Craig Lindsay, and Mike Mulford. This debate proved most illuminating and the Q and A session that followed with audience interaction, was equally of interest.

IN CONCLUSION

At the end of the day, this was a very informative talk which covered each and every aspect of the Calvine mystery. If only we had the missing pieces of the jigsaw, and those are.

1) The two witnesses to step forward.

2) The Pitlochry chemist who processed the Calvine photographs (remember they were six in all)

3) Where are the other five Calvine Photographs?

4) If any reader has knowledge of the above, please get in touch with the author where I will pass this information onto the Calvine team.

END NOTES

Just for the record, fellow Scottish UFOlogist Straiph Wilson placed an advert in a local Pitlochry newspaper which covers this whole area, asking for those hill walkers to come forward, or indeed anyone who had any information on this photograph to come forward, sadly, no one came forward. Whilst I was there, I got interviewed by a well-known television channel, and also by David Clarke himself, who sat me down and asked me initially about Scottish UFO sightings. And then came the question that I was waiting for him to ask, which was. As I was the main UFO researcher in Scotland at that time, why had I not been involved in this case. My answer was three-fold.

1) I didn't learn about this case until 2001 when the story came out in the Daily Mail. At that time, I was living in England and away from Scottish UFOlogy.

2) I had read the small segment in Nick Pope's book, 'Open Skies, Closed Minds' about the Calvine case, but that small paragraph did not pique my interest.

3) When I heard that David was involved in the case, I felt it best to let him carry on with it, as I knew the stake that he had on it and didn't want to tread on his toes (as it were) Looking back, and hindsight is a great thing, even although I lived in England at the time, I should have done my bit, and anything I found out, I should have forwarded onto David.

All in all, it had been a wonderful weekend. I met some great people, like Straiph Wilson, Graeme Rendall, Chris Grant, (who, incidentally, gave me a 3D printed model of the Calvine UFO) Giles Stevens, and a number of people came up to me at the close of the lecture to tell me about their own UFO experiences. To be honest, the best thing to come out of this event, was the event being filmed by SKY Television, which, if presented properly, will show how massive this case really is, and perhaps, who knows, 'might' draw out these elusive two witnesses. But if those two witnesses have been 'got at' by the suits! (You know what I mean) they may have been silenced not to say anything. But say anything about what? That it was an extraterrestrial craft, or just a secret black budget prototype craft that was being test flown! Take your pick. I'm sure this case has more to it than meets the eye!

THE BLUE LIGHT!

Hi Malcolm,

"My name is Danny Davies. I hope you don't mind me dropping you a wee email. Firstly, I would like to say I really enjoyed your book on the Sauchie poltergeist. It was a very interesting read. I have read Guy Lyon Playfair's book on the Enfield haunting, and also the South Shields poltergeist case, and I count your book as one of the best".

"I was also reading an article in which you mentioned UFOs over Fife and Tayside. In the article, it mentions an incident in Crieff in 1954. I found this of particular interest because I used to live in Crieff from 1989-1995. When I was a young boy about 8 years old (1993) we were living in a newly built house, and myself, along with my identical brother Chris, had a really bizarre experience. It was a Saturday night around 10:00pm. My brother Chris thought he heard a noise outside our bedroom window. We had bunk beds at the time. Chris got up from his bottom bunk and looked out the window. The very moment he opened the curtains; a light filled the room. I was on the top bunk and witnessed it also. It was a real strange blue, white light which covered the full window. Needless to say, my brother and I were caught off guard, and found the incident rather unsettling. We also both felt a weird sensation as we witnessed it. After seeing the light, we ran downstairs to tell our parents. The strange thing was, that our parents were sitting in the room below our bedroom. They were sitting beside the window, and we were shocked that they never saw the bright light. My parents suggested it may be someone playing a prank, but both my brother and I knew deep down there was something odd about it. I should also add that I had no interest in the paranormal at this time. However, after this event I became very interested in paranormal phenomena and later went on to study psychology and parapsychology. Not long after the incident my mum passed away due to cancer, and I have always wondered if there was a connection between the light and my mum's passing. Crieff had a very strange energy to it. I believe there are energy lines which run through the town. I know many people who have had weird experiences there, such as UFO sightings, poltergeist events, and other weird things happen when they lived in Crieff. I always believed the phenomena was interconnected. I left Crieff in 1995, but that event really did shape my thinking and how I viewed the world. I have had numerous other weird experiences throughout the years, but that incident in Crieff was really weird. Sorry if I rambled on in that email there! it's not a story I have shared with many people, but it left a big impression on me and still does. Anyway, keep up the good work and like I said your book was excellent".

Kind Regards, Danny Davies.

WHAT COULD IT HAVE BEEN?

Hi Malcolm,

"Here is a UFO sighting that I had back in 2001 in Dundee while I was a Security Guard on night shift working at DERL (Dundee Energy Recycling Limited) one bitterly cold morning around 6:00am. I was opening the main gates to the plant to let the milkman make his morning delivery, and as he was talking to me sorting the milk out, the pair of us were gobsmacked as we looked into the sky and observed a craft in the sky above us. We were both stunned as this craft was just hovering above us and had no noise to it. It had plenty of lights, revealing some kind of triangular shape. It sat stationary for a couple of minutes then moved off slowly before shooting off in an instant. The two of us just thought it must be some kind of military craft, or perhaps even a police spotting craft, but it was the triangular shape to it that still sticks out, plus it was just hovering. If it was military, it may have been some kind of stealth craft?"

Yours truly. David Drummond.

Author's Comment. We now take our UFOlogical journey further north again, where once more, strange UFO tales await us.

Artist impression of Robert Ferguson's Inglewood UFO sighting. Early 1980's

Artist impression of Robert Ferguson's garden UFO 16th November 2024

**Close up of William Allison's Ben Vorlich UFO.
24th October 2014 (c) William Allison**

Full photograph. William Allison Ben Vorlich UFO 24th October 2014 (c) William Allison.

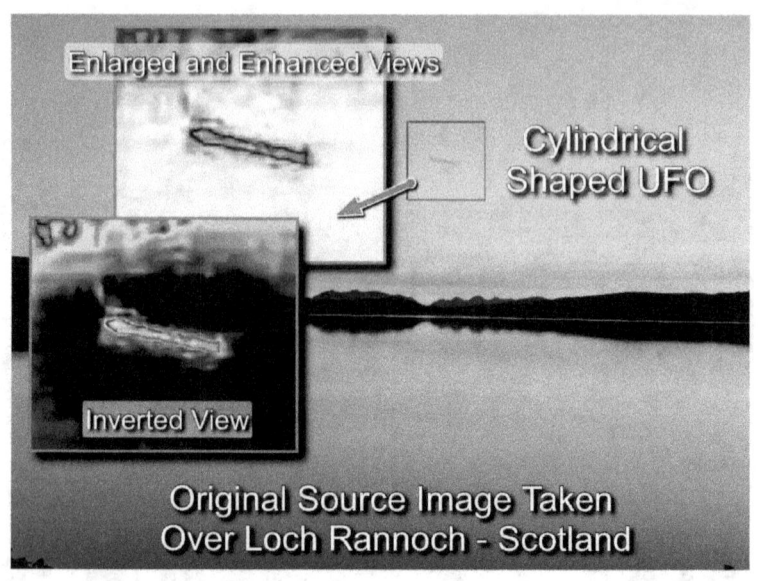

**Tony Steen UFO Photograph with enhancements.
17th September 2020**

CHAPTER EIGHT

Aberdeenshire, Northeast and West Scotland

UFO SPENT FOUR HOURS HOVERING ABOVE OUR FAMILY HOME!

This was the statement from the Daily Mail dated 18th October 2012 which stated that a rural farm in Aberdeenshire Scotland had been 'visited' by a strange craft. Prior to the story breaking, I was contacted by BBC Radio Aberdeen who sent me the video footage taken by the witness to which they requested that I give a statement as to what I thought it could be. Upon viewing the footage, I must admit that I was quite impressed, more so because if truth be told, I was expecting to see those dam Chinese Lanterns. The footage I saw, clearly did not look like Chinese Lanters. Anyway, here in part, is what the Daily Mail had to say about this sighting.

Morag Ritchie (50) was woken in the middle of the night by flashing lights coming into her bedroom. The grandmother of one woke her family up and her daughter's fiancé caught the shocking images of four blinking lights on video. Morag stated,

"We live in a very rural area, so I never have my curtains closed and I like looking at the night sky. I just woke up all of a sudden and looked out of the window to see all these twinkling lights, they looked like they were moving. I was quite apprehensive about it. I'm standing there looking at it, and I'm thinking "is it watching me?", so I went around the house telling everyone and they all came to have a look."

The Mail goes on to state that Mrs Ritchie described seeing a circular object which was hovering and spinning near her home in Fraserburgh, Aberdeenshire. She further stated.

"My husband is a fisherman and he's spent many hours looking up at the night sky, so he was quite sceptical when I told him, but even he admitted it was strange when he saw them.

Eventually we all went back to bed. I woke up a further two times, the second time was about four hours later, and it was still there, but when I next woke up it was daylight, and they had gone. It was there for so long that even all the way out here, someone else must have seen it, but perhaps they've been too shy to come forward about it."

The Mail states that Morag's daughter, Cara, 27, got out of bed to feed her baby in the early hours of Saturday morning when she first became aware about the sighting. She said,

"At first, I thought it was just a plane, but my mum said it had been there for a few hours and there was no noise or anything. I was quite mesmerised by it all to be honest although my fiancé Scott, was pretty scared. He was smoking at the back door where you could see the lights from, and he was genuinely frightened. He kept the door half open, so he wasn't actually fully outside".

Cara went on to say,

"I didn't really believe in UFOs or anything like that beforehand. You hear lots of stories, but you don't really believe them, but this was really really strange. After seeing what I've seen, I'm genuinely wondering if there are actually aliens out there now".

Needless to say, my phone was soon ringing off the hook with calls from the Scottish Sun, the Daily Record, and a few others. I stated to the Mail that although 95 per cent of all UFO reports can be explained, I was baffled by the footage Scott had captured. I further stated to the Mail, that I'd looked at the footage, and there appears to be four lights in a line intermittently flashing which could be anything but nonetheless is strange. Many UFO sightings I went on, were actually Chinese lanterns, but this sighting did not have the elements of those. I continued by stating that this case was very interesting to a researcher like me, but at the moment we wouldn't have any answers for a couple of weeks, at least until I had conducted my Investigations where I hoped to have found out if there were any other sightings or aircraft in the area at the time. Civil Aviation Authority spokesman Tony Finnegan said to the Mail,

"It could be a light aircraft or military aircraft, but at 2:00am in the morning, it's unlikely to be civilian. We aren't able to find out what aircraft were in the area at the time, but there was increased activity of northern lights last week, so I suppose they would be a possibility."

Well, it's obvious that Tony hadn't seen the footage or he wouldn't have said that! I interviewed Morag over the phone, and I asked her to send me an e-mail with more information. This is what she had to say.

Hi Malcolm,

"I am glad that you have asked me about this as it has intrigued us as a family since we all witnessed it. I live in a rural area just outside Fraserburgh. I don't close my curtains at night as I don't have any neighbours to worry about, and I find the night sky quite comforting to look at as I go to sleep. Anyway, I woke in the early hours of Saturday morning (13th October 2012) about 2.30 - 3am for whatever reason I'm not sure. As I lay awake, I noticed what I thought to be a very bright star, but the more I looked at it, I realised that it was quite unusual. So, I got up and looked out the window and the more I looked at this, I thought that this is not a star. It seemed to kind of hover about but not really moving from my line of view. It seemed to me to be more of a spinning object. I then went through to the living room where my son in law had just gone there to feed his new baby and told him to come and look, then my daughter and my husband also got up and came to see. They went outside and tried to video it on their iPhone".

"I eventually went back to sleep only to waken again at sporadic intervals through the night and it still seemed to just be hovering about. I actually felt quite unnerved, wondering if someone or something was watching me as I slept (maybe a bit imaginative but unsettling all the same.) There was no sound when we were out looking at it, so it was not a plane nor a

helicopter. I think between sleep and wakening it was there for a good 3/4 hours. The last time I saw it was just as daylight came in. When I finally got up about 08.30am it was gone".

I asked Morag exactly where this sighting occurred, and she stated that her home lies between the towns of Fraserburgh and Mensie. I posted some details on my Facebook page and received a comment from UFO Portugal who commented on my post by saying.

"I was checking through my aerial control program effectively and there were no civilian aircraft on the date and time mentioned."

What we have to bear in mind reader, is that R.A.F. Buchan is not so far away from Fraserburgh, and one could be tempted to say that they might have been test flying some kind of new craft over the area but that of course is pure speculation on my part. Plus, we have to bear in mind that the witness said tis object was stationary. Could it have been the Northern Lights? I would imagine that the witnesses were well used to seeing this in their area, especially as where they live, they have no light pollution, so we should discount that. I could speculate that it could have been a bright star or planet, but surely the witness would have recognised this as a star due to where she lived and the uncluttered vista that she had of the area?

I never did find out the cause of this sighting. What didn't help was not receiving anything back from the authorities.

RIDDLE OF THE GREEN MAN

No sooner had the furore died down on the Morag Ritchie UFO story, then along came another starling photograph which blazed across the Scottish Press. The headline in the Scottish Daily Record of October 23rd 2012 stated, *'Riddle Of The Green Man'*. The story contained a photograph of the outside of the witness's house, but with the added bonus of what appeared to be, a 'green man'! For me, the photograph didn't show a green man, but more of a distorted green light. The story goes that Gary and Amanda Linney from Collieston in Aberdeenshire Scotland, said the strange figure was seen running away from their cottage as they tried out a new camera. (25 miles away from where Morag Ritchie filmed her spectacular UFO) Former policeman Gary, 52, was quoted in the Daily Record, that there was no explanation for the figure. He went on.

"It looks like a little green man running. It just disperses into the surface of the road. If you look closely, you can see a head. It's very surreal. I was a policeman and a pilot for 20 years and have never seen anything like this before."

We learn that hotel owners Gary and Amanda, 46, tried to recreate the picture but so far haven't seen the strange light since. The couple stated to the Daily Record that this was nothing unusual for them, as apparently, they have experienced a number of paranormal happenings at the Slains Estate house. Gary and Amanda who have three children stated.

"This wasn't a reflection. We live in two old cottages, and my children have seen orbs floating around and heard footsteps. It's usually around the staircase."

Amanda, 45, who was also interviewed by the Daily Record, stated that staff at their hotel which is also thought to be haunted, suggested the ghostly figure may have come from there. She stated.

"I have no idea what it was. We have used the same setting, taken photos in the same location and in different locations and nothing has appeared again. We have experienced a lot of strange things since we took over the place two years ago. The staff think something spooky had followed me home that night."

Author's Comment. The press report and photograph of this sighting can be found in the photographic section of this book.

FLYING SAUCER HOVERS OVER A FOREST

In November 2012, another interesting piece of video footage reached the Scottish tabloids, this time above Perthshire. The news agency SWNS stated that a major UFO investigation was underway after a man filmed a mysterious oval shaped object hovering over a forest. The story goes on to relate, that chef Adrian Musat, 40, was stunned when he saw the spooky white light floating over the woodland through his window at night. We learn that he quickly grabbed his video camera and recorded the mysterious light. He sent his video tape off to the British UFO Research Association (BUFORA). News agency SWNS stated the witness as saying.

"I have never seen anything like it. I watch out the window every day and we have a beautiful view, but I have never seen such a strange thing. It didn't make any noise. The flashing UFO was flying above Clunie Wood near Loch Fiskally, and was about five metres wide and its colours were constantly changing".

We learn from the story that Adrian first saw the object from his home at 7.30am on the morning of Bonfire Night before it reappeared 10 hours later. Since this amazing sighting, Adrian has kept a watch at his window most nights in an effort to hopefully see it again. The article stated that Matt Lyons of BUFORA, has launched an investigation into Adrian's footage and will be speaking to him in the near future to gather a wider understanding of the incident.

THIS WAS NO HALLUCINATION!

Hi Malcolm,

"Having read in the Daily Mail about a lady in Fraserburgh seeing what she thought was a UFO and noting your comments, I wonder if the following is if interest to you?"

"I live in a rural area in Moray some fifty miles to the west of Fraserburgh. About a week ago (14th October 2012) at 8.30pm I was walking my dogs in the fields adjacent to the house. It was a clear starlit night, and as there is little light pollution in this area, it was a delight to just enjoy the panorama of the night sky. I saw coming towards me what I took to be the lights of an RAF Tornado, not unusual as RAF Lossiemouth is only about twenty miles away. However, as it drew nearer and passed over my head, I saw a different picture".

"The 'object's' silhouette was similar in shape, roughly triangular, to that of a military plane, but the unusual thing was, the whole plane, for want of a better word, appeared to be lit up in an unusual way. I can only describe this as an orange/red glow, rather like a piece of steel that has just come out of a blast furnace. There was no sound, although it did not appear to be flying at any great height. I watched in complete amazement until it passed out of sight. As I puzzled on this, I saw in the distance, two more similar lights approaching, so I ran into the house to get my wife who also joined me. This time the objects approached travelling side by side with some little distance between them. Again, travelling silently and at no great height. They followed the same course as the first object, but I saw one of them make a slight adjustment to its course as if to keep the same distance between the two of them. This was then followed shortly after by another single object following the same course, and, unbelievably, by a further two again travelling side by side. We were both left without any rational explanation".

"To those who would tell me it was ' The Northern Lights ' I would say absolute rubbish. I've seen them many times before, and this was nothing like that. Weather balloons? Well do they fly in formation and make adjustments to maintain distance? We thought they may have been test missiles fired from a submarine or ship at sea in some exercise, but I have been at the launch of the space shuttle in America and there was a distinct lack of flame, smoke or noise. I can come up with no rational explanation for this".

"Now I understand that you need to establish the credibility of your 'witness' and can only offer in explanation that my wife and I were both police officers in England with some 45 years of police experience. We've seen it, done it and also got the tee shirt, so any suggestion of hallucination or confusion needs to be well tested. I leave you with these thoughts but, as an ex-detective, I hate not having an answer to this".

Sincerely John Van Rossen.

THE ELECTRIC UFO

Hi Malcolm,

"It was the 19th of September 2020 at 04.42 in the morning. Since birth I have had this sixth sense and couldn't sleep due to a feeling of a spirit visiting me. Suddenly I heard a crackling electricity like sound coming from outside. I immediately looked out the window and saw what I can only describe as a light which looked like a Catherine wheel fire work which was spiralling across the sky. I grabbed my phone and took a picture. I didn't even think to take a video, I don't know why. It then just turned into a bright light which kind of just stayed there then disappeared. It was very bright and was a reddish colour illuminating from one edge. No smells, just a sound of hovering and electric crackling. Time went very fast, and I fell asleep straight after. I tried to wake my partner during this sighting so he could see it, but he couldn't be woken. It was all so fast though. The size was smaller than the moon. In terms of the night sky, it was very clear, and the atmosphere very still for a September morning. It was rather warm for the time of year. There was no clouds, and I couldn't see the moon as it must have been to the front of my property at that time, it's in the back of my property in the evening. There were a few stars but no constellations I recognised".

"In my lifetime, I have often had strange experiences which can be mostly accounted for. In my dreams I often see the future. I have dreamt about many people unexpectedly dying, and everything in my dream and what happens to them in my dream, comes true, and it's always approximately 14 days before. My Granda was a psychic and often had the same experiences. He comes to me in my dreams and tells me things before they happen. I always tell my mum or dad or someone what I dream so that it can be verified. I have had three near death experiences and my granda always came and told me it would happen in the days previous. Not that I can change this happening, but so that I am prepared. He always says to believe in the greater powers, and these things are meant to be, and that I will be OK. When my father was dying, I asked him to come to me, and he did. I asked my granda to save him, and suddenly the atmosphere changed in the room, and I just knew my dad would be OK. I mean it's not everyday someone comes back from having complete kidney and liver failure, especially someone who has had crippling diabetes for 40 years".

"I also have frequent dreams about space. I am on a spaceship looking back at the earth and crying for it because I will be away for a long time. When I wake up, I am always unwell or fatigued for days or weeks on end. These dreams are so strange because they only have people that I know who have passed, and no one else. These people all tell me things that also come true. I know this all sounds completely insane, but I honestly have such a strange feeling that it is all true. I discuss this with my immediate family but no one else for fear of being ridiculed. My whole life I have also sensed spirits and have a strong belief in God, although I also keep that private, the holy spirit especially. I was brought up Mormon, although I don't follow the religion now. I still believe in everything it taught me".

Many thanks, Emily Robertson.

Author's Comment. We conclude our journey through Scotland, by traveling through the Scottish Highlands and Islands. After which, I have updates for the reader on two famous Scottish UFO Incidents. More of which later.

Daily Record 12th October 2012

Little green man photograph taken by Amanda Linney

October 2012

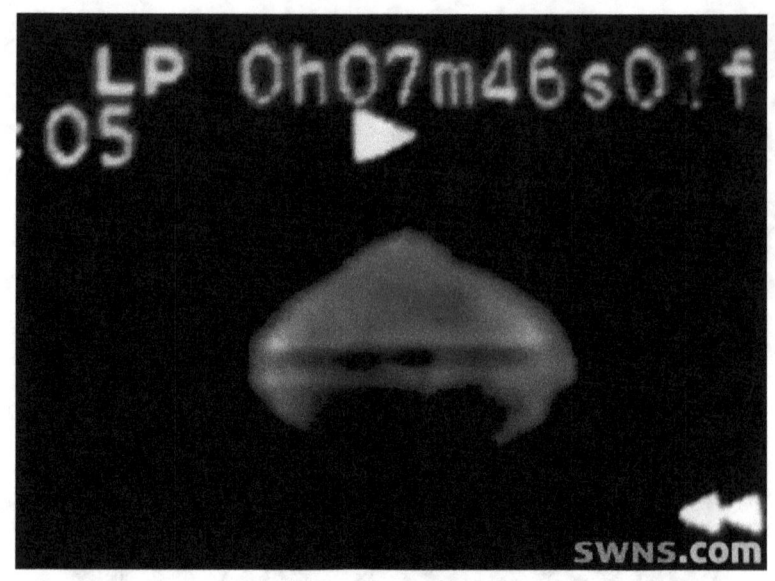

Adrian Musat still from his video showing a UFO

CHAPTER NINE

Scottish Highlands and Islands

A FLYING COW OR A 'SCREEN MEMORY'!

Hi Malcolm,

"I'd emphasise that my wee story is just that, wee, alongside a few weird incidents throughout my life. Centrally though, I'm just interested in a core incident that happened as a child, and whether or not anyone has seen anything to what I myself saw. Not a massive deal, I'm a busy professional/parent, but it's really bugged me through the years. It occurred in Western Scotland, around 1976-78. I can't remember the year exactly, but I was only around six or seven years old, maybe younger. I shared a room with my little brother, whose bed ran parallel to mine on my right-hand side. To the right of him, ran the wall of the front of our house, and the room window, which sat above the bottom of his bed (we stayed in the bottom storey of an old fashioned three-tiered tenement). To my left, was my open bedroom door, looking across a short hall and down slightly at my parent's room. Their bedroom door was open".

"One night I found myself completely awake in the wee hours. I started to peer about the room. In glancing over to my brother, I caught sight of the room window, somewhat off the foot of my brother's bed. I froze instantly. A huge 'head' was looking through the windowpanes. It seemed to be looking around. The 'shape', or angle of its form, which was a large head set on a hint of underlying 'shoulders', moved as a face might in 'scanning' the room. I was frozen with terror. And being a somewhat serious child, I worked my way through a little checklist in my mind. The face was largely silhouetted against the glow of the streetlights to the back. It was behind the window frame, on the street side. The window frame was one of the old ones, encompassing about 24 small single paned glass pieces. The little framed wooden squares ran in front of the form. How could this be I thought?

After all, the window ledge was some 14-feet or so off the ground. A cat? A big bird? An owl maybe?

Yet, it was a very large unmistakably round 'head'. The thing that terrified me though, was the head had black horns! Or what I took to be horns, curling up around the left and right sides. I know how that sounds. And no, I am not a religious person. I remember thinking it was like a 'Viking's helmet' at the top".

"Suddenly the face seemed to 'lock', stopping dead in its movement. It was looking directly at me, that was the thought at least, although I could not discern any facial features. I shot under the covers, and remember so very vividly crying, and nipping myself continuously 'in case I was dreaming'. I plucked up the courage to look out the covers, and towards my parent's room. I called out to them, but they were both asleep. I remember their quiet faces distinctly, completely still above the covers edge. I shouted at them, but they were just completely out of it. And I remember the fact they didn't respond was very upsetting. Back under the blankets I went. I thought 'maybe it's gone'. I counted down, and forced myself to look out again, this time directly at the window. Opening my eyes, the form was still there, completely locked on me, although it was bobbing a tad not completely still. I went back under the covers and sobbed. I remember sobbing a lot. I only stopped again when something, reasonably heavy, pressed down just beneath my feet. Something was sitting at the foot of my bed. And I say sitting, because it was on the edge of the end of the bed. My last confident memory was as I've described. I was frozen with fear, adrenaline pumping through me. My next memory as insane as it sounds, was looking down at my bed from the bottom-left (opposite the window) corner of the room, but that at least is a very brief, hazy, memory. I wonder whether I've just dreamed that bit in the intervening years to be honest. What's odd though, I was in no fit state just to turn off and fall asleep. But the next moment, it's morning. Funnily enough, I very much remember how I angrily scolded my parents, as soon as I got up and ran into our living room. They only served to make me more frustrated by laughing and telling me it might have been 'a cow'. 'How can a cow come up to the bedroom window?' I protested, *"was it a flying cow!"*

"This event has really stayed with me. Around this age I developed a burning and enduring interest in astronomy. Before I knew anything about abductions or UFOs etc. I'd recall the story to my closest friends at Halloween. It was my 'scary story'. It also happened to be the truth. However, as an adult in full disclosure, I've read up quite a bit on UFOlogy etc. From a logical standpoint, I've always maintained that the natural extension of Drake's equation surely meant there were around a dozen or so intelligences that had survived long enough in our galaxy, existing in open knowledge of our existence in turn. But I know that's also a very 'nuts and bolts' view too. This is my core story. A brief wee thing, but something that's stayed with me all these years. I absolutely know it happened. I have also had just a few odd little things occurring at different points in my life. Even smaller than this event. And to be honest, a little bizarre. I was wondering whether there was any resource or anything I could reference? I'd be fascinated if someone has a similar experience in and around that time in Scotland".

Sincerely, Colin Evans.

Author's Comment. I quickly got in touch with Colin where I stated.

Hi Colin,

"Firstly, many thanks for sharing your story with me. This incident clearly has left a lasting impression on you. As you are familiar to a degree, with the UFO subject and abductions, like me, I'm sure you can see the parallels here. That said, a round head with horns is different. Some UFOlogists might speculate that this could have been a 'screen memory', to divert your attention away from what was actually there. Some might say a small grey being! All speculation on my part. It would be interesting to know if you have had any further such episodes, as usually there are more than one. Your experience is consistent with other such tales, (apart that is from the horned head) As for 1976-1978, I don't think I have any similar reports on file".

Regards. Malcolm Robinson.

Colin replied.

"Indeed. A few other things have happened. Like waking up one morning in my small rural house near Linlithgow and finding my ear bloodied, with a large black chunk of putty like stuff on my pillow. Or chasing down voices in a room where my sleeping baby daughter lay sleeping. The problem is, I'm doomed to consider such things through the prism of what I've read as an adult. I first read about abductions in a book by Edith Fiore, must have been the 90s. I remember the cover having a profound effect on me. Nevertheless, I was relating and trying to make sense of that core incident long, long before any knowledge of that space. In fact, I'm deeply sceptical of the 'industry' surrounding UFOlogy. Invariably, this will attract people who desire money and/or attention. Nevertheless, in my opinion, I think the phenomenon at its core, to be real. I think I've a pretty good BS detector and hold myself to high standards".

Sincerely, Colin Evans.

THE SILENT UFO

Hello Malcolm,

"I live in Kilcreggan Argyll, not far from Faslane Naval Base where I served for twenty years in the submarine service. I am now 68 and probably have a few years left. Many years ago, after finishing a back shift 16:00 – 23:59hrs teaching officers in a simulator, I drove home along the coast road and came into a village called Rosneath. There, above a stand of old trees at approximately 120 feet above ground level and 500 feet ahead of me, was a UFO. I stopped my car and got out and continued to view it for approximately 30/45 seconds. Initially, I thought it was cigar shaped but realised that the angle from it to me gave that impression, and in fact it was classic saucer shaped around forty feet in circumference. It had lights but was basically dark grey. There was no noise of any kind. Total silence. Because I knew this event was important, I strained to absorb everything I could and was immediately aware that the village seemed very still. I expected someone walking a dog or something. The atmosphere was very strange. It was about 12.30am. The object remained motionless for a while and then started to move away from my position silently until out of view".

"I arrived home five minutes later and told my wife what I had seen, and we agreed to not mention it for the work I did was considered sensitive, and my bosses would think me crazy. I wouldn't believe it either! However, the next weekend I was standing at the bar in a local hotel when I overheard the word 'flying saucer' from a couple of guys at the end of the bar. It turns out that the chef at that hotel had been out walking on the hillside above the village and had seen a 'flying saucer' sitting there two days after my event. It bugs me now that I didn't question him, looking for details but I didn't. So, opportunity lost. I believe it was circa 1976. That's it Malcolm, it was real for sure".

Regards, Andy Peters.

Author's Comment. A big part of my early life was walking around the shores of Loch Ness interviewing a number of people who claimed to have witnessed 'Nessie'. One such man was Frank Searle. For readers who want to learn more about Frank Searle, I have devoted a full chapter about him in my book, 'The *'Monsters of Loch Ness, The History and the Mystery'*, available on Amazon. For now, though, let me take you back to 1982 when I turned up to his base camp at Foyers on the shores of Loch Ness.

UFO OVER LOCH NESS!

I remember that glorious summer's day in 1982 when I conducted an interview with 'Nessie' researcher Frank Searle. What I really wanted to know that day, was the time when Frank took an astonishing photograph of a UFO which swooped down over Loch Ness near his base camp at Foyers and screamed away into the morning sky. Frank refused point blank to discuss that picture with me and said that he would terminate the interview if I continued to bring it up, strange or what! Some weeks after I had visited Frank, I wrote to him, thinking that he might now be in a better frame of mind to tell me about the day that he photographed a UFO flying over his base camp. In his letter back to me (the days before e-mail eh!) he had this to say.

"Hello, nice to hear from you. But as for UFOs, well I'm interested in all unusual subjects, but you must realise that I get 25,000 visitors a year for my Loch Ness Project. I answer about 2,200 letters every year on the same subject. There's no way that I will get involved with UFOs. I'd get bogged down. At the moment I am without a girl Friday. It's taking me all my time to keep up with the mail, talk with visitors etc. And I am out in my boat from 5am till 10am. So, I just don't have time to discuss other subjects you see. Even when I find a new girl Friday it won't be on. Sorry, but that's how it is"

All best Frank Searle.

Thankfully I have kept the newspaper clipping (Daily Record Monday December 2nd, 1974) which shows Frank's UFO photograph. Here in part is what Frank had to say to the Daily Record about what happened that day.

"I was halfway across Loch Ness in my boat, when suddenly I saw this 'thing' coming from the direction of the new hydro electric station at Foyers. It was travelling about the speed of a jet and at around 2,000 feet when suddenly it shot away westwards over Meall Fuar-mhonaidh. (*) It was only in my viewfinder for a few seconds".

(*) In Gaelic the mountain is known as, the 'Mountain of the cold moor' and is 699 metres in height.

Frank sent his UFO photograph to a Dr Fred Backman who, according to this newspaper report, was a scientist at Evanston near Chicago (I'm thinking that this could possibly be the branch of MUFON 'Mutual UFO Network' who have a base at Evanston, Illinois) Mr Backman was quoted as saying.

"Mr Searle's photographs are good and sharp. But on the other hand, is it very easy to make a sharp picture which isn't real. I don't doubt his word, but it is impossible to say anything positive because there is no background but blank sky"

And that's all we know. This scientist, Mr Blackman, as far as I can tell, never submitted any further information about this photograph, or if he did, I never came across it. I've checked the internet but alas didn't come up with anything. It's also interesting to note that Mr Blackman was quoted as saying *"Mr Searle's 'photographs"* (were there more than one!) So, I guess the only person who knows what really happened that day, is the man himself, Frank Searle, and sadly he is no longer with us, as he died in Fleetwood England on the 26th of March 2005. I think it's fair to point out that Frank Searle's UFO photograph, looks suspiciously like the photographs that Swiss Farmer Billy Meir has taken. A lot of people believe that Billy Meir has faked his UFO photographs. Check him out on Google. Either Frank took a real bona fide photograph of a UFO that day, or, just like his 'Nessie' photographs, it is nothing but a fake. Yes, Frank did fake his 'Nessie' photographs.

Author's Comment. Frank Searle's photograph of a UFO can be found in the photographic section of this book along with Billy Meir's UFO, they look almost identical! The following case file comes from the research by Albert S. Rosales. This case file was initially featured in the British publication, Flying Saucer Review.

Location: Portree Bay, Isle of Skye, Scotland.
Date. 2001. Time. Dusk.

The witness, a bird watcher, was exploring the area known as Murdo's Well. He was at the base of the headland of Black Rock. It was dusk when he wandered away from his group for a few minutes. He was then startled by a grey naked figure running right past him. It had a bald head with big eyes that shone as yellow beams. The 'naked man' was about four foot tall and 'moved weirdly' like he had hunched up shoulders, far more pronounced than normal humans. He ran at double the normal human speed up the hill to two other similar grey figures. The witness could see the grass pop up again after each footstep which suggested it was physically there. After sighting the humanoids, the witness was quite disorientated, suffering some memory loss. When the bird watcher returned to his friends, a girl in the group said, *"Oh my God, you look like you need a hug,"* She then hugged him which was totally out of character for her. His memory then came back spontaneously, and he realized he had been missing for 30 minutes.

Original source: Flying Saucer Review 55.3 pp. 14-15. Drawing of this strange looking naked man, can be found in the photographic section of this book.

Author's Comment. I now present to you in the following chapter, some controversial updates on the Polmont Reservoir UFO photograph. It looks like things were not quite what they were made out to be, as you are about to find out!

Frank Searle UFO Foyers Loch Ness 1974

Isle of Sky creature 2001

CHAPTER TEN

Updates on the Polmont Reservoir UFO Photograph
Was it real? Was it Faked? Or was it something else?

Author's Comment. Part of what follows below, was printed in the Outer Limits Magazine published by Chris Evers of which I am associate editor. There was some disturbing new evidence that came to my attention which I felt should be put out in the public domain. Here is what I wrote.

Well, what do UFO researchers do? They research of course. If a piece of information becomes available that casts a different light on a specific UFO case, then one must clearly look at it and give it some respect. I've researched this subject all my life, and I have always said, that if I ever uncovered that a specific case which we all believed at the time to be true as a real bona fide UFO sighting but later on, found out some further information which called it into question, that I'd shout from the rooftops. Well, I am now going to shout from the rooftops.

Before we get into the update I should point out to you the reader that what follows is **NOT** set in stone, it is for the most part only speculation (I repeat, only speculation) but it would be remiss of me not to bring it to your attention. So here we go. Here is a piece of information regarding a classic Scottish UFO case which at the very least should be made aware to people it may be unfounded and for the moment only hearsay, but it must be presented. The case I'm referring to is the Polmont Reservoir UFO Incident.

First and foremost, here is how I presented the case in my first book, *'UFO Case Files of Scotland Volume 1'*, after which we shall look at some information which will cast some new light on this case.

UFO PHOTOGRAPHED OVER THE BRITISH PETROLEUM PLANT IN GRANGEMOUTH?

I've said many times before, that it is extremely easy to fake a photograph and claim that it represents either a ghost or a UFO. When one is researching the UFO subject, you tend to find that from time to time, someone will approach you with what they claim is a photograph of a UFO. Of course, having witness testimony backed up with a photograph of a UFO is extremely valuable and one must look very carefully at not only the claims of the witness, but to ensure that proper analysis of their photograph is undertaken as well. Such a photograph came to my attention during the early years of my Investigation into the Bonnybridge UFO phenomena. Phil Trevis is an aspiring musician who plays guitar in a local Grangemouth rock band, but on the night of November 12th, 1991 (before the Bonnybridge wave exploded) was taking photographs with a friend for a project about photography. In a written statement to the author, Philip had this to say about his sighting.

"My friend and I were taking photographs of the B.P. Chemicals Plant in Grangemouth from Polmont Reservoir, Central Scotland when we noticed a dim, or rather two small dim flashing lights over by the two flashing pylons at Kincardine Bridge. We watched the object which we thought was a helicopter, fly slowly over the bridge to above the brightly lit Grangemouth Stadium. We watched it hover for about five minutes. It was then that we noticed that the 'craft' wasn't making any noise. Normally if it was a helicopter, you would hear the rotor blades. It then turned around and faced our direction. It was roughly 2,OOO feet above the ground. Then it dipped and increased dramatically in speed. At the point of the photograph, it was about 2OO to 3OO feet directly above. It was then that we heard the light pulsing 'hum' of the object. My friend and I were quite shaken at the time but afterwards had an overwhelming sense of excitement. Since then, I have shown only a handful of people my photograph and have also destroyed the negative. I have no reason for destroying the negative, but now obviously regret my actions". Phil Trevis.

The actual photograph was handed over to me by a friend of the photographer's at an SPI meeting held in Stirling. It was taken by a Halina 35mm camera, using Kodak 24 exposure on gold film. What one should bear in mind whilst looking at this strange photograph, is that what you are actually looking at, is the underside of the object. Because when this strange device was above both of the startled witnesses, Philip had to actually bend over backwards in order to take his photograph. In the photograph you can see that the middle of the object appears to be concave. Various bright white lights are seen shining out from this circular object which creates a sort of halo effect in the sky around it. So, what did our Investigations uncover, was there a natural explanation to account for this photograph? I firstly contacted the local police to see if any members of the public had contacted their station with a similar sighting, no one had. I then submitted many letters to the various Scottish Airports to see if perhaps some kind of aircraft or helicopter had been flying in this area on the night in question. Prestwick Airport at Atlantic House in Ayrshire replied in June 1995 by stating that,

(A) Records for the period in question were no longer held.

(B) It was improbable that a Military Aircraft flew over Grangemouth on the night in question.

(C) Gas Venting often takes place at this petro-chemical plant, an occurrence which could appear alarming.

Both witnesses were well aware what this 'gas venting' looked like, and this most certainly was not what they both had witnessed. Aberdeen Airport were not able to offer any explanations, as were both Edinburgh and Glasgow. The Ministry of Defence in London replied that because this sighting was of no defence significance, they were unable to assist, (now where have I heard this before)! But what if anything could the B.P. plant offer in terms of information. This plant, which is extremely explosive, is a beautiful sight when lit up at night, and looking at it from a distance, one could be forgiven for thinking that they were looking at Las Vegas such is the enormity and brightness of this complex. In a letter received by the author from a Mr Bill Moore, press officer for B.P. Chemicals dated 9th June 1995, Bill stated, and I quote.

"I can confirm that helicopters carry out pipeline inspection duties on behalf of B.P. Chemicals. These flights occur at fortnightly intervals and only take place during daylight hours at weekends. I should point out that the helicopters do not tend to fly over the site as they are more concerned with following the separate pipeline routes connecting Wilton and Mossmorran to Grangemouth. Micro-lights or controlled kites with cameras do not fly over the complex. I have checked our records, and there is no indication of any aircraft having flown over the Grangemouth complex on the 12th of November 1991".
Bill Moore.

In a further letter, this time from a Mr K.W. Smith, Estates & Pipelines Coordinator for B.P. Oil at the Grangemouth Plant, he stated and confirmed that B.P. Oil do not use micro-lights or any other controlled flying devices to inspect pipes, and that air space immediately above the B.P. Petrochemical complex is a 'restricted area' to aircraft. He went on to state that according to a limited search by him, he could find no evidence of anything unusual on the night in question. After these checks and several others, it was plain to see that nothing conventional was to blame for what both witnesses saw. Analysis on the photograph proved very little and did not help to prove the case either way, and as we know, the witness destroyed the negative for reasons which even now, he can't fully understand. In fact, he was actually going to destroy the photograph as well but was talked out of it by a friend. Having spoken to Philip on a number of occasions, I still have no reason to doubt his honesty, and I do believe that what he and his friend saw that night, was something totally unexplainable by rational means. Sadly, Phil's friend passed away in a motor accident, and so therefore I was unable to obtain any clarification to Phil's story. The Phil Trevis photograph is clearly unusual and is most certainly part and parcel of the Bonnybridge phenomena. The area in which he took his photograph, is only several miles away from Bonnybridge itself. An unusual photograph then and one of the very few photographs that we have which claims to show UFO activity over Scotland. Or was it?

In 2017 I received some information which cast doubt on this photograph.

THE FLY IN THE OINTMENT!
SOME NEW INFORMATION THAT COULD CAST DOUBT ON THIS PHOTOGRAPH

After this spectacular photograph hit the press and was in the public domain, I received a few emails from a friend of Phil Trevis who informed me that maybe I should look at this case in a new light, and that he had some information to give me which he thought I should know. The following are segments from a few emails sent to me by Lee R MacLachlan. Here is what he had to say.

"I can clear up one event that I've mentioned on posts in the past to you. I'm referring to the Phil Trevis UFO from Grangemouth Polmont Woods. I believe I know the truth behind his photo and its origin. and I'd be delighted to discuss it with you if you're interested".

Needless to say, I emailed Lee back saying yes, I'd be very interested to hear what he had to say, he replied with.

"Well, I've known Phil since about 1996, and being a good friend of his for a number of years from that period, I got to know he liked to be in the limelight. Another friend of ours had commented on that photograph, saying he had spoken to Phil about a college thing he was doing about photographing light subjects in the dark. He had spoken about photographing lights in a dark room. I was really into UFO's as well as Phil, in fact more so, as I believe I saw 'something' myself years later. Anyway. I believe the photo of his UFO, wasn't even taken from

outside. I believe it was from a bass guitar amplifier's power light which I had saw in his bedroom many times. It was red, as it was the power light, which had a flat spot on it and a black ring round it which was cracked. I believe the photo was a close up of the light for a college thing he was doing"

"I don't want you to think that this is 100% concrete as I've never heard Phil admitting it was fake, but I know for certain that the photo was taken while he was doing the study. He claimed the photo was taken right above him and he had shown me the exact spot the photo was taken from. The location is nicknamed the 'heli pad'. It's right next to the BP chemicals and refinery which is a massive complex with a no-fly zone. Phil never went into too much detail with me when I asked about it. I believe this is because he knew I shared an interest, and I knew that any craft at all being in that air space would have been spotted, no matter the time of day by staff at the B.P. complex knowing it is a no-fly zone. He also claimed that the craft flew out over the River Forth. There are many bridges crossing that all around that area, I cannot believe that no one else spotted this, as those bridges have traffic, trains etc going all day and night and are always busy. The B.P. complex staff have to be outside as well as inside 24/7. Phil is well known for stories, and I believe personally that this is exactly what he has told. Just a fabricated story. I don't know how much investigation took place to prove otherwise, like I say, I have not heard from Phil that it was a hoax, but it is what I believe".

THE OTHER WITNESS!

At this point I asked Lee about the other person who was with Phil that night and who also allegedly saw the UFO but had since sadly died in a road traffic accident. Was it true, what could he tell me about it? He responded with.

"No that isn't correct from what I know. Phil never spoke to me about any friend of his that had died. I know many of Phil's old friends better, the ones he would have been associating with at that time. I would have heard about that for sure. If it was a relative then possibly, but I know Phil used to be part of a large *group of friends which he no longer sees. I am friends with many of these people and some from his college days. All I am saying is, from what I have heard of Phil, who only lived about 20 meters away from me, he has lost a lot of friends due to his stories being uncovered. I could be 100% incorrect with all of this, but I do believe things are very coincidental. I even tried to recreate the photo with some of my own equipment and got some very similar results".*

I then informed Lee that Phil still maintains that his UFO photograph was the real deal, and that he was with a colleague whilst taking the photo and could he confirm any of this? Lee replied.

"Yes, I do believe he was at the location at some point, as it was popular place for him and his friends, I also believe he was there for something other than the college project, as it's well known in the area for being a dangerous area to photograph. It is illegal to photograph the B.P. complex and that was his suggestion for being there. Basically, he could not have photographed the B.P. plant and used it to state that's where the UFO photograph was taken. It leads me to question, why break into the grounds of the 'heli pad' which is a Scottish waters site I believe to take photos that he could not have used for the project in the first place. At no other time would him or any friends be carrying a camera, the terrain was too dangerous to be carrying cameras as it would be in some very dark woods. I used to go there with Phil and other friends and hang out there trying to get to that location, it was difficult. It just doesn't add up to me".

Lee went on to say,

"I just can't stress enough though, that I am not saying it is a fake. I'm merely saying, from my knowledge of the local area, the circumstances of that time, his friends, his project, his intended subject or the photoshoot, the lack of witnesses other than Phil, The B.P. complex being a no-fly zone, and the River Forth having a naval base on it, it just doesn't add up with me knowing Phil, and hearing Phil tell stories I knew weren't true because he

would include me in them, I am very suspicious of the whole story".

PHONE CALL FROM LEE, SUNDAY 17TH DECEMBER 2017

Further to the above information which Lee submitted to me via email and text, I set up a telephone conversation with him just to run over again a few salient points from the points that he originally made to me in his e-mails. The following are extracts from that conversation.

"I would also like to say that Phil to my knowledge, never owned a camera, but admittedly he could have borrowed one. His father had a camera but wouldn't let Phil borrow it as it was quite an expensive one. Maybe Phil could have borrowed one from the college. As I've said to you before, Phil stated that he was doing a project called 'light and dark' What really made me think that Phil faked this photo, was one night after a party at Phil's mum and dad's house I drew the short straw of sleeping on the floor in his bedroom, and as I was lying on the floor, I rolled over and was facing his bass guitar amp, and it suddenly occurred to me, that the red light that was on the bass amp, was almost identical to the shape that was on that UFO photo, it was a bulb rather than an led light, and it was within a black bezel. And if I was to put a red light in a dark room, I could recreate that effect quite easily"

"As I say it was a black bezel and there was a wee bit of light shining underneath, as the actual bezel didn't sit on the metal, it was like a metal plate with a black bezel sitting on top of the bulb. So, by that you are going to get a lot of red light which comes through the plastic, and the bezel and the metal plate that the bulb is sticking out from. And when I saw Phil's photo again afterwards, I saw the wee bit of light and I thought that pretty much looks like the reflection off the metal of the bass amp and to me that was like an "oh my God" moment that was in his bedroom before the day and age of mobile phones, so trying to take a similar photo to disprove it would be neigh on impossible".

At this point in our conversation, I asked Lee if he could remember the type of amplifier that he saw that night and he replied with,

"It was a Carlsbro amp, but I can't remember the model because it was a bass amp. I never used a bass amp Phil used to use this amp quite regularly as a guitar amp not so much a bass amp. Phil always wanted to be the centre of attraction and one time at a Def Leppard Concert, Phil approached me and asked me to ask him for his autograph as it would make members of the crowd think that he, (Phil) was some kind of celebrity".

BUT IS LEE HIMSELF MAKING ALL THIS UP!

At this point I asked Lee is 'he' was making all this up about Phil, and that maybe they had parted on bad terms and that he had an axe to grind. I felt that I had to ask Lee this question as I knew that others may think that this was the case. Lee replied.

"What I'm saying is not borne out of any malice, and I'm not looking to get into the newspapers or anything, I just want to get my side out there. Like all things in life, people go their separate ways, and Phil left our band to start a new band. After that, we didn't see each other again, and it's been around 15 years or so since we last saw each other, so no, there was no falling out. As I've said, we did play in a band together and he did leave the band with the drummer to go and start a new band, but I found that a bit of a godsend because I wanted to do something new, I didn't hold a grudge at all. It was just that we kind of drifted apart, two guys that played in a band that got on quite well and just drifted apart"

"I will say that there was a comment made one evening at his house about how to fake a photograph of a UFO for an album cover, and I thought "mmm", The two things didn't connect at the time. Now the thing that most caught my eye was, if you are in a punk band, what are UFOs got to do with that? It wasn't even like we had a song relating to UFOs aliens or anything like that"

It was again during my telephone call with Lee that he opened up and said that he too had witnessed what he believed might be a UFO, Lee stated.

"It was around this time that I did start having a bit of interest in the subject. I initially didn't believe a thing about UFOs until around this time. My mum when she was alive, was visiting her aunty and I was in the house myself and I was standing in the hallway just going down the stairs, when I happened to look out the window, and I saw something in the sky that kind of looked like two black triangles stacked on top of each other like a Christmas tree, and there were beams of light shooting from each point of the triangles, it was a bit bizarre. And I never ever got an answer as to what that could have been. I actually phoned my mum because I was quite freaked out about it, and she said your aunty has just been outside watching the exact same thing! About a month later I spoke to my aunt, and she described the exact same thing as I saw, but she saw it from a different perspective, and she passed away a couple of years ago and we never spoke about it again. But I definitely saw something that night and that made me think that something's not right here"

BUT IS PHIL'S UFO PHOTOGRAPH THE REAL DEAL?

I asked Lee again if there were anything else that made him think that Phil's photograph wasn't the genuine article, he replied with,

"Now I'm not trying to say that this whole event didn't happen, but I don't believe that Phil's photo is genuine. There are no stars in the photo no clouds in the photo, and the red ring that goes around the middle looks more like a reflection. There are a lot of things for me that remain unanswered, but to be fair, the one thing that stops me from saying that the photograph is faked, is that I wasn't there when he took it, and that I don't have a clear copy of that photograph and I am now doing photography myself, and I can tell you that Phil's photo is 100% easy to fake. I started to learn about photography about five years ago, and I don't

know what equipment was readily available back then when Phil took his photograph, other than his dad had an SLR camera. I can do time lapse video with my own camera which cost me two thousand pounds, and the thing that my camera does is just amazing, but back then, during Phil's time, (1991) he would have used a film camera, wind on, click a button, job done, maybe a bit of focusing and a bit of zooming in and out, but that was your limit back then I would have thought"

I should point out that Phil Trevis allegedly took his UFO photograph in 1991 which was one year before the rise of the UFO wave in the nearby town of Bonnybridge which hit the world's headlines in 1992. One could surmise therefore that Phil capitalised on this UFO wave occurring above the town of Bonnybridge and decided to bring this photo to the fore, claiming it as a UFO or, alternatively, the photo wasn't taken in 1991 and when the Bonnybridge UFOs hit the headlines he faked the photo to coincide with this on growing phenomenon to gain some notoriety, but that dear reader, is pure speculation on my part.

MORE LIES!

Lee also had other reservations about Phil as to him telling the truth, and he gave me a 'for instance' when he told me the following story. Lee told me that when Phil left the band and was playing with another band, he had hooked up with a brilliant drummer, probably the best drummer in the area. Now Lee knew this drummer and when he asked this drummer if Phil was playing in a band with him, the drummer replied that it was rubbish, and that Phil had never played in a band with him. Lee at this point thought that Phil was trying to make a name for himself and wanted to be someone. Another reason that Lee believes that the photograph is a fake, is Phil's own testimony itself, in other words, Phil kept changing the story! On one telling of the story, the UFO came from the right then swooped down low over his head then stopped above his head and in the second telling the UFO came from the left and didn't stop above his head and he also said that he saw two beams of light which he thought were thrusters. Now admittedly the human memory can be fallible, and each and every one of us may not always remember things from our past correctly so I'm not putting too much stock on that.

However probably the most damming of all the evidence to suggest that Phil hoaxed the photo, was that Phil himself told Lee that that he never took that photo, that it was 'somebody else that took the photo' but didn't know who it was. And then one day (probably when the Bonnybridge wave was at its height) he turned round to Lee and said, *"Yes I am that person, I took the photo"*. Phil said that the reason he didn't admit to him having taken it straight away, was that he didn't want people to think that he believed in aliens, hence why he never admitted it in the first place. What Lee cannot understand knowing that Phil always wanted to be known for something, is why Phil wasn't shouting from the rooftops and didn't admit to taking the photograph straight away, but as we have read, Phil claimed that he didn't want people thinking that he believed in aliens.

PHOTOGRAPHY COURSE

I asked Lee again if he could recall Phil telling him that he was doing a photography course with a subject title of 'Light & Dark' and he replied with,

"He told me that his dad was an amateur photographer and he once told me that he had asked his dad if he could take a camera to Polmont Woods to take a photograph of the B.P. plant at Grangemouth to which his dad replied that you are not allowed to take photographs of that plant, that it's forbidden it's against the law. As you know, we played together in a band and its very clear in my memory that he brought this up again that he couldn't take photographs of the B.P. plant. So, Phil to my understanding, had no camera not even a point and shoot. He had nothing but his dad's camera. Admittedly he could have borrowed it or stole it or whatever and took that photo, I don't know. But I do know that any time the band mentioned photography we had to find someone with a camera, and when he went to his dad asking for his camera, his dad always said no, maybe he said no because his son's band was a kind of punk rock band and I can imagine

what his dad was thinking, that he would never see his camera again. So, I know that every time he asked his dad to borrow his camera, it was always 'no chance'. So, it made me think, when did he get the equipment to take that photo, it could have been from the college, because the photograph was taken before I knew him. I can confirm that he did comment that he was doing a thing with the college about lights at a previous time but not when I knew him".

At this point I asked Lee as he was in the local music scene if he had heard of anyone speaking about Phil as to where he was or what he was doing these days and he replied.

"Well, I added him as a friend on Facebook, but the page was taken down shortly afterwards or it was blocked"

I then asked Lee a question that I had asked before and that was, was he happy with me naming him in this book? He replied.

"To be honest, it doesn't bother me in the slightest. I am not trying to tell you this story to get any fame or glory from it, but at the same time I have absolutely no fear of anybody contacting me about it, this is my belief, and I have always said from the start that I have no hard evidence that this photo is actually fake, that it's just my opinion, and it's an opinion based on things that I have seen myself. But I can't prove it. I've said before, back in those days' camera technology wasn't that great. My cousin is a freelance photographer, Michael Scofield, and there are various family members that are into photography and various family members that are into politics, so I am not unknown to a camera and photography, but I think that the photo Phil took should, as I've said, show a stars in the background, but there is nothing to show that. The background is sky and even with the brightness of that light there should have bit a bit of blue in the photo, but again that doesn't necessarily mean to say that the photo is fake. It could have been the wrong setting on the camera and that's why there isn't a star and there isn't any more blue in the sky. The more I look at the photograph knowing what I know, my view is that it's a fake. As I say, Phil was known for telling lies, Phil left

his job when I knew him telling the workforce he was going on a world tour with his band, furthest we played was Glasgow. He was a known compulsive liar in our friends' group".

At this point I closed the interview and thanked Lee for being honest and upfront with me and making his feelings known about the photograph.

BUT COULD THERE BE YET ANOTHER EXPLANATION?

Coronal Mass-Solar Flares!

For a number of years, I had seen across the internet, photographs which to all intents and purposes, looked very similar to the Polmont Reservoir UFO photograph. These photographs showed what is known as a coronal mass ejection (CME) Wikipedia tells us that this is a significant release of plasma and magnetic field from the solar corona, and that they often follow solar flares and are normally present during a solar prominence eruption. The plasma, we are told, is released into the solar wind, and can be observed in coronagraph imagery. Wikipedia goes on to tell us (and I quote)

Coronal mass ejections are often associated with other forms of solar activity, but a broadly accepted theoretical understanding of these relationships has not been established. CMEs most often originate from active regions on the Sun's surface, such as groupings of sunspots associated with frequent flares. Near solar maxima the Sun produces about three CMEs every day, whereas near solar minima there is about one CME every five days.
Coronal mass ejections release large quantities of matter and electromagnetic radiation into space above the Sun's surface, either near the corona (sometimes called a solar prominence), The ejected material is a magnetized plasma consisting primarily of electrons and protons. While solar flares are very fast (being electromagnetic radiation), CMEs are relatively slow. Coronal mass ejections are associated with enormous changes and

disturbances in the coronal magnetic field. They are usually observed with a white-light coronagraph.

So dear reader, I'm sure you will agree, that when we put the Polmont Reservoir UFO photograph next to the photograph of a Coronal Mass Ejection, *(see photographic section)* they look mightily similar. It begs the question of course, as Philip was the person to come forward with this photograph, might not the photograph be a version of this coronal flare? Whilst it may look like it, I can't for the life of me see why Phil would use a photo of this nature as a UFO, (but then again!) Furthermore, we have to remind ourselves that this was back in 1991 and yes admittedly the world wide web started on the 6th of August 1991, but there were not so many home computers around at this time to copy things from the internet, and any computers that were around at this time would have been expensive!

BUT WAIT. THERE'S MORE.
WE ARE NOT FINISHED YET!

As I was putting this article together, I trawled the internet as you do, to see if I could find out if I could track Phil Trevis down, and whilst doing so, I came across a forum on this case from Unexplained Mysteries.com posted on January 29th, 2009. Here, word for word, is the text that I took from this forum.

"Hi folks! I am the real Phil Trevis, the guy that took this photo! The original photo was taken off me and is now the property of BUFORA. The photo is real, what it is a photo of I cannot tell you. It was definitely up in the sky. I have looked around at a lot of the comments and yes, I do agree that it can be thought of to look like cups, bowls and anything else. All I can truthfully say is, this was outside in the sky, and I am still in amazement that the picture took so well. It was taken on an old compact 35mm film camera, just what I had in my hand at the time. The craft did move fast, which I have been told has contributed to the graininess of the shot. As far as I know, the photo has made a few rounds around the world's photographic investigation labs and nobody yet, has come up with a reasonable explanation".

"The photo as you see it, looks like it has been cropped slightly, but I will say, 'very slightly'. This is something that you wouldn't really forget in a hurry, so what has been cropped out is just blurred darkness. Someone once told me they thought they saw stars but, from what I can remember of that night, it was pretty cloudy as it had been raining all day! I didn't tell anyone about this photo for a while as I was sure I would be put on a plinth and laughed at! When I did find someone who I thought I could trust, they took it and showed it to Malcolm Robinson, who was then part of a group in Central Scotland that investigated UFOs and other Paranormal incidents. He put various TV, Radio and Magazine companies onto me and I have been filmed, photographed and recorded all over the world because of this photo".

"I wish I knew more of what it was. Investigations about that night gave us info that there was no known air traffic in the area at that time as the airspace above the Chemical Plant is restricted airspace. There were no security records detailing any sighting from ground staff at the plant, nothing from the public to police, nothing! Just over 17 years later, I am still trying to find out the answer to what this is. I would also like to know where the photo actually is and see what these experts really think of it. As far as some reports have told me, they don't see it as a fake. I know it's not a fake, but I prefer other people to make up their own minds. It doesn't annoy me or hurt me to think that people think it's fake! That is their opinion, and they are entitled to that. So, if anyone, somewhere does know what this is, UFO, experimental aircraft, anything, let us know".

Thanks for your time! Phil Trevis.

MALCOLM ROBINSON'S SUMMING UP

Needless to say, I wanted to get Phil Trevis's side of things to balance things out, as it had been many years since we last spoke, probably 1994 or 1996 where we both appeared on the T.V. Show Strange But True? Hosted by Michael Aspel. Sadly, however, both telephone numbers that I had for Phil were no good and neither was the email address that I had for him, so no joy there. I did however find a Facebook page for Phil, and managed to message him, but as of the time of writing, he hasn't come back to me.

I would have loved to have gotten Phil's take on this whether he would stick to his guns and give me the same story as he did all those years ago, or would he come clean and tell me what 'really' happened! Would time have changed his mind and was it time to get the issue off his chest in that he faked the UFO photograph! Of course there might be nothing to get off his chest! Maybe Phil truly **DID** witness a UFO with his friend that night, and all this speculation is but pure hearsay and unfounded and we are doing him a 'massive' dis-service here. Without Phil Trevis's 2025 statement and him having the chance to rebut any of the above, then we are back at square one. The photograph can either be one of the following things.

POSSIBLE EXPLANATIONS

1) A true photograph of what could be a machine/device from somewhere other than this planet.

2) A true photograph, but it's our own technology. But as to why if might be flying over a populated area and close to an oil refinery, we will never know.

3) It was a hoax and may be the red on/off light switch of a Carlsbro bass guitar amplifier.

4) It was a hoax made by altering a plasma photo of a corona discharge from the Sun.

5) Something else!

Until such times as we hear from Phil Trevis to contradict the above, we'll never know, but at the end of the day I hope you the reader can see that by me making this information known, that come what may, we **MUST** place and ensure that any new information on any old UFO or paranormal incident is brought into the public domain, for not to do so, would not be in keeping with further research into either new or historical UFO cases. So, there we have it, true or false? Does this new information change your views on one of Scotland's most amazing UFO photographs? I hope to be in a position in the very near future to track down Phil Trevis and re-interview him in regard to the claims made by Lee R McLachlan. So, stay tuned folks I think this story isn't quite finished yet.

(*) Wikipedia tells us. Grangemouth Refinery was an oil refinery complex located on the Firth of Forth in Grangemouth, Scotland, built by BP but latterly operated by Petroineos. It was the only operating crude oil refinery in Scotland, and with its closure left five remaining refineries in the UK. Grangemouth until that point, was the oldest refinery in the UK, and supplied 65% of Scotland's oil products, including petrol and diesel. The refinery processed its last crude oil in April 2025 and is slated to fully convert to a fuels terminal from July 2025 onwards.

AH BUT WAIT, THERE IS MORE TO COME!
THE POLMONT RESERVOIR UFO PHOTO
(A New and Different Perspective!)

Author's Comment. Just when I thought that I had heard the last of the Polmont Reservoir UFO case, along comes an e-mail that I received on July 15th, 2025, from one Dennis M. Murray who I don't know. He took me to task for not responding to an e-mail that he had sent to an old SPI web site. However, I never received his e-mail, as this site is no longer in use. Anyone who leaves an e-mail request on this old site, received an automatically generated thank you e-mail. Mr Murray thought I was being elusive, I wasn't! Mr Murray stated (when he found my correct e-mail) that as I hadn't responded to his e-mail of 12th October 2022 to discuss his findings that the so called Polmont UFO was in fact an 'eye defect', he would take his findings public. I responded to him by saying that I would be more than happy to discuss his conclusions with him. He replied.

Dear Mr. Robinson,

"Thank you for your response. At this stage, I'm not sure there's any added value in continuing a discussion on this specific topic, as I've already made my findings public".

"I believe Mr. Trevis has not been fully transparent with you in presenting that image. The picture in question is a clinical photograph of an eye exhibiting Transillumination Defects. If he presented this as evidence of a UFO, then it suggests a deliberate misrepresentation. If it were an accidental mix-up, one would expect he had another image of an actual UFO intended for use and had presented that at a later point to correct his mistake".

Please find my report included.
Kind regards, Dennis M. Murray.

Author's Comment. Here is Dennis's report.

THE GRANGEMOUTH "UFO PHOTO"
A Case of Misidentified Ocular Imagery

Author: Dennis M. Murray, Independent UFO Researcher & Technical Analyst

INTRODUCTION

The UFO field has always suffered from sensationalism overshadowing science. A prime example is the Grangemouth UFO photo, touted by investigator Malcolm Robinson as 'the most extraordinary UFO picture' he had ever encountered. Shown to audiences at the Outer Limits Magazine conference in Hull, the image was claimed to depict a structured, glowing, unidentified flying object hovering over Grangemouth, Scotland, in 1991.

As someone committed to evidence-based UFO research, I've examined this image using both photographic analysis and pattern recognition. My conclusion is simple and clear: this is not a UFO. It is a close-up image of a human eye showing transillumination effects in the iris, likely photographed from a medical or optometric context.

WHAT THE IMAGE ACTUALLY SHOWS

Transillumination Defects are areas where light passes through the iris due to atrophy or thinning of the tissue. These defects often appear as glowing spots or 'windows' in clinical images taken under infrared or strong illumination, such as slit lamp photos. In such images, you often see:

☐ A central circular pupil (dark or glowing, depending on lighting).

☐ Bright, symmetrical radial patterns.

☐ A glowing periphery due to the iris backlit by the illuminating source.

All of these features match exactly what appears in the Grangemouth photo.

KEY POINTS OF COMPARISON

Feature	Grangemouth Image	Iris with Transillumination Defects
Central dark or glowing circle	Present – appears as the 'core' of the UFO	Pupil – centered dark circle
Radial glowing patterns	Visible around the core	Radial iris defects illuminated by slit-lamp light
Symmetry and lighting	Highly symmetrical light arcs	Typical of clinical iris photos with ring lighting.
Surface texture	Smooth biological looking shading and gradient	Matches pigmented iris surface under lighting.

One should do a Google search on 'TRANSILLUMINATION DEFECTS' and it will present you with similar pictures.

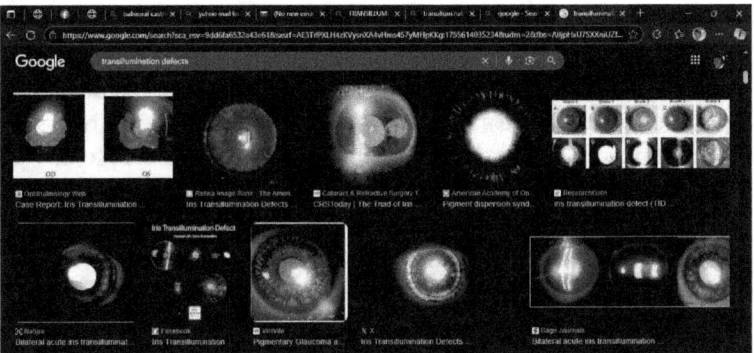

WHY IT MATTERS

Malcolm Robinson may have presented this image in good faith, but this is precisely the kind of error that undermines serious UFO research. Accepting a misidentified medical image as an extraterrestrial craft damages public trust and detracts from real cases that merit investigation.

To date, I have found no verifiable source data for this image tying it to a camera, witness, or photographic negative from the 1991 Grangemouth case. Conversely, I have found nearly identical examples in ophthalmology journals and textbooks on iris pathology. This photo should not be circulating in UFO literature without an accurate, evidence-based explanation.

CONCLUSION

The image shown at the Outer Limits UFO conference is not a spacecraft. It is a clinical photograph of an eye, likely one showing signs of pigment dispersion syndrome or similar iris thinning. While this revelation may be disappointing to some, truth must override sensationalism. In a field already vulnerable to misinformation, we must prioritize technical accuracy and hold public presenters accountable. UFO research deserves the same rigor as any scientific field and that means debunking when the evidence demands it.

MALCOLM ROBINSON COMMENT

Well dear reader, there you have it, photo solved. It's just a defect of someone's eye according to Dennis M. Murray. Look, I'm always open to other possibilities when it comes to any given UFO photo, but I'm unsure about this one. As a serious researcher, if anything comes my way that challenges either a witness statement or in this case, a photograph, then of course I'll listen. It's my job to look at things from all angles. I would not be doing my job properly if I refused to discuss or engage with any alternative explanation. I have kept in touch with Dennis and said that I would be happy to present his findings in this book, (as I have done).

Author's Comment. From Dennis M. Murray back to Lee R. MacLachlan. In a further e-mail that I received from Lee R. MacLachlan in August 2025, he again stated.

Hi Malcolm,

"For years I've been trying to remember the type of amplifier I saw this kind of light on. The closest thing I've found, which is pretty close, is this".

"Back then it wouldn't have been an LED light, but a small incandescent bulb, which meant there had to be a way to change it. That's why these bezels/lenses were designed to be pried open with a screwdriver or sometimes secured with small push-in clips (very much like the clips you get on battery compartments). If you

imagine one of those on a black round bezel with two clip points, then the "lock down" areas could easily allow more light to bleed out when viewed at an angle".

"That's where I think the illusion comes from: those light leaks would appear like 'jets' or 'beams' of light on one side, giving the impression of thrust or propulsion when in reality it was just a mundane quirk of the fixture design. The surrounding black metal would absorb most of the light spill, which is why the glow doesn't expand very far beyond the ring. With these clip style locks, the part you push to release, is generally pressed down lower as it's the part that locks into place. This would possibly mean that the ring would have a section missing at say 75° round to 105°. If that is the case, more light would come from that section. giving you a 'thrusting' effect. To me, that explains the whole thing far more convincingly than a solar flare or eye defect theory. It fits perfectly with how old jewel-style pilot lamps worked on amplifiers and other equipment. I honestly wish I could track down the exact light model itself, but I suspect it may have been a custom piece, or at least one that isn't common anymore".

Best regards, Lee.

As I have stated above, the witness and photographer of this now infamous UFO photograph Phil Trevis, has disappeared. I no longer have his contact details. Needless to say, I would expand on the questions that I have for him (mentioned above) with some new ones, namely.

1) Did you fake this photograph and what it really shows, is the red light of a bass guitar amplifier?

2) Did you fake this photograph by taking a photograph off the internet of a coronal discharge from the sun?

3) Did you fake this photograph by taking a photograph off the internet showing a transillumination defect?

4) Why did you destroy the negative?

5) Did you truly photograph a UFO?

At the end of the day, only one person truly knows if the Polmont Reservoir photograph is of a UFO, and that is the witness and photographer, Phil Trevis. If he ever reads this book, I do hope he will get in touch with me through my contact details at the end of this book, where I would be happy to redress the issue with him.

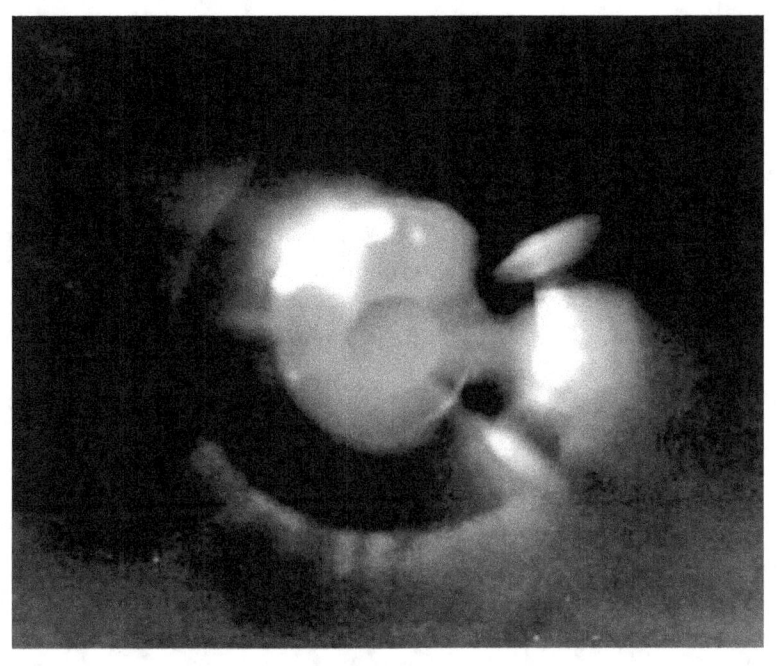

The underside of the Polmont Reservoir UFO (Or is it!)

Phil Trevis

CHAPTER ELEVEN

Updates on the Dechmont Woods UFO Encounter

Author's Comment. Since my book on the Dechmont Woods UFO Incident came out in 2019, I have received a number of e-mails from people each who have had a story to tell me regarding what they have witnessed in the skies in and around Dechmont Woods. It would have been great to have included them in the original book, but at least I can now tell these stories here. Before I do so, let me give those readers who are unaware of this case, the basic facts.

It was on the morning of November 9th, 1979, that forestry foreman Robert (Bob) Taylor, encountered what he described as a hovering domed shaped object in Dechmont Woods near Livingston Central Scotland. Two small three-to-four-foot spiky sphere-shaped objects, descended from the main object, raced towards Bob and pulled him forcibly towards the larger dome shaped object. At this point Bob lost consciousness. Upon waking up, he found that his cloths were all muddy, and that his trousers were torn. Before him on the ground, lay over 40 holes and two ladder like marks. The incident was reported to the local police and was treated as a case of an assault by person (or persons!) unknown. It is the only case in the British Isles that has had a full investigative police and forensic scientific study. I was one of the main researchers of this case at that time and did what I could to try and get an answer as to what Robert Taylor saw. There was never any clear-cut definitive answer to the case, lots of speculations, but never an answer that convinced everyone. Having interviewed Bob a number of times, I was convinced of his sincerity, and as such, I believe that he saw something not of this world. All this is explained in my book, *'The Dechmont Woods UFO Incident'* available on Amazon.

So, this chapter is an update on what people have reported in and around Dechmont Woods, I'm sure you will find what follows, most interesting. I certainly did.

BLACK TRIANGLE OBJECT
NEAR DECHMONT WOODS

There have been many UFO sightings in and around Dechmont Woods over the years. The following is of interest, as it's another one of those large black triangular objects' that was spotted. Witness Lynne Crawford Knight now tells the story.

Hi Malcolm,

"It was around my 14th birthday 19th of November 1991, I can't recall if it was before or after. My mum was driving myself and 3-month-old brother to meet my dad (who had been working in Edinburgh) at a family friend's house in Aller Place, Eliburn. We were on an area of the A899 Livingston to Houston to Ladywell Road, I was sitting in the back seat, my brother was in a rear facing car seat on front passenger seat. It was late, possibly between 8:00pm to 9:00pm but I can't be sure. My mum had got slightly lost but quickly found her way on to the right road after seeing a sign for Eliburn. When I asked her recently, she also remembers seeing the sign for Houston House which also helped guide us in the right direction. We had just come off a slip-road or roundabout, turning left onto the road mum recognised. We had a brief celebration, I think mum was relieved as we were running a bit late by this time, when mum suddenly asked".

"What's that?"

"I looked between the seat through the front windscreen and saw it too. The road was empty, but there was a flyover ahead and directly above it (about a streetlight's height), was a large black triangular craft. The corner nearest us wasn't pointing directly towards us, it was pointing towards our left. There was a white light on each corner of the underside. Mum wound her window down, then slowed the car right down so we could see it, and we came to a halt about 100 yards (rough guess) before it. Mum was mesmerised, and has since said she lost all fear, even although she had her kids with her. I don't know if it was her curiosity or something more, but she just wanted to see it. She opened the car door and started to get out. All my warning bells were going off, and I instinctively grabbed her and begged her to get back into the car. Her response wasn't immediate, but she snapped out of it, got back in, and closed the door. At that point, a ring of white (like a hollow beam) shone down onto the road below it from the middle of the craft, and it started to move towards us. It didn't turn or straighten; the corner was still pointing towards our left. It must've been about 30 feet above us, and about 30 feet wide. It was directly over our car (which was terrifying and still scares me) when suddenly we were distracted by a car coming in the opposite direction. By the time we looked back up, it was zooming off so fast in the direction the corner was pointing in and up. We couldn't follow it properly and it just disappeared. That bit happened so fast, but the moments before, watching it, were almost like slow motion (like when you can't believe a ball is heading for your grandad's greenhouse and you're powerless to stop it!)"

"It only took about five minutes or so after that to reach our destination. We got teased about being late, which we were, so put it down to getting lost. However, we were surprised by 'HOW LATE' we were. It wasn't dramatically later, so it's hard to say whether we lost any time. To be honest I suspect we could try and work it out, but I don't think either of us want to know as the idea is too much. It was so long ago, and we weren't watching our time the same way as we do now, no iPhones etc constantly reminding us. Years later, in late 90's when the X-Files made Ufology more mainstream, there was a new documentary made about Roswell and Area 51. My mum was out at the time, so my dad and I watched it and recorded it for her as we knew she'd be interested (VHS). At one point an eyewitness to the craft being kept in an Area 51 hangar, described what he had seen, and an image was shown. It was 'exactly' like we had witnessed, and I was nearly yelling at the telly! My dad and I decided to watch it with my mum without telling her about it, to see whether she reacted the same way. She did. Oh, I should mention, although it seemed silent, we couldn't hear a noise, but we could 'feel a noise', almost like a lower frequency we couldn't quite pick up".

Author's Comment. Now let's not forget, they said that they were only about 100 yards away from this strange black triangular craft which 'appeared' to be hovering about the flyover. (similar to Ray Procek's UFO above Castlecarry Viaduct near the UFO town of Bonnybridge) She then states that a 'hollow beam' shot down from the middle of the craft which 'appeared' to come towards their car. (Similar to the triangular UFO seen near Newton of Falkland of which it put down two similar columns of white light onto the ground) Then there is what 'appears' to be a time discrepancy. Did they just get lost? Or did something else happen that night? Staying with the Dechmont Woods area, the following is something that the author just had to try.

IF YOU DON'T TRY, YOU'LL NEVER KNOW!

Who would have thought that I would still be working on one of Scotland's biggest ever UFO cases 44 years on? But that is what happened when SPI's medium Steven Bird and I descended on Dechmont Woods near Livingston Central Scotland on April 23rd, 2023, to try, what some would say, was an 'off the wall' research project, but more of that in a moment.

OFF THE WALL RESEARCH, OR A GREAT IDEA!

So, this brings me to a new investigative study into this case. An investigation, that certainly we at SPI had never tried before. What follows, will no doubt cause many a raised eyebrow amongst many UFOlogists, both here in the U.K. and overseas, and to some, this research project may seem off the wall, if not futile in the extreme and downright stupid. But let us remember, when one is doing any investigation into fantastic claims, then one should always think out of the box. We should ask ourselves, 'what else needs to be done to solve this investigation'? What are we missing? What can we bring to the table that might provide further information in clearing up this 44-year-old mystery? So, what am I talking about here? What is so controversial that Malcolm Robinson and Steven Bird had in mind to hopefully provide further answers to this age-old mystery? Well, we decided to metal detect the ground where Robert Taylor's UFO had hovered, not only that, but for SPI's medium Steven Bird to contact the spirit of Robert Taylor to ask him questions about that day and boy did we get some interesting information.

Look, I know a lot of people reading this won't believe a thing about what is to follow. Yes, it is controversial, yes, it is 'off the wall'. But look, in this complicated world of UFOlogy and spirit, there is no harm in using any tools available to try and get some answers. Not to use any tools just because some people might say they are foolish, should not detract from their use. Get all the cards out on the table, leave them there for people to look at. So, I ask you now, to park your scepticism whilst reading the following report, and just accept that all avenues of investigation should be explored, for in not doing so is not doing any case, never mind the Dechmont Woods case, any justice. OK, sit back, strap up and enjoy the controversial ride.

LET'S START AT THE BEGINNING
MEETING STEVEN BIRD

When I came back to Scotland after 23 years living in England, I decided to start up some local UFO and paranormal meetings at my hometown in Sauchie Clackmannanshire, Central Scotland. Fellow researcher Ron Halliday brought along one gentleman by the name of Steven Bird who I would later learn, was a gifted psychic medium. We soon became friends, and in due course Steven assisted SPI by coming along on our investigations and lending his mediumistic abilities to a few of our cases. During the course of one of my local lectures, Steven said that the spirit of Robert (Bob) Taylor was with him, and was enjoying my lecture, although I was surprised, I wasn't perturbed by this, as being a Spiritualist myself, I was firmly of the conviction that there is a life after death.

Anyway, let's move the story on. I broached the subject of metal detecting the part of Dechmont Woods where Robert Taylor saw his UFO with both Ron and Steven. Now, as far as I know, metal detecting at the UFO scene in Dechmont Woods has never been done before, if it has, and yes, there is every likelihood that it has, I wasn't aware of it. I had recently come into the possession of a metal detector and had tried it out and found a few things, which admittedly, were a load of junk, tin cans and the like. But I had the idea that *"Hey, why not, let's give this a try at Dechmont, you just never know"*. Both Steven and Ron liked the idea and were well up for it. I am a member of the National Council of Metal Detecting (the NCMD) as I felt that I should join up with a reputable body. As it turned out, Ron sadly couldn't join us on the day as he had a prior engagement. I should also point out at this juncture, that for a good few months leading up to us going to Dechmont Woods, Bob Taylor had made his spirit presence aware to Steven and was telling Steven that about metal being found in the trees, or a tree at the scene where he had his encounter with this large object. Bob was insistent that we would definitely find metal in either trees or a tree at the site, but more of this later.

METAL DETECTING AT THE DECHMONT WOODS UFO SITE

So, on the morning of Sunday the 23rd of April 2023, Steven Bird picked me up from my home at Sauchie Central Scotland and we drove towards our destination which was the car park near Deans Community High School. This car park gives easy access into Dechmont Woods. Whilst we were driving, Steven said that the spirit of Bob Taylor was with us in the car, and that he was sitting in the back seat and was pleased that we were engaging in this activity. Now, what you the reader should know, is that Steven Bird, prior to moving from England to Scotland, had never heard of the Dechmont Woods case. His main passion was proving that the spirit lives on. Steven is a platform medium and provides proof of Life After Death to churches up and down Scotland. It should also be noted that Steven has also had a number of UFO sightings himself.

It wasn't until Steven met Ron Halliday and I, that we furnished him with the Dechmont Woods Incident. He has never visited the site himself, and although he has driven through Livingston due to his day job in sales, he never knew how to get to the area. There was never any need to. All I told Steven on the journey to Dechmont, was that we needed to park up at a car park near a school, I wasn't going to tell him anymore and that it was up to his spirit friends to get him there. And here's the rub, Steven had an ace up his sleeve in the spirit of Robert (Bob) Taylor, the sole witness to the Dechmont Woods UFO. As we approached the town of Deans (a town that Steven has never driven in before) The spirit of Bob Taylor was telling Steven where each and every turn off was. I, sitting in the passenger seat, kept stum. At one point Bob was telling Steven to turn left, but stupidly I broke my silence and said, *"No go right"*. Well, we got lost. Had we gone the way Bob told us, he would have been spot on. From then on, Steven listened to what Bob had to say and within a few minutes we were pulling into the car park near Deans Community School. Quite incredible.

Apart from our intention to use my metal detector and Steven's mediumistic abilities, we also planned to do a few EVP experiments, (Electronic Voice Phenomena) For the uninitiated, this is where sometimes researchers can obtain spirit voices on tape. Before we alighted the car, Steven decided to try an EVP experiment even although he now didn't feel Robert's spirit presence in the car anymore. Steven quite rightly said, that for any spirit to come near the Earth plane, takes up a lot of energy, and can be quite draining, but nonetheless, we decided to give it a try. After reviewing the recording on my iPhone, all we could hear were our own voices, sadly Robert's voice wasn't there. We alighted the car and I reiterated to Steven that I was not going to tell him which path to go to get to the scene of the incident, he was going in blind so to speak. I kept his attention away from the marker posts which state 'UFO trail this way'.

As we got to the top of the rise, there were footpath trails leading off in different directions. I asked Steven, *"OK, which way now my friend"?* To which he replied, *"Bob's telling me go right"*. Bob had by this time came back and was now telling Steven which way to go. Now remember dear reader, Steven had never been to Dechmont Woods before, and for those who have, you will know that there are footpath trails leading off in a number of directions. So, we passed Deer Hill on our right and came in front of one part of the woods, at which point again, there were trails leading off in different directions. I again asked, *"OK Steve, where now"? "We turn right"* he quickly said. So far, he was spot on. We trundled on through the woods where Steven was insistent that we go the way Bob was telling us to. Then suddenly Steven stopped dead in his tracks. I asked him if he was alright, to which he replied that he was taking on Bob's condition that he experienced on the way back to his home that day after he saw the object in the woods. He felt Bob's fear of what he had seen. Steven said that his legs felt heavy, thankfully the condition eased, and Steven was able to continue walking down the forestry ride, and before too long, we were standing in front of the scene of the famous 1979 encounter.

THE AREA HAS CHANGED A LOT SINCE 1979

I stated to Steven that the site that he was now looking at, was very different to the way it looked way back in 1979. Today, the trees are much taller and have encroached on the area. Of course, we now have at the site, the stone cairn and some signage. For those not in the know, the stone cairn and plaque was requested to be placed there by SPI to commemorate this incident. And with the help of the Livingston Development Corporation, they duly placed it there back in 1993. Standing next to the cairn was the signage board detailing the Dechmont Woods UFO incident. Again, I Malcolm Robinson, had badgered the West Lothian Council to put up this signage at the site, along with other marker posts and signage to allow members of the public to find the area. (Which I have to say, shamefully, I am very proud of.)

INTENSE ENERGY AT THE SITE!

As soon as Steven walked into the area beneath where this hovering UFO was situated back in 1979, he said that all his senses were tingling, that even now, here in 2023, there was still a residue of intense 'energy' permeating the area. It wasn't a spiritual energy he asserted, but something very different. Before long, Steven was walking around the area reiterating about this energy and again sensing the fear that Bob Taylor experienced on that day. One thing that I found most interesting and thought that Steven had got wrong, was the location where Robert fell unconscious to the ground. I've always been led to believe that the area where he fell was near the cairn, not 20 yards further into the clearing on the right hand side. Steven continued by saying that the two spiky spheres that had descended from the object were rolling about in a different area to the generally accepted version of events which was the main clearing. He said that they were also rolling about further over to the right of the clearing as you stand looking at it from the cairn. Now of course, this may well have been the case. Once Bob lost consciousness, these spiky spheres could have been rolling all over the place, and not just in the central part of the clearing. Another astonishing statement from Steven, again not in keeping with the official version of events, was when he told me that Bob was saying to him, that he now recalled seeing the object when he regained consciousness, and saw it lift up into the sky where it disappeared at a terrific speed. As stated, in the official narrative, that was not the case. Bob states that when he regained consciousness the larger object was gone as were the two spiky spheres. So, what are we to make of this? You either accept it as the testimony from the spirit of Robert (Bob) Taylor or you don't. I did say at the start that this would be controversial and that there would be some who would not accept this. We also tried some more EVP experiments at the site but did not pick up anything.

FALSE SIGNALS

As Steven was walking around the site 'tuning in', I got on with my metal detecting of the site. Needless to say, I was getting many hits from my metal detector, all of which were little bits of tinfoil and a few beer tins. This was to be expected as thousands of people have visited this site from not just the U.K. but from overseas as well, and as such, the litter/debris that they have left behind over the years, has infiltrated into the soil. To be honest, I could have dug up all the hits from my detector, but this would have taken me all day. More frustrating, was the fact that my metal detector was picking up 'false signals' Detectorists call this the 'Halo Effect', this is caused by iron objects in the soil which contains moisture. Some type of soil contains magnetic properties, and this can lead to some metal detector devices giving false readings of mineralisation's in the soil. Although the ground was not soaking wet, there had been intermittent rain showers that morning. Of course, it is the duty of every metal detectorist to ensure that any hole/plug that we make, gets carefully replaced and patted down. This I did with the few holes that I did dig. At the site of the Dechmont Woods Incident I interviewed Steven to get his early psychic impressions. Here is what he said.

INTERVIEW ON SITE WITH STEVEN BIRD

Abbreviations (MR) Malcolm Robinson. (SB) Steven Bird.

(SB) *"I'm tingling like you wouldn't believe".*

(MR) *"It's the 23rd of April 2023, I'm here in Dechmont Woods with SPI's medium Steven Bird and he is going to tell us shortly what he has psychically been picking up. Steven, we are standing here in the epicentre of where this event happened way back in November 1979. Now you mentioned coming down the forestry ride about what you were feeling. Could you just reiterate what that was, and what you are getting just now"?*

(SB) *"Bob was with you and me in the car most of the way over here, and although I work on the road, and I do know where Deans is but before I came to Scotland, I had never heard of the Dechmont Incident. I spoke to Bob a number of times during your lectures, so I got to know him a wee bit even although he has passed. When we were coming here, he actually took us to an alternative path through a different school that would have taken us up to the same route. But he got us here with a combination of second left third left etc and he was giving me the directions to actually get here. Now I didn't look at the signposts on the way in. Now I am drawn to the right-hand side of this field, this tree area (points to area) But this log that is lying down here and this area, really means something to Bob as well. But when we were walking down the path just up there, I was drawn to the path of the middle path of the three to come back out, and it was the scariest walk that he had ever had. He was limping, and he said he had a cut on his right leg, and he had a slight pulled muscle, and he was slightly worried about getting home* because he wasn't compos mentis and his whole world had been turned upside down. He was worried about his wife and his dog, and there was a lot of fear going around in his mind. Nothing made sense anymore. He was just wanting to get home and get home safely. There was a small doubt in his mind that he wasn't going to. What he had seen that day, cut him right down to the core".

"I am on maximum tingle at this point for want of a better phrase. I am seeing the shape of Bob lying on the ground, and its right about this area, round about where that moss and stump is. I'm seeing him, and he is opening his eyes. He just doesn't know what is going on. The object is still with him at this point. He is extremely frightened, and very soon after he wakes up, he saw that the object was still there, but I feel that it was on its way to leaving. Apart from the things that we already know about the story, he wasn't sure if he saw it when he woke up, but he is telling me that 'he did'. When he was here, he wasn't sure entirely about the end of it, but now he is telling me that yes, he did see it, and he saw it go, but he didn't see it go, if that makes sense. It was there, and then it wasn't there. And what he did tell me, a number of months ago at one of your lectures, that there was 'something' in the trees. It wasn't on the ground; it was in the trees. So, I am now going to start looking and feeling my way around here and see if I can find anything. So that's all I can tell you just now, other than this area, still has a massive energy. If you bring a hundred mediums here, a hundred of them will pick it up. They will feel it, it is palpable. It's still here. I don't know what kind or type of energy it is. It doesn't feel like a spirit energy, it feels like, well I'm going to use the word, 'cosmic'. Like something has disturbed the very energy in this area, and it's still here".

(MR) "That's amazing Steven. Steven thanks very much. So, what I feel you should do now, is to walk around and get a feel for this place and do your thing, whilst I will take some photographs. I should point out that this is something that SPI had to do. We had to come back here and try something different. I'll be trying my metal detector shortly; Steven is going to try and tune in as well. As far as I know, this site has never been metal detected before, now it may well have, but we don't know. So, it *will be a good exercise just to say, 'well we've done it' and also bringing forward Steven and his mediumistic abilities, we may, or we may not get anything. What I can safely say is, that Bob has been with Steven on the journey here in the car and also coming down the forestry ride. I'm switching off the recording now, and its now time to see if we find anything".*

MALCOLM, I HAVE BEEN VINDICATED

At this point I left Steven to do his thing, and that was tune into the area whilst I swept the area with my metal detector. A few minutes later I heard Steven excitedly shout out that I should come over and see this. Steven had a big smile across his face and said that he was vindicated. He asked me to look down at the fallen tree trunk lying across the grass. At first, I saw nothing, then Steven asked me to look closer, and as I did so, I became aware of two coins that had been hammered into the trunk of the tree. Initially I didn't see the significance of this, and my thoughts were interrupted by Steven as he excitedly asked me to remember what he had been saying to me for weeks, and that was that Bob Taylor had been telling him to look for something metal in the trees, or a tree, and when that was found it would be proof that Bob's spirit had been with Steven and that he was communicating direct with the spirit of Bob Taylor. As I looked down at these coins hammered into the tree, I could see the meaning behind the message. I must admit, I had thought (somewhat naively) that we might be looking for some debris from the object that Bob had seen that day that had somehow came off the object and found itself lodged into a tree. Well, it wasn't that, that's for sure, but I guess the significance of this human find, was equally bizarre and encouraging in the sense of how the message had come about.

CLOSING WORDS

At the end of the day, there will be those who will scoff at this approach and who will say that there is no value in what we did that day. I tend to disagree. With this type of research, one must always look to cover all bases, for not to do so is not in keeping with trying to find answers. Yes, I agree, maybe this psychic and metal detecting approach might be off the wall, and we are perhaps bringing together one mystery with another. I accept that, but I still think that it was something to try. Yes, I could have dug up all those metal detecting contacts that I had, but as you have learned above, every contact that I did get was purely debris. However, I can assure you that I will be back, hopefully with Ron Halliday, where we will both metal detect the area good and proper, but more importantly, we will ensure that we will leave the ground the way we found it, and there will be no signs of soil disturbance.

Just as a footnote. Readers of my book on the Dechmont Woods UFO Incident, may recall that when SPI organised the cairn ceremony at the site back in 1993, SPI's then psychic, Helen Walters, witnessed a red ball weaving in and out of the trees at the site. She also witnessed a grey alien's face suddenly appear in the trees as well. So, I would say that there is a place for psychic mediums to attend, not just the Dechmont Woods site, but perhaps any significant UFO site and see what they pick up. Their testimony might never be accepted, but what they will be doing, is presenting another piece of the puzzle that in due course, may prove relevant. So, an interesting day, with interesting results. I'm glad we did it.

WHAT WAS THE ARMY DOING IN DECHMONT WOODS?

Author's Comment. Again, staying with the Dechmont Woods event, how about this for a revelation! Being in the public eye, I receive numerous e-mails from people the world over, some of whom have stories to tell me about this famous Scottish event. But none came so close to making me sit up, as the e-mail that I received in September 2023 from Harry Cartmill, a Labour District Councillor serving the Bathgate and surrounding communities. Here is what he had to tell me.

Hi Malcolm,

"It was good to meet you at the Bonnybridge sky watch last week. My clear recollection of the Bob Taylor Dechmont Woods Incident started by hearing both T.V. and radio news reports on the evening of it happening. As a 13-year-old boy it was fascinating and exciting in equal measures. My late aunt Jean Russell was in charge of the payroll within the Water Board and immediately recognised Bob Taylor from all the reports. She described him as a reliable employee, a Church Elder, and indeed someone who lived a quiet unassuming law-abiding life. From memory, the incident took place on a Friday (unless we skipped school for a couple of hours!) The next morning after my paper round, I hastily cycled from Bathgate with a couple of friends to the site in Dechmont Woods. Having played golf many times at Livingston Golf Club (now Deer Park Golf and Country Club and where I actually worked for three years back in the early 2000's) I knew roughly where to go. As we approached the site, two Army personnel (both dressed in green sweaters and black berets) sternly told us to stay back, they may have been part of a bomb disposal unit or may have been drafted in from Redford or Dreghorn Barracks in Edinburgh. I didn't see a regimental emblem so regrettably can't identify which Army department they belonged to. Anecdotally I had heard that Army units were seen travelling through Dechmont Village on the afternoon of the incident, so it looks like some sort of military activity was triggered".

"The next day (I think a Sunday as the sun was setting) we cycled back to the site this time thankfully, no Army presence. We clearly saw burn marks on the ground and 'scrape marks' also. At around the time of the Dechmont Woods incident, there was a report in the West Lothian Courier that Barney Gallacher, father of famous golfer Bernard Gallacher, had seen a strange craft in the sky, this may be in your book (which I'd love to read) but if not, Courier archives would provide you with the story. As I mentioned, I worked around 20 years ago for the Muir Group who own and run Deer Park Golf and Country Club, quite often we had people arrive asking about Bob Taylor and hoping to visit the site. When time allowed, I was happy to take them to see

where it happened. It amazed me that some of these people came from the U.S.A. Canada, and even Australia to see the site. I hope this is helpful to you".

With Kind Regards, Harry Cartmill.

Author's Comment. Well, that certainly puts a new spin on the Dechmont Woods UFO case doesn't it! Who were these two army people? Were they really army personnel? Could they just have been adults who had nothing at all to do with the army, wearing what appeared to be army type clothing which included black berets? Harry said that he had heard that army units were seen driving through Dechmont Village. Whilst many years have elapsed since Harry saw these two men in Dechmont Woods getting told to 'stay away', it is my intention to try and see if I can find any other information on this most intriguing account.

DID WITNESSES SEE THE SAME UFO AS BOB TAYLOR ON THE VERY SAME DAY?

Hi Malcolm,

"My partner Jennifer contacted you on Facebook, thanks for the response. The Dechmont incident has intrigued me all these years, however I have only relayed my story to family members. Back then I was 17 and worked in a meat processing plant in Broxburn, West Lothian and used car share to make our journey. On the morning in question (November 9th, 1979) myself and 3/4 colleagues were travelling east on A8, approaching Dechmont. As we passed the entrance to the old Bangour Hospital, we observed a glowing orange circular object around 200 yards away to our right, the object was also travelling east, parallel to our car, and it was moving horizontally along the top of the tree line for roughly 50 yards before it dipped below tree line and out of our view. In my opinion, it appeared in a controlled descent, roughly about the same speed as an aircraft about to touch down. I would assess the time to be either 06:45 or 07:45 as it was still dark".

"When I got home that night, my dad informed me that he and others had seen a strange light travelling eastwards at altitude

above Bathgate (4 miles west of Dechmont). Then obviously the media was full of stories about the forestry worker. I've researched his story, and his sighting was assessed to be 10:30am the same morning. Our sighting I would say, is roughly 500 yards east of where the information plaque is situated in Dechmont Woods, and I am in no doubt it is one and the same incident. Hope this adds to or helps your research, I would say it definitely adds credence to his story".
Regards, Brian Thomson.

Author's Comment. In a further e-mail that I received from Brian, he stated.

"It is certainly an intriguing case. I have to say back in 1979, I was sceptical about Robert Taylor's account, I thought he had seen the same thing as I did and fabricated the rest of the story, but having recently watched his interviews, I have to concede he comes across very sincerely. I actually attempted to reinvestigate the criminal case (I am a retired CID West Lothian officer) but hit a brick wall trying to recover the relevant paperwork. I think the paperwork just got lost, Livingston Police Station was relocated a few years ago, and I assume only important case work was retained. It would have been just hard copy files back in 1979, so virtually impossible to trace back. I just fancied getting a read through the details but alas. Please feel free to use my experience in your book if you feel it's worthwhile, and I will make a point of reading the book and attending your seminar if you return to Deans".
Regards, Brian Thompson.

Author's Comment. I can't stress enough that people have to realise that there were a number of UFO sightings in the days preceding Robert Taylor's account, and also a number of UFO sightings in the days that followed. A number of these accounts are told in my book, *'The Dechmont Woods UFO Incident'* available on Amazon. The following account is from yet another witness who claims to have seen a UFO the very same day as witness Robert Taylor.

I SAW ROBERT TAYLOR'S UFO!

Hi Malcolm,

"Just to let you know that I was staying at Kenmore Avenue in Deans Livingston and saw a UFO heading towards Dechmont Hill the previous evening that it was reported. The Robert Taylor sighting. The object I saw was heading straight towards Dechmont Hill and it was moving almost silently very low above my house. I was shocked when it was on radio forth news the following day. I thought the guy must be nuts reporting this, especially as most of the population still believed in the "duck and cover" survival method in the event of a nuclear missile strike! Anyway, I have always kept quiet about my sighting, but poor Robert Taylor did have a second witness, and I should have backed him up, and I have always felt very guilty about not doing so. But I was always very aware of how the controlled media works and knew that it would be a pointless gesture".

Author's Comment. Needless to say, when I received this e-mail, I just had to know more. So, I asked him to reply to the following questions, which were.

1) Can you confirm the date of your sighting?
2) What time was your sighting?
3) What did the object you saw, look like. Try and be as precise as possible.
4) Any noise?
5) Any colours?
6) How long did you see the object for?
7) If you held a 5 pence piece at arm's length, would that cover the object, or would the object be bigger than a five pence piece held at arm's length?
8) Was the object high up?
9) Was the object below cloud cover?
10) To your knowledge, did anyone else see the object either (a) with you or (b) when you might have spoken about it to others.?

The witness Tim Reynolds (pseudonym) replied.

Hi Malcolm,

"Thanks for getting back to me. The first thing I want to make clear is that I do not want any publicity. Here are the answers to your questions"

1) "It was the evening before Robert Taylors story hit radio forth. November 1979. I cannot tell you the day as I would have to look that up, but I was at work and was shocked when the following lunchtime radio forth mentioned his story".

2) "The time would have been around 8:00pm (ish). I was having a coffee and a cigarette on my back steps as to be honest, unlike my wife, I never did spend much time watching the nonsense on the T.V. There were very few stations at the time".

3) "This is difficult. I do not want to suffer from a false memory syndrome, but it seemed longer than wider".

4) "Very little noise. More a quite swooshing sound. Not an engine noise that's for sure".

5) "It seemed black to me, but then the sky was dark then too being November. Deans was in the early stages; it was a kind of pioneer town. I went back to see the area 15 years later and it had completely changed".

6) "Only a few seconds. So, as I say, I was quite stunned to see something I have never experienced before. Any planes I had seen were always in the distance flying east to west from Edinburgh airport or west to east depending on the wind".

7) "5 pence, are you kidding? It was much bigger than a CD case".

8) "Very low, possibly around 70 feet high. Thats why I thought whatever it was, it was heading straight into lower Dechmont Woods"

9) *"I did not see any clouds"*

10) *"I mentioned it to my wife at the time, but she was busy watching the television, and frankly, didn't seem to pay any attention. I have only ever talked about it to a small amount of people. Whatever I saw certainly had no natural explanation that's for sure. Good luck and best of luck with your research".*
Regards Tim Reynolds.

Author's Comment. Following on from the above, here we have another person, who, at the time was just a schoolboy and saw something strange in the sky the same day as Bob Taylor. Here is what he wrote to me.

WAS IT BOB TAYLOR'S UFO WE SAW?

Hi Malcolm,

"Loved your Dechmont Woods UFO book. My brother was at your talk a couple years ago in Deans. I live in the USA now. My brother Derek Cosgrove and I were picked up from school (Deans Primary) that day and were going to our cousins' house for the weekend (East Kilbride) I was only eight years old at the time. I remember it was a Friday, and we were on a half day from school due to Remembrance Day We left around lunchtime. My dad didn't drive, so we were picked up by my uncle at Deans primary school (just over a mile from Dechmont) In the car was my uncle, my mum, my brother and myself, (dad was coming after work) I remember my mum pointing out something in the sky when we were leaving. Mum said it was 'following us' (her words) I can remember seeing a kind of white ball with a kind of streak, sort of like a comet trail. This happened just after we left the school at 12 noon and were about to get onto the M8. It was on the left-hand side of the car, so it was either West or South from us".

"At the time - there were these 'tripod' things on the road heading to Bathgate - Near where NEC - I believe they were oil rig training platforms. They looked like the tripods from war of the worlds, and my mum made a joke that the ball was related to the tripods. The time would have been just an hour or two after

the incident at Dechmont. We knew nothing of the story until the Monday back at school (when it was all we could talk about). I didn't even think about the white ball until our mum mentioned it that afternoon after school"

Regards, Alwyn Cosgrove.

Author's Comment. Alwyn's brother Derek replied to me with his recollection of that day. He said.

Hi Malcolm,

"I'm Alwyn's brother, and I figured I'd add in what I remember of that day. I was only four years old back then, so my memory of the actual day is not great. I still remember us being in the car and seeing the ball in the sky though. Whenever the story has come up with my friends, I've always said we saw something in the sky that day. And while I'm mostly told to shut up, I'm 50 years old now and still saying it, "We seen something in the sky that day". I don't have as much detail as my brother, but from my memory, the ball was more orange in colour than white. Sorry I can't give you more about the actual day".

The following account is also interesting, but sadly it's a story that I can't confirm (much as I have tried) That said, I thought it would be interesting at the very least, to bring the story out into the open, for if it's true, then it would have provided an interesting piece of the puzzle to the Dechmont Woods story. See what you make of this

DID SHE MEET ROBERT TAYLOR AS HE STAGGERED HOME!

Hi Malcolm,

"I watched a UFO investigation program last night which featured the Dechmont Woods case. I had never heard of this incident myself. Today I talked to members of a family who moved to Livingston shortly after that time".

"My friend said this to me, "Our neighbour Mary Burnside, said she had seen the object". He then said they made a fool of Mary over this. So, I contacted the friend's mother. My friend's mother said that Mary was met by Mr Taylor coming back from the woods, he came up to her, and he said, "Did you see that"? Mary said that she did see it but did not want to mention it to him. My friend's mother could not remember Mary's surname but said she lived alone next door. It was her son who said that her full name was Mary Burnside, and she lived next door. Was Mary Burnside just a crazy storyteller or was she a witness. Also, the program I saw showed a nighttime or dusk re-enactment of the incident, but the mother of my friend says it occurred early morning".

"My friend's family moved from Livingston to the Falkirk area in the 1980s so lost contact with the neighbour. They did live in a new council estate not far from where the golf course is now and near the hill at that time. I am not sure how long the golf course has been there, and the mother could not remember a golf course. They did not know Robert Taylor but had heard about the incident. They went walks to the woods themselves at times and did not see anything unusual. The mother wants me to take her to the hill and woods the next time I am visiting Scotland. She may be able to show me where she lived and where Mary the neighbour lived at the time. The family still hold the belief that their neighbour and Robert Taylor must have hallucinated or imagined it. Their neighbour would likely be in her 70's now but her name may have changed if she got married. So, she may had been a witness to something but did not want to get involved. Reports said he lost his ability to speak for a few hours after he woke up. So, he must have just made gestures to her on the path. It would be interesting to hear her account. If I find anything else out, I will keep you updated".

Sincerely, Norrie Roscoe.

Author's Comment. I occasionally contacted Norrie on e-mail to see if he had heard anything else, but he had nothing else to ad. It would be great if we ever managed to contact Mary Burnside, get her story of meeting Robert as he came back from the woods in his distressed state. The thing is, surely there would have been more witnesses who had seen Robert Taylor staggering back to his home that day in a dishevelled state, but other than the account above, I've not heard from anyone. OK, so Mary saw Robert staggering home on the day of the incident, wouldn't it be great if we actually had a witness who was there on the day of the incident and saw the whole thing? Well, wait for it, **'WE DO'**? Back in 2022 I had a lady contact me with the following information. This is what she said.

I WAS THERE; I SAW THE WHOLE THING?

"You asked me to email you about my account of what I saw that day. I was five years old, going out with my sister and a couple of her friends. We headed up towards Dechmont, got no idea why, as I was just following my sister and her friends. We went through the woods, but we weren't sure if we were allowed, so we were being careful not to be seen as we thought we were in trouble for being somewhere we weren't supposed to be. We heard a truck pull up behind us, and above us we saw lights coming towards the trees. We thought it was a helicopter coming to tell us off for being in the woods. I remember running, across the bumps of muck where the trees had been planted. I remember falling on my knees a couple of times as the ground was unsteady and there were rows of bumps which made it harder to run. I never thought anything more about it till years later, when I heard the story, then I told my husband that I was going to point it out on a map where it happened. He checked, and I got the exact spot of where it was when we saw the lights coming down".

Author's Comment. I quickly e-mailed the witness, Toni Castle asking some more questions and stated.

Hi Toni,

"Many thanks for your quick reply, I really appreciate it. Thanks also for your recollection of that morning's event along with your sister. I know that we are talking 43 years ago now. Can I ask, why you and your sister with friends, were up at Dechmont Law that morning? Did your parents know you were

there? Should you have been at primary school at that time? It's just that your sighting is very important, more so, as I was not aware that there were any other people in the woods at that time. Also, you said you saw lights coming down, did you see those lights attached to any object? It would be great if your sister and friends could get in touch with me, but I appreciate it that your friends that day, may well have moved away from the area".

"With very best wishes, and thanks again for getting in touch". Malcolm Robinson.

She replied.

"I can't remember why we were there, but we always went out on little adventures. Most days out on our bikes or going to places that where scary and interesting. I think we were taking a short cut through the woods. If it had a fence, then we climbed it and that's when you know you're not supposed to be there. I just checked the date, and it was a Saturday in 1979, so we would not have been at school, so that answers why we were all out. We were kids running through the woods and thought we were in trouble. The guy may have not seen us, as in those days we were fast runners. I recall that there were a lot of tree branches in the way when we saw it. It was also rotating. As I was always with my sister, my mum and dad never worried. They were usually in the football social club in Deans on a Saturday and Sunday. I can remember the lights were bright, and the thing was turning as it was landing. The lights seem to be flush with it. So not sticking out. We were very scared and ran for our lives".

Hope that helps. Toni Castle.

Author's Comment. I pointed out to Toni, that the event was on a Friday, and as such, she should have been at Primary school, perhaps she got her dates mixed up! She replied.

"We would have been at school as can't see why we would not be on that date. (Friday November 9th, 1979) It could have been after school, that would be the only reason I can think of".

Author's Comment. I sent a number of e-mails after this, asking more questions. I needed to hear from her sister and two friends for them to get in touch with me, but I never heard back. I also called the telephone number that I had for her back in 2022 and briefly explained who I was and why I was calling, but the phone was put down on me. Admittedly when I asked if she was Toni Castle, she did say 'no'.

ANOTHER SIGHTING AROUND THE SAME TIME OF BOB'S

Author's Comment. After my book on the Dechmont Woods UFO Incident was published, I had a number of people contacting me regarding their own UFO sightings, either on the same day, or days afterwards. One gentleman, Keith Carlyon told me the following.

Hi Malcolm,

"I have a feeling it was the Thursday night Same day as Bob's encounter. I was at a dress rehearsal for a pantomime when there was a light which hovered outside Howden Park Centre for a good 20 minutes, the whole cast were out watching it. I'm 100% sure that it wasn't a plane or helicopter. Then, after our rehearsal, the light was still there! It followed us home. As we approached the Deer Park roundabout, there was a massive bright light in the sky that was shooting about, back and forward, it followed my dad's car on the approach, every time he stopped, the light did too, we drove, the light followed us. It stopped above my dad's car. My mum has always been adamant that it was a UFO. This light then shot north faster than anything I've ever seen. This sighting has stuck with me all my days. Sadly, I know now, that the time that Bob saw his UFO, did not coincide with the time of what we had seen. I'll never forget it. You can imagine when we read the next day about Bob's encounter. Again, our sighting and time don't coincide. I should point out that my mum and dad were church elders, they didn't drink. I was 11 years old when this happened, and I can assure you that on this night

something strange was in the sky, 100%" Regards, Keith Carlyon.

Author's Comment. Robert Taylor's sighting was on a Friday morning around 10:30am. Keith's sighting was on the Thursday night. Was this the same object or something different? Robert saw a structured object, whilst he and his parents and members of the pantomime, saw a very bright light which apparently swooped downwards towards Keith's dad's car.

MY FATHER TOOK THE GROUND PHOTOGRAPHS

Hi Malcolm,

"I've just watched a YouTube stream (Zohar Stargate TV) of an event in Scotland where you talk about the Robert Taylor incident. You mention two emails from a source regarding the two military installations in and around Livingston, you did not mention the emailers name, however, the content of said emails, match exactly the details given to me by my late father, his initials were A.S. He is also mentioned and has photos in the official BUFORA report. He was a senior archivist for several large organisations. He has stated that there are other photos that he has never released but still has the negatives. Unfortunately, he was survived by his wife, who I have no contact with, so have no way of obtaining said negatives, although I assume they still exist in the ownership of his widow".

"I was fortunate to work with PC Bill Douglas for six years at Livingston up until his retirement and also spoke to Lester Knibb on my frequent trips to Howden Hall. According to my father, the photos used on Arthur C. Clarke's Mysterious World TV programme that Inspector Ian Wark used, were his, as they were better than the police's photos. They were also used in one of Jenny Randles publications, although this was done by two other individuals who claimed the photos were theirs! I had the reply letter from the publisher stating that this would be rectified in any future publications. My father had always stated that he never wanted monetary gain from his photos just credit. The mystery lives on".

"I still remember seeing the photos he took and hearing about the incident. I was 11 at the time, although it was many years after when he spoke about the MoD installation which is now Deans industrial estate. I've seen pictures with the railway spur going into it from the Livingston North rail line. When I worked at Livingston Police Station, one of the Incident branch officers who remembered the case, tried to pull the file, only to find it completely empty, that was in 2000. My dad was always very cryptic and cagey when talking about the incident, and it was my view that he knew a lot more than he ever let on or told me. People know the truth about what happened. I think the two emails if they came from my father or not, (it is the same info he gave me) are trying to point to the real truth".
Regards, Graeme S.

Author's Comment. I then asked Graeme, who, by the tone of his letter, appears to be Alistair Sutherland's son, what he thought had happened? He replied.

"To be honest I don't know. I think given the info regarding the MoD, the way he tried to steer me in that direction, the fact that I worked for Ferranti Defence Systems Ltd in the 1980's and saw military developments that were 20 years in advance (and these were not even really top secret) I think this might be one possibility". (A secret aircraft project? Author's interjection)

"My father was a Police Officer in the 1960's. He might have been many things, but he did have integrity. My interest in UFO's, astronomy, authors such as Graham's Hancock, Robert Bouval, Eric Von Daniken all stemmed from him, so I would say he was not a sceptic or debunker or denier. I remember being 7 years old (1975) and being taken to Roslyn Chapel looking for something that I thought at the time was the bones of Jesus. I was told stories of The Apprentice Pillar, and went looking for a room down in the depths of the chapel (sound familiar?) Going to Loch Ness (I remember him talking with friends and him making sketches of a plesiosaur shaped fin) That is why I take the info of some now defunct military hardware experiment a little more seriously. He definitely knew something but wouldn't say. It's just a pity his wife never wanted children and actively put up barriers

to me having contact as an adult, otherwise I might be in possession of the negatives now. After speaking to Bill and other officers involved, I do agree with what they have said. There was definitely something heavy on the ground. It didn't get there through the woods, as there would have been signs. Hallucinations don't leave marks on the ground that match Robert's account of the event. The way the trousers were damaged match the account given. Bill told me "There was something heavy in the clearing, then there wasn't. It could only have left the clearing by going upwards". I hope some of the info and background I've given on Alistair helps you to understand the information that was given to me was the same info given to you via two emails. Whether that was him or not, is the direction he wished to convey but was unwilling to say".

Kind regards Graeme S.

TRESS BLAIR AND BOB TAYLOR'S TROUSERS!

Author's Comment. As we know, this subject is riddled with many people who have many claims. I for one will never throw the baby out with the bathwater. In other words, I'll listen to anyone who has a story to tell me after which, I'll make a judgement. Does that mean my judgement will be correct? Not necessarily as it will still only be my own impression. The reason I say this is that Tress Blair (or Wooshwa as she prefers to be called) who I have written about earlier in this book, states that she is not from here (Planet Earth) that her real home is in the stars on a planet called Sucruma. Before I get into the time when she held Robert Taylor's ripped trousers to see if she could psychically pick anything up, I'd just like you the reader, to read what she said about who she is. In an e-mail to me she said.

Hi Malcolm,

"I am happy to answer your questions, but some I may not have the answers to as yet, as we are not told everything. Firstly, I can record my language and my singing and have done a few times. Secondly there is no mention of a God with the epitora species they are not like humans. They live many lifetimes and

the atmosphere around them is colder than ours. Also, they have no need for money. They are from the 7th dimension around from the sun, but it can get very black at time's, I don't know why. They are telepathic, no speaking is required, you just look into each other's eyes, they are gentle healing people from Sucruma. Everything will be in my book when I finally get round to finishing it, and then I've been told, the work will begin. Epta emr eca ebow ima las ecaya per ematora emala, a little of my language".
Tress (Wooshwa)

Author's Comment. So, as I always like to test people to satisfy my own curiosity, I decided to see if Tress (Wooshwa) could hold Robert Taylor's ripped trousers and see if she could psychically pick up anything from them. Now admittedly this is in no way, a scientific test, for she knew all about what happened with the witness and his encounter. But nonetheless, I decided to let her try and see what she could pick up (if anything) from the ripped trousers. This experiment was done at the Premier Inn in Castleford England on Saturday the 17th of August 2019. (We had just left the Close Encounters UFO conference, in Pontefract) Attending this session, were, Bill Rooke, his wife Victoria, myself Malcolm Robinson, and Chris Evers, the conference organiser. The following is what Tress (Wooshwa) wrote about that experiment.

"After Malcolm Robinson's talk about Bob Taylor at the conference in Pontefract, we met up at the Hotel and I had the opportunity to see the trousers that Bob Taylor wore the night he was abducted. When the trousers were taken out of the plastic bag, I had an immediate sense of association, and my nose starting to run. I asked Chris to lay the trousers out in front of me, and when I tried to put my hands on the trousers, there was a force that was pushing me away. I tried several times to place my hands on the trousers but felt there was a strong energy resisting me. I was very aware that my nose was still running, and I started to feel shaky and was becoming a bit hazy".

"As the feelings subsided, I was standing inside a space pod. The interior of this pod was dimly lit, but I could see that it had

amazing ocean blue coloured walls with a light cream colour above. To the far end it was completely dark black, so I couldn't make out what was over there. In front of me and to the right, at about my shoulder height, there was a round ended countertop protruding at right angles from the wall, and below I saw Bob's dog lying, very still, asleep. On the left of the pod, I could see a tall, very shiny, silver table. It was boxed in and had symbols around the base. On this table I could see Bob, but only from his chest downwards, as his head was tilted backwards. At each side of the table there were three small beings, I could only see the top of the three at the far side, as the table was between us, but I could clearly see the three nearest me and they seemed to be levitating about half a metre off the floor in order to reach the table".

"I became aware that they had taken blood from his feet or ankle. As time went on, I noticed the atmosphere was becoming oppressive in the pod. As I looked around my surroundings, I noticed how still everything was, and how measured their movements were. As I was watching what was going on, all six of them, in unison, suddenly looked up at me realising I was in their presence. I knew I had to leave, but could see no way out, so I had to force myself backwards the way I had entered. I had to make several attempts before I was out of the pod and back in the room. When I left the Pod, I could smell a metallic like smell, and felt completely exhausted, almost falling to my knees. As I looked over the room, I saw Bob Taylor for an instant, sitting beside the window. I felt that I had been in the pod for hours. This was not Psychometry as I did not touch the trousers but was in fact anomalous cognition "Remote Viewing".

Sincerely, Tress Blair. (Wooshwa)

Author's Comment. Well, what are we to make off that? I have tried this experiment before with other people with interesting results. These experiments were featured in my book, *'The Dechmont Woods UFO Incident'* so I won't repeat them again here. What I will say, and I'm sure Tress (Wooshwa) won't mind me saying so, that many will take this with a pinch of salt. It's not truly evidence as such, all it is, is someone who states that they have this ability to 'tune in' to objects and items and can provide information about them. It's as if these very trousers have somehow stored the emotions of that eventful morning like some sort of VHS magnetic tape, and through Tress's psychic ability, she has psychically attuned herself into what happened 'after' Robet Taylor lost consciousness. It's circumstantial at best, and although what she 'saw' can't be proved, it's all part of the Dechmont Woods story, and for what it's worth, I felt it best to include it here.

DOWSING ROBERT TAYLOR'S TROUSERS
Author's Comment

Back in May 2014 when I lived in Hastings in East Sussex England, I became aware of a UFO Conference that was being held in my hometown, which was a bit of a surprise. A bigger surprise was the cost of a ticket which was £45:00, I almost fell off my chair. (Admittedly that price did include a meal and entertainment at a nearby hotel) So sadly, I decided to give it a miss. However, someone mentioned my name to one of the organisers and that I should have a 'special invite' to attend, 'free of charge' and before you could say 'Jack Robinson' (no relation) I was walking through the doors of this well attended conference. So, what has this to do with the Dechmont Woods Incident I hear you ask, well keep sitting quiet and we'll get to it. Firstly, let me tell you a little bit about who was organising it. It was a group calling themselves AMMACH (Anomalous Mind Management Abductee Contactee Helpline) Their web site (in part) states the following.

A.M.M.A.C.H

AMMACH started life on the 23rd January 2011, by Joanne Summerscales and Miles Johnston who have both had a long-term interest in, and are researchers of, the many fields and subjects, such as suppressed advanced technology, the unaddressed history of humanity/genetics, alternative energy systems, health/illness management and the extensive area of UFOlogical/ET experience, including the Exopolitical arena, which seeks full official disclosure. Which will, when it happens, have a profound impact on every area of life; the social, religious, political and economical. We also document an experiencer's story for research purposes, to educate and inform the people, to put into words a greater awareness of the human experience, which is an integral part of what AMMACH seeks to do.

So dear reader, I was 'invited' along to their event where I was specifically asked to bring along Robert Taylor's ripped trousers (the witness of whom we have read about above) What happened was, that during a break in the conference, Robert Taylor's ripped trousers were unceremoniously placed across two tables where Geoffrey Crockford and a couple of other dowsers did a number of different tests on the trousers. What they were looking for, I can't recall, but they didn't get much, other than what they described to me, were 'zinc traces' around the tears in the trousers. Zinc, we are told, acts as an antioxidant by helping to protect cells from damage and is involved in the normal functioning of our immune system. Whilst these tests were a little disappointing in that nothing major came up on them (and I say that in the light of quite an astonishing presentation that Geoffrey and his college Nigel Hughes gave at the conference) The Bi-Location team have dowsed the landing site at Rendlesham Forest, and not only did they find some trace elements left in the soil from this UFO? But they got a holographic shape of the entire craft of which they showed on slides to the audience. They say that they can go to any worldwide site where a UFO has landed, and prove if something truly did indeed land, and recreate what the craft looked like. Yes, controversial for sure, and I can't convey the full aspect of what and how this is all done here in these few words. But basically, what they are saying is that you and I, and everyone on this planet, leave trace elements wherever we go. Dead skin from our bodies, sweat on door handles etc. But when something 'alien' leaves trace deposits, then that is totally different from normal man-made effects, or DNA if you like. So, I must admit I did have high hopes of some kind of trace elements on the trousers, and other than some zinc and some statements about berries and something to do with trees there was nothing. Since that day on May 31st, 2014, I've not heard a lot about AMMACH although there are some interesting video clips of Joanne Summerscales interviewing UFO abductees. For the record, the text that follows was taken from one of their flyers which gives you a little bit more about who they are and the work they do. It states.

THE BIOLOCATION TEAM – FORENSIC DOWSING

A Key to the Reality of Extra-terrestrial Life with Geoff Crockford and Nigel Hughes.

Biolocation techniques are likely to be the key to observing and collecting evidence of extra-terrestrial activity in the solar system. This activity appears undetectable by conventional astronomy. A research program using the techniques has been collecting science-based evidence since July 2011.

Geoffrey Crockford's background is scientific research and postgraduate teaching. Before attending London University, he worked for the Atomic Energy Authority at Harwell. After graduating, he joined the Medical Research Council and later in his university career moved to the Department of Occupational Health at the London School of Hygiene and Tropical Medicine. In 1988 he became an independent science consultant with a worldwide clientele of major organisations and companies.

Nigel Hughes, a University of London science graduate following University Nigel worked in several scientific posts before entering a career in Civil Aviation as a pilot. He flew as a jet captain for a major European airline and was a commercial flight instructor and examiner. After a flying career of 24 years, he retired from aviation becoming a business and education consultant.

So dear reader, let us move on shall we with our next case file, which admittedly is not Scottish, its German. That said, what the witness saw, was strikingly similar to those spiky spheres that Robert Taylor saw in Dechmont Woods as they rushed towards him. Steve Morgan now takes up the story.

A SIMILAR SPIKED BALL!

Dear Malcolm,

"I saw a report about the Livingston incident shown on National Geographic channel this week which left me feeling pretty overwhelmed. I recognised the drawings and descriptions of the smaller 'red sea mine' looking objects. During the summer of 1965, I was in the garden at home in Osnabruck, Germany, I was aged 7. I looked upwards and saw a red ball with long rods protruding, exactly as shown in the programme (I later described it as a 'red sea mine' myself). The only difference was I saw a black square panel, which I took to be a window and watched awhile, expecting a face to appear. It was silent and remained perfectly still, hovering approximately 75 feet above, and slightly forward of where I stood. I went into the house and told my father. We went in the garden, but it was no longer there, it had gone. I remember all the details really clearly and can still picture it against the blue cloudless sky. I never spoke of it again with my father and have only occasionally spoken of it with a handful of people close to me. After seeing the TV programme, it really validated my experience and for me leaves me in no doubt that Mr Bob Taylor account is genuine, and very real, and not the result of imagination or hallucination as offered as a possible theory on the programme. I have never written about this, but the programme did leave me with a strong wish to share my experience with you or Mr Taylor's family. I served with the Royal Air Force for 18 years and now work with the Police as a forensic practitioner and have always considered myself as very practical man and not one given to speculation. Thank you for taking time to read this, but as I said the programme re-opened an old memory and I had to tell someone".
Yours Sincerely Mr Steve Morgan.

Author's Comment. The witness doesn't really say how many rod-like extensions the sphere that he saw had. Plus, I should point out, Robert Taylor never said that those two spiky spheres that he witnessed rushing towards him were red in colour.

He said they were a dull grey with the texture of emery paper. (Emery paper is a type of abrasive paper used for rubbing and polishing metal) Still, it does make one wonder if this was something similar to what Robert Taylor saw that day. But we ain't finished yet, below is yet another witness who saw something similar to witness Robert Taylor. Here is what he had to say.

DID WE SEE ROBERT TAYLOR'S UFO?

Hi Malcolm,

"Just watched an episode about the Robert Taylor encounter on TV and thought you may be interested to know, that I and some work colleagues of mine, witnessed an object that same day. Our sighting was at the same locus. Basically, I was 17 years old at the time and was travelling to work at the Halls of Broxburn along with three other passengers in the car. I recall the time being either 07:40 or possibly 06:40, I cannot remember what our start time was, but I would err more towards the former time. We were driving along the A89 Bathgate to Edinburgh Road. I believe Dechmont Woods sits between A89 and M8 so if you look at map, we were just passing the junction for old Bangour Hospital (The junction would be to our left-hand side, ie north) about 300 metres west of turning for Dechmont Village itself. Anyway, suddenly this object appeared to our right, travelling in the same direction and level with the tree line for around 50 metres and thereafter disappeared below the tree line. There was no explosion or impact apparent. We were no more than 100 metres from this object, and I would have described it as a glowing orange circular meteor type object, although the trajectory would have discounted it being a meteor in my opinion. In addition, it was not travelling fast as it was tracking the speed of our car, maybe 50mph maximum and the object disappeared into trees on our right (south) as we approached Dechmont. When I got home that night, I heard further reports from locals, who described an object travelling eastwards at height over the town of Bathgate and the times of these sightings coincided with our slightly later sighting. I later learned of the

forestry worker event, and at the time, thought he was a crank who had seen the same incident and embellished it a bit. Now I'm not so sure. I believe the object landed in Dechmont Woods, not sure exactly where the forestry worker's sighting was, or how far Dechmont Wood stretches, but that's what we saw. I would gauge this object as the size of a small car".

Thanks Brian Hall.

Author's Comment. Do lie detectors work? Does one's body language give away what really is going on with a certain situation? Well, there are some people that can tell, just by looking at someone and their body language, if they are being truthful or not. One such man, Drew McAdam, made the West Lothian Herald and Post back on Wednesday the 25th of November 2009. Here is that newspaper report. Titled, *'Alien assault was no hoax'*.

'A body language expert has said the West Lothian man who claimed he was 'assaulted' by aliens 30 years ago was telling the truth. Human lie detector Drew McAdam believes 'without doubt' that forestry worker Bob Taylor's account of the infamous UFO incident in woods on Dechmont Law was true after studying his body language in a video documentary. Mr Taylor said he was attacked by two strange spheres with protruding spikes in the woods in 1979 in what is thought to be one of the world's most genuine sightings of UFOs. Scotland's foremost mind reader Mr McAdam, 54, from West Calder, believes a new documentary unveils the truth behind the myth. The popular entertainer was trained by the army's intelligence corps in body language techniques and was the dreaded 'Interrogator' on TV's Trisha Show to illicit confessions out of participants'.

'During the 1979 incident, the 3-foot-wide spheres attached themselves to Mr Taylor after dropping from a 20-foot sphere-like object, ripping his trousers and rendering him unconscious for 20 minutes. Mr Taylor died in 2007, aged 88, but Waterborn Productions Ltd have produced a film that contains footage of interviews with some of the personalities involved in the story at the time, and Mr McAdam has now used his unique talents to determine whether the saga was a hoax or not'.

"*I expected to uncover body language suggesting that the whole thing was a hoax or a lie,*". said Mr McAdam, who reads non-verbal cues, micro-expressions and body language to uncover lies'.

"*However, I can categorically state that at no time is there any evidence of deception from any of these people. Not once. When Bob Taylor recounts the incident, he is clearly accessing actual memory, not his imagination. His body language is open. There is no fluctuation in his paralanguage, and his open-palmed gestures suggest a man simply recounting what happened*".

'Among the people interviewed in the documentary include Mr Taylor's work colleagues, police and sceptic Steuart Campbell, who wrote the book, The UFO Mystery Solved. Mr McAdam said:

"*Based on my expertise and experience of body language, my view is that the interviewees were telling it exactly as it was. This was no hoax.*"

'However, Steuart Campbell demonstrates textbook closed body language, self-caressing and all the 'tells' of a person in discomfort, offering an explanation about which he, himself, harbours grave doubts'.

"*He may dismiss the whole thing with scientific theories, but his body language is saying something different. Did aliens land on Dechmont Law 30 years ago? We'll probably never know. But thanks to the footage we can still view the interviews and sort out the nonsense from the fact*".

'Mr Campbell responded by saying'.

"*I certainly was comfortable, although that's not a word I would use. I think that this so-called body-language expert has mistaken scientific caution for discomfort. At all times, I only ever say what I believe and am sure is correct. However, he's right about Bob Taylor, who everyone agrees is an honest person. He surely tells the truth, but of course it's what he believes to be the truth. What he saw and indeed if he saw anything at all is disputable. I think I tried to make clear in the film*".

THE DECHMONT WOODS 'DOGMAN'!

Staying with Dechmont Woods, here is a story that will blow your socks off. By now the reader will be aware of the Dechmont Woods story, but what a lot of people don't know however, is the fact that not only does Dechmont Woods have this remarkable UFO encounter, but it also hosts an unearthly 'being' known simply as, 'the Dog Man'! as witness Mark Wilson found out. I'll let Mark tell you what happened.

"It was middle of November 2021, about 9:00pm My neighbour and I went up to Dechmont Woods with my huskies. We parked up in Deans Industrial Estate and walked over the motorway bridge and up into the woods. At the start of the woods there is a path, and as soon as we walked in, my dogs got a scent of something and pulled us over to one side. As they were sniffing about, I saw a streak of light about 100, 150 meters in front of me, go across the path and back into woods behind us. I said to my pal that 'something' ran across the path ahead. I shinned my torch, and in the torch light, I saw big orange eyes staring back at us which I thought might be a deer, but most wild animals run a mile away when there are a pack of dogs around"

"I kept shining my torch whilst walking towards it. Now remember I've got five big huskies, and this thing stood its ground. I got up parallel to it, mesmerised by its big orange staring eyes. This was not a deer. I was a foot away staring at it. It stood and stared back. It was at least 6 feet tall with a dog like face, but more of a beak for a mouth. I said, "You ain't no deer", and slowly walked back down the path. It just stood and watched me. My pal said, "What the f**k is that". Both of us headed back down the path and out of the woods. I looked back and it was stood on the path. You could see the body. It looked all black but stood at least six feet tall then it was gone. The funny thing is, it never made a noise. Now I grew up in a farm, I know all the animals. I was a keen fisherman and hunted in my younger days. I've been all over Scotland camping. I've seen a lot of strange stuff and let me tell you, this was scary. My dogs would not go near it, and they never get frightened".

Author's Comment. Well, what are we to make of that? The reader should consider that there have been many sightings of this so called 'Dog Man' throughout the world with a plethora of cases throughout the British Isles, and I would urge the reader to check on the internet about such cases. This will allow you to see that clearly there is something going on here. Of course, you read in the newspapers about sensational reports about this so called 'Dog Man'. And whilst doing research on this topic to back up Mark Wilson's account, I came across a report in the British tabloid, the Daily Star (27th February 2021) with a piece by Deputy news editor Sophie Bateman. She reports.

Brit haunted by terrifying 'dogman' since childhood tells spooky cryptid sighting tale

'Colin Keelty, a British man, claims to have had multiple run-ins with an enormous dog-human hybrid in rural areas of the UK throughout his life, and is 'open-minded' that there could be a supernatural explanation. 'When Cryptids Call', is a new podcast hosted by cryptozoology expert Lee Solway that features listeners calling in with their spookiest paranormal experiences in the UK. A recent episode featured an eerie tale from Colin Keelty, who says he's had run-ins with a 'dogman', an enormous mythical creature thought to be a dog-human hybrid. On October 4th, 1990, he was backpacking his way from East Hull to Hornsey and came across a park in Hatfield. He was walking down the lane at about 8:30pm with a full moon that lit the place up like daylight, when he spied something strange in a gap under a hedge row. Colin explained'.

"I kept looking at it, like is it a cow? Is it a deer? It just looked like a dog's back legs, but then I thought, hold on, where's its front legs?"

'At that moment a friend happened to be driving past and offered him a lift, and when he got in and looked back at the field, he could see this dog standing there'.

"I said 'look, look, there's a dog standing in the gate hole". He just looked at me and said "Col, you're working a lot of hours, get some rest'."

'Colin went on'.

"To be honest I had nightmares after that. For years I kept waking up, not every night obviously, but some months would go by, and I'd have another one. And the recurring nightmare is this thing jumped out of the gate and just ripped me to shreds. And I woke up screaming some nights, with sweat. Even though I'm into that, I just could not believe what I saw".

'From then on, he became obsessed with going on solo expeditions to try to catch another glimpse of the creature but kept it under wraps from his family until September 2015'.

After his sighting of the 'dogman' in the field, Colin became obsessed with tracking it down. One morning he was exploring some private woods when he found an enormous 'pile of poo' indicating a large creature had been in the area recently and that was only the first strange thing'.

"As I was coming to the stream I thought, 'what's that smell? Oh man that is putrid, really foul'. Then I hear this big thud, thud, thud. I thought what the heck's that? So, I stopped, and this thing stopped".

'He assumed it was one of the men who work in the forest so called out but got no answer. He kept walking and the thuds kept following him. Could Colin have come across the legendary dogman in the woods'?

"All this time the hairs on the back of my neck stood up. The smell was putrid. I got on all fours to see through the bracken, then I got back up and it got back up. I stated walking slowly and this thing was following me, then I speeded up and it speeded up. I thought, bloody hell what is this thing? When I got to the end of the bracken it bowed off to the right of me, and I was going to the left. When I got to the end, I just glanced over and there's this... I *don't know what the heck it was. I don't know what to say. It was huge, hairy. Why I thought it was a dogman is because of the smell".*

'He was terrified when he spotted the enormous hairy creature in the woods. Colin's convinced it wasn't a prankster wearing a costume because nobody knew I was going to be there, they're private woods, nobody walks through there. He couldn't make out the creature's face'.

"All I could see was a mass and hair. I wish I'd got my phone out and took pictures of this large thing. It wasn't human, I know that. Another thing was when I was going into the woods, you could hear animals moving around, but just as I got in, everything went silent like there was a giant bubble. It was real weird".

'It wasn't Colin's first sighting of a cryptid, having seen 'something' twice as a child and again while out walking in Goathland North Yorkshire with his wife. Colin said'.

"About half a mile into these woods she said, "I'm scared". She said there's something up front we shouldn't see. I said, "stop being stupid", but she grabbed my hand, which was unusual at the time because we weren't getting on. But there was definitely something in these woods, and once we got out you could feel the relief".

'Colin's also seen 'strange things' while out driving at night but says modern dash-cams are ill-equipped to capture the lightning-fast creatures he's seen run in front of his car. Having been dogged by unexplained sightings of an enormous creature his whole life, he's still unsure of the truth behind it all'.

"I like to think these things are real, but I'm open-minded about the supernatural. I do really think these things move about the country through green belts [areas of untamed wilderness]. *I've had loads of stories of factories where there's a green belt out the back and something's gone crashing through, something*

large that we can't explain bigger than a deer, massive and black".

Author's Comment. Samantha finished off her article on Colin's encounter by stating, and I quote, *'Only 30% of the UK's total landmass is urbanised, with the rest made up of farmland, marshes and forest'.* Makes you wonder eh!

I'll give you one more 'Dog Man' account before we move on. This one comes through the Coast-to-Coast American radio show's internet news channel. It's from October 10th, 2024, and was written up by Tim Binnall entitled, *'Couple Reports Dogman Encounter at Infamous 'Haunted' British Forest'.* He relates.

'A British couple says that they were left profoundly shaken by a terrifying encounter with a Dogman that was lurking in a forest infamous for incidents of high strangeness. Coming to light by way of a local media report last week, the unsettling incident happened this past July as the unnamed husband and wife were walking through the notorious Cannock Chase Forest area in Staffordshire in England where all manner of weird events are said to have occurred over the years. In this instance, the couple claim, they were visiting a cemetery within the site when they noticed a putrid smell in the air. Initially thinking it might be from a dead deer, their assessment was quickly upended when they caught sight of its source: a bipedal canine creature'.

"We both saw something in the distance moving between the gravestones. It must have been eight feet tall, and it was incredibly broad".

'Recounting the chilling experience, the witness noted that the eerie interloper was 'covered in hair like a giant wolf' and moved around on two feet. When he wondered aloud to his wife what they were seeing, the man said, the creature seemingly realized that it was being watched, which led to a truly frightening face-off between the couple and the canine cryptid'.

"It turned around instantly and locked its eyes on us. They were big and yellow, and the creature had huge teeth, like nothing we'd ever seen before. It was the single most terrifying thing I've ever witnessed in my life. My wife is so distraught she won't even talk about it".

'Putting a fitting punctuation on the Dogman sighting, the witness said the otherworldly creature unleashed a haunting howl before fleeing the scene. Remarkably, Cannock Chase was the setting for a similarly strange encounter that occurred at around the same time as the couple's experience this past summer when a man walking his dog says that he was approached by a 'Black Eyed Kid' entity at the creepy haunted forest'.

Author's Comment. So, just two accounts of the hundreds if not thousands of reports of a Dog Man like creature throughout the world. The vast majority of which are consistent with each other. Clearly Mark Wilson in the Dechmont account, is of the opinion that this was something that 'shouldn't have been there. And although he still to this day goes into the woods with his husky dogs, he is always on the look out for this 'unearthly thing', hoping that it stays out of his way. Mark has also witnessed a UFO in the so called 'Falkirk Triangle' which I recounted in my first book, *'UFO Case Files of Scotland (Volume 1)* available on Amazon. I feel that I should give this account again, so that you the reader, can see that Mark has indeed, had his fair share of strange happenings. Here is what happened on that eventful day. Mark was 25 years of age at the time of his sighting. He states.

BUZZED BY A UFO ON THE M9 MOTORWAY

"It was Boxing Day, 26th December 1994, and the time was about O5:4Oam. We were on our way home from Stirling travelling on the M.9 Motorway. Jane my girlfriend and I, noticed a large bright glowing light of which at first we didn't take much notice of. But when we got right into Grangemouth, we noticed that this light wasn't moving, it was hovering over near Bonnybridge. We noticed as we travelled further up the

motorway, that it was moving towards us, it was as if it had a magnet on the car and it was staying at the same distance away from us but travelling along at the same speed. I took the car up to 90 mph and this object kept pace. When we slowed down, it slowed down too. We were both very scared at this time. It was at the right-hand side of our car, and then, just like a speeding bullet, it shot over to the left-hand side of our car. A few seconds later it again shot over to the right-hand side of the car then again back to the left-hand side where it remained. The object then shot straight up into the sky and was gone in seconds"
Mark Wilson.

Author's Comment. In Mark's drawing that he supplied to the author, we can see that the object they both witnessed is shaped like a box with sloping sides and which was jet black in colour. Clearly then, this was not a conventional object, no wings tail fins or any other appendages were noted. It had come from a distance, then swooped down onto the two unfortunate witnesses. Is the British Government and the Ministry of Defence seriously trying to tell us that incidents like this are not threatening to its citizens?

NATIONAL MUSEUM OF SCOTLAND REFUSES RIPPED TROUSERS!

Some people know that I have here at my home in Sauchie, Clackmannanshire, Scotland, probably one of the most important pieces of evidence when it comes to a particular UFO incident. I have in my possession, the ripped trousers that Robert (Bob) Taylor wore when he encountered a UFO in Dechmont Woods near Livingston back in 1979. Let me explain.

As we have learned in this chapter, the witness, Robert (Bob) Talyor, claims that his trousers were ripped by two small devices that were emitted from a larger object in a clearing in Dechmont Woods back in 1979. The trousers show a large tear on the right-hand side, and another large tear on the left-hand side. These trousers have appeared on countless television documentaries across the world and were forensically tested by Police Scotland who agree with the witness, that these rips were made by a mechanical pull upwards. (I have all the police records on this case) This is the only case in the British Isles that has had a full-blown police and forensic investigation. I wrote about this incident in my book *'The Dechmont Woods UFO Incident'* (available on Amazon) After the police investigation, the trousers were given to Philip Mantle of the British UFO Research Association. Philip then kindly passed the trousers onto me, as he quite rightly stated, *"They belonged in Scotland, and not in England"*.

SO WHY A MUSEUM?

None of us, including you dear reader, are on this Earth for very long, and it would be remiss of me not to ensure that all my UFO and Paranormal research goes to the right location after I have passed on. All my life's work should not end up in a skip. When I pass away, most, if not all my UFO and Paranormal research, is going to a Swedish researcher by the name of Clas Svahn who has promised to display all my research work along with my personal collection of books and magazines that I have collected over the years in his museum in Sweden. Clas is a journalist and President of UFO Sverige. However, there is one piece of UFOlogical history that I did not want to leave Scotland, and that was the ripped trousers that witness Robert Taylor wore on that eventful November morning of 1979. Indeed, it was agreed by myself and Robert's daughter Anne, that come what may, these trousers must never leave Scotland for foreign shores, a promise I heartedly agreed upon.

I felt that the National Museum of Scotland in Edinburgh would be the perfect location to display these trousers. Not only are these exhibits from around the world displayed there, but the museum include some of the ancient artefacts and exhibits from Scottish history which are a joy to behold. I've spent many hours in this museum looking at a multitude of historic items. And yes, although this item (Robert Taylor's ripped trousers) would be somewhat 'off the wall' shall we say, it is nonetheless part of Scottish history, albeit a strange one. But I felt that it still deserved a place in the halls of this museum, along with information relating to what it was all about. So, I decided that I would contact the museum of Scotland in Edinburgh with my proposal. The following is part of an e-mail that I sent to the Museum of Scotland.

Re: Item for the Museum of Scotland

Hi Barbara,

"The item that I would like to be displayed in the museum of Scotland is certainly different from your other exhibits. It is a pair of trousers, but not any trousers, trousers with a history which I feel would warrant a place in your wonderful museum".

I went on to explain all about the incident and the furore that was associated with it. I gave all the facts of the case and a whole lot more. I further stated.

"I have all the police files on this case that I can give you. I can put you in touch with one of the police officers who investigated this case, and I can provide you with numerous links to television programmes on this famous incident. I honestly believe, that as Scotland's biggest UFO incident, this would prove a big attraction to your museum".

"Yes, it is a weird item for the museum, but it's now part of Scottish history, albeit a strange history, but I honestly believe, that this Scottish relic, deserves a small place in your museum where people can look at these rips in the trousers, learn about the story and wonder. If you type into Google or You Tube. The Livingston UFO Incident or Dechmont Woods UFO incident, you will see a wealth of videos and information about this case. I have attached a number of items which will inform you more about this fascinating case. Should you require any further information, I would be only too glad to assist".

With very best wishes.
Malcolm Robinson.
(Founder Strange Phenomena Investigations (U.K.)

SO, WHAT WAS THE OUTCOME?

Well, this was the reply that I received.

Dear Mr Robinson,

"Thank you for your email".
"I regret that NMS are unable to accept your offer on this occasion as we already have similar examples to these in our collection, and as an institution we must collect representatively". "I apologise that we are unable to help you in this instance, however if you have any further enquiries please do not hesitate to get in touch".

With kind regards, Laura Kondrataite.

Departmental Administrator, Scottish History & Archaeology, National Museums Scotland, Chambers Street, Edinburgh, EH1 1JF

Author's Comment. Wait a minute, did they just say that they had 'similar exhibits in their collection'! I doubt it very much. Yes, I accept that it might have been a bizarre request, but HISTORY IS HISTORY, no matter what aspect of history we are speaking about. Needless to say, I was a bit peeved by that, so to stir it up with hopes of public attention, I notified one of my media contacts, Oliver Norton of the Scottish Sun newspaper about my dilemma with the National Museum of Scotland. Like me, he was surprised that they had turned their noses up at this historic Scottish gift and quickly got in touch with the museum. In a full page spread that appeared in the Scottish Sun Newspaper on Sunday February 2nd, 2025, the museum spokesperson apologised for saying that they had 'similar' exhibits on show and said.

"This was a mistake. We are offered objects as donations to the National Collection all the time, and we don't have the space or capacity to accept them all".

Not to be outdone, a colleague of mine, Willy Devlin, wrote off to one Matthew Hume, who looked after exhibits at a museum near Linlithgow. Matthew replied.

Dear Willy,

"Thank you for your email which has been passed on to me as the Volunteer Curator of the Museum. Bob Taylor's trousers are indeed a fascinating artefact, and I agree that they should ideally be displayed in this county. However, we are bound by our collecting policy which states that we can only take items into the permanent collection which relate to Linlithgow and the immediate area. I am slightly puzzled by your reference to the Bennie Museum it implies that the trousers would belong to them and be loaned to us for permanent display. Permanent loans are not entered into by accredited museums, and I would have thought that the Bennie would be the most logical place to display the trousers in any case, as Dechmont would fall within their collecting policy. Given the significance of the item to the West Lothian area, and the fact that Bob Taylor was an employee of Livingston Development Corporation at the time of the incident, perhaps you might feel it appropriate to offer the trousers to the West Lothian Council Museums and Archive Service, who are responsible for the collections of the former Development Corporation. The email address is museums@westlothian.gov.uk We would still be happy to discuss displaying the trousers on a temporary basis in the future, perhaps as part of an exhibition, if you feel that this would be of interest. Please do get back in touch with me if you have any questions or further information which you think would be relevant.
Regards. Matt Hume.

Author's Comment. Whilst the above does provide an opportunity, I am still on the look out for somewhere permanent to showcase these famous ripped trousers. Perhaps you, dear reader, have a suggestion. My good friend and fellow UFO researcher Philip Mantle is, I believe, donating all his UFO files to a British museum. At the end of the day, we must ensure that researchers files are kept for future generations to look at. It may be a crazy subject to some, but come what may, UFOs are real, and UFOlogical items, whatever they may be, deserve their place in history.

THE DECHMONT WOODS SKY WATCH.
9th October 2021

Author's Comment. What is featured below, is a write up that I did for my Facebook site regarding an SPI sky watch in Dechmont Woods.

What a night, what a fantastic night we all had at last night's SPI Sky Watch in Dechmont Woods, scene of one of Scotland's biggest UFO encounters, where forestry worker Robert (Bob) Taylor, encountered a hovering dome shape object above a small grassy field. This past week Scotland has been subjected to torrential rain, so if truth be told, I was thinking that our sky watch would be a wash out, (if you would excuse the pun). But lo and behold, the rain had stopped, the skies had cleared, and the conditions looked perfect. I had journeyed to Deans along with one of my daughters (Karen) and her boyfriend Garry McKenzie who was driving. When we arrived at the car park near the woods at 9:45pm, and upon exiting the car, I looked sky wards and was met by a multitude of stars sprinkled over a velvet background, a wonderful sight to behold. This was a sky watchers dream, providing conditions that all sky watchers hope for.

Soon other cars started to arrive, and I was approached by a gentleman shining his torch in my face so I couldn't see who it was, then he spoke, *"Alright Malcky"?* He lowered the torch, and it was none other than Garry Wood, one of the witnesses in Scotland's other major UFO event, (The A70 UFO Incident) It was great to see Garry again. Soon we were joined by other sky watchers some of whom I have known for some time, others I didn't know, and some of which were at SPI's last sky watch held in Bonnybridge a few months ago. At this point, we were joined by a Dutch television crew who I had agreed to see at the sky watch who had arrived in their large van. And, after some introductions, they miked me up for sound where I then spoke to the assembled skywatchers thanking them for coming along, and to be careful as we trek through the woods, as due to the recent rain in the past few days, pathways would be muddy. The last thing I wanted was anyone slipping and falling and injuring themselves. As it would turn out, the pathways were not that bad, I was very surprised.

After a 15-minute walk to the site of the Robert Taylor incident, I gathered the sky watchers together and spoke about this impressive case and some of the theories that were banded about to explain it. I then brought out the famous ripped trousers, the trousers that Robert Taylor wore on that eventful day showing the rips at both sides near the pockets. I passed the trousers around for people to hold and feel what I believe is a piece of historic UFOlogical history. During my short talk, the sky watchers and I were being filmed by the Dutch TV crew. After my talk at the site and waiting for some stragglers who phoned up lost (you know who you are, lol) we moved to another area in the woods, away from the main site to continue our sky watch. It was a small field but had a commanding view of the skyline. At first the cloud cover had rolled in, but thankfully after about 10 minutes, the skies were clear again, which provided everyone an expanse of sky to gaze at. At this point I gave another short talk about why groups like SPI conduct sky watches, all of which was filmed by Dutch Television. Then I asked a good friend of mine, Tress Blair, who also goes by the name of Wooshwa and has captured some really strange light anomalies on camera, to do her thing. Now what she does is controversial folks, but at the end of the day, I will always give people time to do what they have to do. And what she does is to try and bring what she calls her 'celestial visitors' to the party, in other words, make UFOs appear. She does this by a strange kind of singing and utters some strange language, all quite intriguing. All the assembled sky watchers looked in her direction as she called out to the stars. When she had finished, I asked her if she felt that her 'sky friends' were near, she replied that they were very near. Now admittedly none of those assembled saw anything, but then again, she is psychic, so maybe she is tuning in to something that we couldn't see. That's not a get out clause, but a fact! Indeed, Tress turned round to me and asked if I had seen a nearby bush move, as three alien entities were standing there looking at all of us assembled. I couldn't see anything, maybe I was on the wrong wavelength! Let me say loud and clear here, I believe Tress Blair in what she does.

I then said to those assembled to flash their torches into the night sky. This was something that famed Arthur Shuttlewood (now deceased) did many times on Cradle Hill and Starr Hill near Warminster England where, after doing so, he was astonished to get bursts of light come down from the sky. Well, we all tried this, and got nothing. One gentleman had brought along to the sky watch, a very powerful green laser light, which he drew patterns with across the night sky. Then suddenly I heard my name being shouted out loud, that they had seen something very bizarre in the night sky. One lady had witnessed a sudden burst of white light appear between two stars that formed the Plough constellation. This was not a shooting star (although a few shooting stars were observed on the night). This was something totally different. It only lasted a few seconds and was gone, a few other people also witnessed this.

After another hour or so, I decided to wrap it up. The sky had been kind to us, and the rain stayed away, and incredibly for October, it wasn't really cold. The time was nearing 02:00am as we headed out the forest and back to our cars at the edge of Dechmont Woods. It had been a great night, and apart from that one strange burst of light in the sky, nothing else was reported. Nonetheless, the experience of being back at Dechmont Woods with a crowd of lovely like-minded souls, proved, at least for me, a night of magical memories. I just hope that the Dutch TV people do our sky watch justice and do not take the proverbial! Incidentally, this Dutch TV crew have been filing at various 'UFO hot spots' across Europe, and earlier in the week they filmed my good friend Ron Halliday at Norwood Castle, unfortunately Ron couldn't make our sky watch. So, a great night, with some great memories.

ROBERT TAYLOR'S PASSING

Sadly, Robert Taylor the witness in the Dechmont Woods encounter is no longer with us, and when I heard about his passing, I wrote the following on my Facebook.

It is my sad duty to report that Close Encounter witness Robert (Bob) Taylor sadly passed to spirit on Wednesday the 14th of March 2007 due to Bronchial pneumonia. His family and friends were with him when he passed to spirit. A week before he died, Bob's family read out to him, my concise article about his case from the January edition of UFO Data magazine edited by Russel Callaghan, Bob smiled and stated that this was EXACTLY how it happened, and he was very pleased in my reporting of the event. Bob's family were also pleased with the article in UFO Data as they have supported their father's claims knowing him as a truthful reliable and honest father who would certainly not have made up a story such as this. I felt it only right to mention the passing of Bob to the UFO Community, because at the end of the day, having worked on this case, I can safely say that this was a classic, there is no two ways about it. Very seldom do you come across a case such as this, that has a witness so truthful and honest, and, through no fault of his, was propelled into what could only be called 'the Twilight Zone' something so far removed from his day-to-day reality. Something that he wasn't looking for. Something, that to the day he died, he stated, 'DID' happen. Cases like Bob's keep me at the forefront of the UFO subject, simply because of working with the witness, meeting his family, getting to know them and the whole story. This case will always stand the test of time as one of Scotland's most alluring and fascinating UFO cases. It goes without saying that Bob Taylor will be sadly missed, but if anyone now knows the mystery to the UFO Enigma, it will now certainly be Bob. Robert's funeral will be on Wednesday the 21st of March.

Incidentally dear reader, I was the very first 'outsider' to whom the family told of Robert's passing, which I felt truly humbled at. I do hope that this chapter which contains new information regarding UFO sightings in and around Dechmont

Woods (Including the strange 'Dogman' encounter) shows you that other people, apart from Robert Taylor, were witnessing strange objects in the sky either at the same time as he was, or in the hours before and after. Validation is always a good thing when we can show that Robert Taylor's UFO sighting wasn't a 'one off' event, other people saw things that day as well. Whilst compiling this chapter, I came across an audio recording that I did with Robert Taylor dated January 19th, 1992, where I informed him about the Livingston Development Corporation had placed a stone cairn with a plaque to commemorate his encounter, and I asked him what he felt about it. He replied.

"Well, I don't really know. I'm not really fussy one way or the other. They haven't mentioned it to me or got in touch with me".

Bob then asked if the cairn was actually on the spot where he saw this object, I replied that it was. I then said to Bob that myself and other members of SPI would be holding our own event at the cairn to commemorate the encounter and asked him if he would like to come along. He stated.

"Oh, I don't know. I don't want to get into all that newspaper business again".

I then asked him, if, all these years later, any other memories had surfaced from that day. He replied with.

"No. My memory of that event is just as clear today, as it was then. I described it as a 'vehicle' and not as a 'flying saucer', but it certainly landed and took off there".

Bob then kindly asked if I was still into all this business which I stated I was, and that it was his encounter that really propelled me into the study of UFOs. I kept in touch with Bob over the years, and he never deviated from his original story. I've spoken to a number of people who knew Bob personally, and each and every one of them said to me that he was as genuine as the day is long. I still, to this day, regularly get asked to appear on television, radio and pod casts to discuss this case. One thing is for sure; this is certainly one of Scotland's biggest ever mysteries, and one in which I am so proud to have been a part of.

Steven Bird points to the metal in the fallen tree. Dechmont dig 23rd April 2023

Steven Bird and Malcolm Robinson Dechmont Dig 23rd April 2023

Two metal coins in the fallen tree. Dechmont Woods 23rd April 2023

The Spheres Dechmont Woods Case (c) Explorers Web Site

Transparent UFO (c) Explorers Web Site

Mark Wilson with one of his husky dogs.

Mock up of Dogman creature seen in Dechmont Woods by Mark Wilson in November 2021

Dechmont Woods Orb (c) Tress Blair

Toni Castle's sketch of what she saw whilst Bob Taylor had his UFO experience in 1979

CHAPTER TWELVE
SUMMING UP

Well, there we have it, we have reached the end of the book. I do hope that some of the cases featured in this book have raised an eyebrow with you, and made you re-evaluate that things are not always what they seem. UFO sightings are still ongoing throughout the skies of this world, but are we any nearer in trying to understand fully what's going on? Over the past ten or so years, we have seen a major shift from the powers that be in the United States, in that they are now sitting up and taking more notice of what's going on, mainly due to the UFO sightings witnessed and filmed by Navy pilots from the USS Theordore Roosevelt, the USS Princeton, and the USS Nimitz. Plus, we have had the Congressional Hearings into UFOs and even the NASA panel of experts looking into the UFO enigma. It all adds up to the fact that the subject of UFOs, (or UAPs as the Americans prefer to call them) is now finally being recognised as a legitimate topic of conversation, and not before time! Needless to say, there are many more UFO sightings that have been witnessed across the Scottish skies, and what I have featured in this volume (as well as the other two volumes) are but a few. I am always interested to hear from UFO witnesses who have had a sighting, and if that's you! Then please get in touch with me through the details at the end of this book.

At this stage of the book, maybe we should address the elephant in the room, and by that, I mean the, *'What If'* scenario? What if one day we finally did have 'open contact' from another race of beings not of planet Earth? Let me now take you through some of the things that we should be contemplating.

THE WHAT IF SCENARIO!

(1) What would happen if we had open contact with an alien species?

(2) Does the Government have protocols regarding any 'first contact' with an alien species? Indeed, do the various Government of the world know more than they are letting on!

(3) Are we truly aware of the implications of an E.T. presence on Earth on religion?

(4) What would an open disclosure do to the various churches of the world?

(5) Probably more alarming would be the use of alien technology falling into 'one' single country's hands. Would that one single country then control the world?

(6) Would an alien civilisation take over planet Earth, would we be the slaves?

(7) Would an alien presence impact on mental health?

(8) What would happen to the World's economy?

(9) Would traditional industries start falling by the wayside?

(10) Would we be dealing with friendly aliens, or aliens with a deceitful covert agenda?

(11) Would 'their' very presence on Earth give us a new pandemic with viruses that we can't control?

(12) Would the introduction of an alien race be beneficial to human society? For instance, would they help mankind move further to the stars?

(13) Or, would an alien race decimate the human race. Decimate our society. Decimate our culture and decimate what we, as the human race have built up since the Earth was formed?

(14) What if one day all this becomes reality, will mankind be prepared? Have we an action plan? Or will our ignorance of the UFO enigma be our downfall?

(17) If aliens truly landed on planet Earth, who would be 'master race'!

The above are legitimate topics that we all should concern ourselves with. For they 'might' pose a considerable concern to mankind. It may never happen of course, but mankind should have something in place should it do so. As a researcher, it still puzzles me as to 'why'? Why don't we have open contact? Why are we still having abductions? I get asked these questions many times by the media, and there is no definitive answer that I can provide. Speculations yes, but no definitive answer. I doubt very much is there is anyone anywhere, who has the true answer. All we know for sure, is that strange aerial vehicles are visiting our planet, and, on occasions, are taking people without their consent for some form of medical or clinical procedure. That worries me, as it should you. Researchers like myself are here to get answers, and that can be no easy task. It still surprises me that this subject continues to get ridiculed by the media and yet many people world-wide are traumatised by what they experience. I do hope that in my lifetime we get the answer that has eluded us for so long. Moreover, I hope that the answer is a peaceful one, and not something that has unscrupulous desires on humankind, for if that is the case, then who knows what awaits the future of mankind's existence on planet Earth.

REFERENCES

Brit haunted by terrifying 'dogman' since childhood tells spooky cryptid sighting tale - Daily Star

https://www.coasttocoastam.com/article/couple-reports-dogman-encounter-at-infamous-haunted-british-forest/

Three UFO sightings in Dumfries and Galloway over past three years - Daily Record

Close Encounters of the Dumfries Kind - Daily Record

Why do humans have bones instead of cartilage like sharks? (theconversation.com)

Cairnpapple Hill - Wikipedia

The WHEEL CARaVAN PARK & CAMPSITE - Home

NASA satellite captures sun-diving comet during solar explosion - CBS News

FURTHER READING

The following books on UFOs, are, I would suggest, a good place to start your continued study. Most of these books can be found on Amazon.

Above Top Secret. Tim Good. Publisher: William Morrow; Reprint edition (20 Sept. 1989) ISBN-13: 978-0688092023

Abducted. Anne Andrew, Jean Ritchie. Paperback: 320 pages. Publisher: Headline Book Publishing; New edition (3 Jun. 1999) ISBN-13: 978-0747259138

A Passage Through Eternity. Philip Kinsella. Paperback: 280 pages. Publisher: Independently published (2nd Feb. 2018) ISBN-13: 978-1977067289

Electric UFOs. Albert Budden, Blandford Books, 1998. ISBN: 07-137-268-57

Haunted Skies. (Various volumes cataloguing UFO sightings throughout the U.K. from 1939 through to present day. By John Hanson & Dawn Holloway. E-mail John at info@hauntedskies.co.uk

Livingston Enigma (Dechmont Law). A Tectonic Approach, John Dykslag (Self Published) 2007.

LightQuest. Andrew Collins. Paperback: 416 pages. Publisher: Eagle Wing Books, Inc. (2012) ISBN-13: 978-0940829497

McX. (Scottish X Files). Ron Halliday. B&W Publishing, Edinburgh, ISBN: 1-873631-77-4

Of No Defence Significance? John M Jenkins. The Pen-Y-Coe Press (1997) ISBN. 0-9531984-0-5.

Pascagoula-The Closest Encounter. Calvin Parker. (Flying Disc Press) ISBN: 9781-9829-95843.

Sky Crash. Jenny Randles, Brenda Butler, Dot Street. Paperback: 400 pages. Publisher: Harper Collins Publishers Ltd; New edition (22 May 1986) ISBN-13: 978-0586066782

The UFO Handbook. Alan Hendry. Publisher: Doubleday; First Edition (1 Aug. 1979) ISBN-13: 978-0385143486

The Truth Agenda. Andy Thomas. Paperback: 386 pages. Publisher: Vital Signs Publishing; Revised edition (1 Jun. 2011) ISBN-13: 978-0955060816

The UFO Mystery Solved. Steuart Campbell. Explicit Books Edinburgh ISBN: 0-9521512-0-0

The Dechmont Law UFO. Phil Fenton. Newstar Publishing 2012.

The Dechmont Woods UFO Incident. Malcolm Robinson. (February 2019) ISBN: 978-0-244-15911-5

The Falkland Hill UFO Incident. Malcolm Robinson. (October 2022) ISBN: 9798-3516-822-04

The A70 UFO Incident. Malcolm Robinson. (February 2022) ASIN: BO9RG7RXR1

The Bonnybridge UFO Enigma. (A Modern Day Mystery) Ron Halliday and Malcolm Robinson. (March 2025). ISBN: 978-1-917778-02-2

The UFOLOGY Umbrella. Jason Gleaves. Flying Disc Press. ISBN: 9781-793-055-002.

UFO Encounters. Jason Gleaves. Flying Disc Press. (2022) ISBN: 9798-4043-74971.

UFO Case Files of Scotland (Volume 1) Malcolm Robinson Publish Nation. (October 2009) ISBN: 978-1-907126-02-04

UFO Case Files of Scotland (Volume 2) Malcolm Robinson Publish Nation. (December 2017) ISBN: 978-0-244-95154-2

UFO Scotland. Ron Halliday, B&W Publishing Edinburgh, (1998). ISBN: 1-873631-839

UFO Study. Jenny Randles. Hardcover: 208 pages. Publisher: Robert Hale Ltd; First Edition (11 May 1981) ISBN-13: 978-0709188643

UFO Landings. (Philip Mantle) Flying Disc Press. (2020) ISBN: 9798-654-537-966

Without Consent. Philip Mantle. Publisher: Fortune Books Ltd (2002) ASIN: B00I63L8YU

You Can't Tell The People. Georgina Bruni. Paperback: 496 pages. Publisher: Sidgwick & Jackson; Main Market edition (9 Nov. 2001) ISBN-13: 978-0330390217

Zones of Strangeness. Peter A McCue. Paperback: 560 pages. Publisher: Author House UK (28 Feb. 2012) ISBN-10: 9781456778422

ABOUT THE AUTHOR
MALCOLM ROBINSON

Malcolm Robinson has been interested in the strange world of UFOs and the paranormal for as long as he can remember, and in 1979 he formed his own research society, entitled, Strange Phenomena Investigations, (SPI). The aims of SPI are to collect, research, and publish, accounts relating to most aspects of strange phenomena, and to purposely endevour to try and come up with some answers to account for what at present eludes us. SPI are the oldest UFO and Paranormal research group still operating in Scotland.

MALCOLM'S TELEVISION WORK

Scottish Television News (STV) – Independent Television Network (ITN) – BBC Reporting Scotland – Channel 5 – Sightings (U.S. T.V. Show) – Japanese Television – German Television – Mexican Television – Australian Television – Dutch Television – Italian Television – Strange But True? (With Michael Aspel) – Grampian Television – GMTV (with Eammon Holmes and Lorraine Kelly - The Disney Channel – Loose Lips (with Melinda Messenger and Richard Arnold. - SKY Discovery Channel – SKY History Channel – ITV This Morning (with Philip Schofield and Amanda Holden) – SKY News with Kay Burley. The Unexplained with William Shatner. Ancient Aliens, Weird Britain (with Andy McGrath) and many more.

DOCUMENTARY MOVIES
(That feature Malcolm Robinson)

The Pentagon UFO Files (2022) Space Force, The Dawn of Galactic Warfare (2022) Aliens at Loch Ness (2022) The Dechmont Woods Case (2023) Loch Ness, They Created A Monster (2023) The Loch Ness Monster, 'Hunting The Truth' (2023) UFO Government Files Declassified (2023)

RADIO

BBC Radio Scotland. - Radio Clyde – Talk FM – BBC Northsound – BBC Radio 4 – Central FM – The Howard Hughes show – Coast to Coast with Art Bell and George Noory – The Whitley Streiber Show. And many others, both here in the U.K. and overseas.

ARTICLES

Articles by Malcolm have appeared in many of the world's UFO and Paranormal magazines. Malcolm has assisted many of the U.K's National and Regional newspapers in connection with stories concerning ghosts, poltergeists, and UFOs.

INFO

Malcolm was the very first Scottish UFO researcher to speak in the following countries, United States of America, (Laughlin Nevada). France (Strasbourg) Holland (Utrecht) Ireland (Carrick on Shannon & Galway) Malcolm is also one of the few people on this planet to have gone down into the depths of Loch Ness in a submarine. Malcolm is an international author and lecturer and is the associate editor of the Outer Limits Magazine. Malcolm is the first Scotsman to give a lecture on UFOs and the Paranormal on a cruise ship, when he presented three lectures to holiday makers on board the Marella Discovery on an East Coast cruise of the USA and Canada in October 2023.

AWARDS

2017. UFO & Paranormal researcher of the year. Given at the Paraforce Conference in Witham, Essex, England.

2019. 40 Years Continuous operations of SPI. Given at the Outer Limits Conference in Hull, Yorkshire, England.

2021. The Tartan Skull Award. Presented at the Scottish UFO & Paranormal Conference (over Skype)

TO CONTACT MALCOLM ROBINSON

Research group Strange Phenomena Investigations (SPI) are always interested to hear from anyone who believe that they may have had a UFO or paranormal experience or indeed may have a photograph or piece of film footage which may appear to show something paranormal. If so, please contact Malcolm Robinson at the details below. (all submissions will be treated in confidence)

Malcolm Robinson.

You can e-mail the author direct at malckyspi@yahoo.com
Facebook: www.facebook.com/malcolm.robinson2
You Tube:
https://www.youtube.com/@malcolmrobinsonufoparanorm9006

My thanks to each and everyone of you who hold this book in your hands. All I would ask of you, is to keep your interest going, and always understand that there are still things that mankind don't understand, and for us not to fully explore these 'things', would not be in keeping with man's understanding of himself, and his place in the cosmos.

www.ingramcontent.com/pod-product-compliance
Lightning Source LLC
Chambersburg PA
CBHW052012070526
44584CB00016B/1724